Smoothing Out Financial Uncertainties

You may not be able to control the markets, but that doesn't mean you're at their mercy. Here are some ways you can protect yourself against life's financial uncertainties (along with a few notes on where you can find more information in this book):

- Plan for life's certainties and prepare for life's uncertainties (covered throughout the book).

- Invest in and protect your ability to earn money; it's likely your most valuable asset (Strategies #4, #6, and #7).

- Adequately insure yourself, your stuff, and your income stream (Strategies #5 through #8).

- Minimize or eliminate debt (Strategy #11), and focus on building a great credit score (Strategy #12).

- Maintain an emergency reserve fund (Strategy #10).

- Invest for your goals, time horizon, and risk tolerance (covered throughout).

- Diversify your portfolio across a broad mix of asset classes (covered throughout).

- Monitor and rebalance your portfolio to maintain your target asset allocation (Strategy #41).

Your Risk Profile

Consider the following to determine your personal risk profile.

- **Risk capacity:** How much risk *should* you take, assuming a worst-case scenario? Take into account your age and family situation, your income, and your other assets and resources. Keeping these factors in mind, how much risk should you take to achieve your goals?

- **Risk tolerance:** How much risk *can* you take? Consider your ability to stick with your investment plan without losing sleep or getting stressed out. Do not take on any more risk than you can comfortably tolerate.

- **Risk required:** How much risk *must* you take? You are exposed to certain risks whether you like it or not. However, many financial risks can be minimized or avoided. To do so usually means that you must accept a lower return on your investments. To meet your personal goals and objectives in the time frame you'd like, you need to take some risks, but take no more risk than you must to achieve your goals.

Calculating Interest

Years Until Goal	3% Average Inflation: Multiply Cost By	4% Average Inflation: Multiply Cost By
5	1.16	1.22
10	1.34	1.48
15	1.56	1.80
20	1.81	2.19
25	2.09	2.67
30	2.43	3.24

Investing in an Uncertain Economy For Dummies®

Web Resources to Help Find or Check Out a Financial Advisor

The following Web sites can help you in your search for a financial advisor:

- **Financial Industry Regulatory Authority:** www.finra.org (click on Broker Check) The Financial Industry Regulatory Authority (FINRA) is the new name for the National Association of Securities Dealers (NASD). If a financial advisor earns commissions on the sale of investment products they must be registered with FINRA. The Broker Check tool on the FINRA site can be informative but it is limited. Don't rely on this tool as your only method of checking out a financial advisor.

- **Securities and Exchange Commission (SEC):** www.sec.gov People who get paid to give advice about investments generally must register with either the SEC or the state securities agency where they have their principal place of business. Be sure to request and read any prospective advisors' ADV forms. The Form ADV has two parts. Part I, which you can access at www.sec.gov/answers/publicdocs.htm has information about the advisor's business and may list problems the advisor has had with regulators or clients. However, the advisor is not required to report some things that you'd view as essential information in selecting an advisor. Part II outlines the advisor's investment services, fees, and investment strategies. Ask any prospective advisor for their ADV Part II and make sure that you read and understand what it says.

- **Certified Financial Planner:** www.cfp.net/search The Certified Financial Planner or CFP designation is the most widely recognized educational credential for financial advisors and planners. Visit www.cfp.net/search to locate a CFP practitioner in your area.

- **National Association of Personal Financial Advisors:** www.napfa.org/consumer/ The National Association of Personal Financial Advisors (NAPFA) is the country's largest membership organization of Fee-Only® financial advisors. To qualify for membership in NAPFA an advisor must provide comprehensive financial planning services, adhere to the organization's Fiduciary Oath, maintain all required licenses and registrations as a financial advisor, submit a comprehensive financial plan for peer review, and charge their clients exclusively on a Fee-Only® basis.

- **Garrett Planning Network:** www.garrettplanningnetwork.com The Garrett Planning Network is the country's premier membership organization of Fee-Only® financial advisors who focus on providing competent objective advice to people from all walks of life. Members must be CFP professionals or in process of obtaining their CFP designation, abide by the CFP Code of Ethics and Professional Standards and the NAPFA Fiduciary Oath. Garrett advisors are prohibited from imposing any minimum fees, income, or asset requirements on the majority of their client engagements.

For Dummies: Bestselling Book Series for Beginners

Investing in an Uncertain Economy

FOR DUMMIES®

by Sheryl Garrett and
Garrett Planning Network

WILEY

Wiley Publishing, Inc.

Investing in an Uncertain Economy For Dummies®

Published by
Wiley Publishing, Inc.
111 River St.
Hoboken, NJ 07030-5774
www.wiley.com

WILEY

About the Author

Sheryl Garrett, CFP, founder of The Garrett Planning Network, Inc., has been dubbed "The All-American Planner," possibly because of her zealous mission to "help make competent, objective financial advice accessible to all people." Sheryl's fresh approach as a financial advisor working with clients on an hourly, as-needed, fee-only basis has evolved into an international network of like-minded financial advisors, the Garrett Planning Network. This book is a collaborative effort brought to you by more than 70 professional financial advisors who are members of the Garrett Planning Network (www.garrettplanningnetwork.com).

Sheryl has also been honored to work with the House Subcommittee on Financial Services regarding predatory lending regulation, financial literacy, and Social Security reform. She also works as a consultant and expert witness in lawsuits against financial advisors who rendered questionable or inappropriate financial advice.

She has authored, coauthored, or served as a technical editor on more than a dozen books and several magazine columns. These books include *Garrett's Guide to Financial Planning* (National Underwriter), *Just Give Me the Answer$* (Dearborn Trade), *Money Without Matrimony* (Dearborn Trade), *Personal Finance Workbook For Dummies* (Wiley), and *A Family's Guide to the Military For Dummies* (Wiley).

As a vocal advocate for financial education, Sheryl has frequently been interviewed on CNNfn, Bloomberg, ABC World News Now, and Fox-TV; NPR's *All Things Considered and Marketplace*; and in *Business Week, Newsweek, Time, Forbes, Kiplinger Personal Finance, Money, Smart Money, MarketWatch, U.S. News & World Report, Glamour, Parade, Better Homes and Gardens, the New York Times, USA Today,* and *the Wall Street Journal.* For four years straight, Sheryl was recognized by *Investment Advisor magazine* as "One of the Top 25 Most Influential People in Financial Planning." The National Association of Personal Financial Advisors (NAPFA) honored Garrett with the prestigious *Robert J. Underwood Distinguished Service Award* for her contributions to the development of the financial planning profession.

Dedication

On behalf of the members of the Garrett Planning Network, I dedicate this book to you, the reader. Our goal is to help answer your questions and empower you to make smarter financial decisions so that your most cherished life goals become reality.

Author's Acknowledgments

The passion and devotion of my colleagues in the Garrett Planning Network made this book possible. We all share the mission to help make competent, objective financial advice accessible to all people. This book is an extension of that mission.

Thank you to Jeff Alderfer, David Anderson, Diane Blackwelder, Kevin Brosious, Barbara Camaglia, Kay Conheady, Peggy and Chad Creveling, Helga Cuthbert, Debbra Dillon, Paul Dolce, Jake Engle, Christine Falvello, Cynthia Freedman, Eileen Freiburger, Robert Friedland, Deidra Fulton, Gwen Gepfert, Garry Good, Angela Grillo, Kathy Hankard, Katherine Holden, Will Humphrey, Ben Jennings, Kim Jones, Jean Keener, Derek Kennedy, Michael Knight, Cheryl Krueger, Derek Lenington, Charles Levin, Jennifer Luzzatto, Roland Mariano, Warren McIntyre, Herb Montgomery, Thomas Nowak, Robert Oliver, Kevin OíReilly, Michael Oswalt, Abigail Pons, Dylan Ross, Brooke Salvini, Martha Schilling, Corry Sheffler, Brian R. Smith, Bruce Sneed, Janice Swenor, James Taylor, Denisa Tova, Gigi Turbow Marx, Neil Vannoy, John Vyge, Liane Warcup, and Richard Weimert. Without your insight and contributions, this book would not have been possible.

My collaborative and support team, including Shawnda Hubbard, Jamie Breeden, Thomas Arconti, John Belluardo, Rick DeChaineau, William Keffer, Buz Livingston, David McPherson, Kevin Sale, Louise Schroeder, and Michael Terry, were indispensible. Thank you all for your endless energy and steadfast devotion to this project.

I'd be remiss not to acknowledge the army of folks involved in this project at Wiley Publishing. Thank you for taking on this challenge and for having faith that we could deliver.

Publisher's Acknowledgments

We're proud of this book; please send us your comments through our Dummies online registration form located at www.dummies.com/register/.

Some of the people who helped bring this book to market include the following:

Acquisitions, Editorial, and Media Development

Senior Project Editors: Tim Gallan, Christina Guthrie

Acquisitions Editor: Mike Baker

Senior Copy Editors: Sarah Faulkner, Danielle Voirol

Assistant Editor: Erin Calligan Mooney

Technical Editor: Joe Nierman

Editorial Managers: Christine Meloy Beck, Michelle Hacker

Editorial Assistants: Joe Niesen, Jennette ElNaggar, David Lutton

Cover Photos: © Brand X Pictures

Cartoons: Rich Tennant (www.the5thwave.com)

Composition Services

Project Coordinator: Katherine Key

Layout and Graphics: Christine Williams

Proofreaders: Laura Albert, Joni Heredia

Indexer: Broccoli Information Management

Special Help: Elizabeth Rea

Publishing and Editorial for Consumer Dummies

    Diane Graves Steele, Vice President and Publisher, Consumer Dummies

    Kristin Ferguson-Wagstaffe, Product Development Director, Consumer Dummies

    Ensley Eikenburg, Associate Publisher, Travel

    Kelly Regan, Editorial Director, Travel

Publishing for Technology Dummies

    Andy Cummings, Vice President and Publisher, Dummies Technology/General User

Composition Services

    Gerry Fahey, Vice President of Production Services

    Debbie Stailey, Director of Composition Services

Contents at a Glance

Introduction

· ·

*T*he only certainty in investing — and probably in life — is *uncertainty.* That can make investing seem like an adventure; however, it's more like a transcontinental expedition than a day trip to an amusement park. You can't anticipate the turbulent waters or the snowstorms you may encounter along the way, but you'll reach your destination if you plan ahead and prepare for all potentialities.

If you're feeling uneasy about the current economic environment or your ability to protect yourself and your nest egg, you're not alone. You're living in truly interesting and uncertain times. Treat this book as your survival guide — it can help you limit your ris2ks, plan for the long term and the short term, and invest in ways that let you sleep comfortably at night, no matter what the markets throw your way.

About This Book

Over 70 professional financial advisors collaborated to bring you *Investing in an Uncertain Economy For Dummies.* It's designed as a reference guide, so don't worry if you don't have the time or inclination to read it from cover to cover. This one-of-a-kind resource contains over 80 individual strategies to address the risks you face, plan for life's certainties, and prepare for the uncertainties of any economy.

The book contains seven parts, each focusing on an investing theme — accumulating wealth, preparing for retirement, and so on. Focus on the strategies or part that addresses your specific need at this time. Then refer back to this book whenever you have additional questions or areas about your personal financial life for which you need some guidance.

Conventions Used in This Book

While writing this book, we used a few conventions to make your life just a bit easier. Here's what you can expect:

- ✔ We use *italics* when we define a word or phrase that's important to understanding a topic. And when we get especially excited, we may throw in some italics for extra emphasis.

- ✔ When you see text in **bold,** you can expect it to be either a step in a numbered list or a key word in a bulleted list.

- ✔ All Web addresses appear in `monofont`.

✔ When this book was printed, some Web addresses may have needed to break across two lines of text. If that happened, know that we haven't put in any extra characters (such as hyphens) to indicate the break. So when using one of these Web addresses, just type in exactly what you see in this book and ignore the line break.

✔ Gray shaded boxes, otherwise known as *sidebars,* contain interesting but nonessential information. Feel free to skip 'em if you're short on time.

Foolish Assumptions

To provide the tools and advice you need, we made some of the following assumptions:

✔ You recognize the need to become more informed about the financial markets and your personal finances. You don't want to become a victim of self-serving sales pitches, and you need answers now.

✔ You have some interest in taking a more active and productive role in managing your personal financial life, or you at least want to make sure you don't do anything really stupid or get ripped off.

✔ You have access to the Internet, whether at home, work, or your local library.

How This Book Is Organized

Investing in an Uncertain Economy For Dummies is organized into seven distinct parts, each covering a major area involving your financial life. Here's a summary of what you can find in each part.

Part I: Laying a Solid Foundation

Before you start pulling money out of current investments or pouring money into new ones, you should make sure you have the right mindset toward your finances, investments, and the market at large. This part gives you an historical perspective of market cycles, helps you assess your finances and goals, and reviews some financial strategies to help you get a good foundation in investing.

Part II: Using Investment Vehicles and Accounts throughout the Economic Cycle

The investment marketplace offers lots of options — as well as futures, commodities, stocks, bonds, mutual funds, exchange-traded funds, cash accounts, retirement accounts, and more! This part gives you an overview of your choices and explains when certain types of vehicles or accounts may be right for you.

Part III: Demystifying Risk: Accumulating and Protecting Wealth

It's easy to think that the only risk involved with investing is losing value when the market goes down. However, other risks — emotional reactions, inflation, job loss, and so on — are major financial risks you have to consider in your planning. In this part, you explore types of risk, gauge your risk tolerance, and discover how to design a portfolio that allows you to limit risk while still getting the returns you need to meet your goals.

Part IV: Investing for Accumulators

This part helps you save and accumulate money for your emergency fund, major purchases, and goals such as college education and retirement. It also outlines various investment vehicles and strategies tailored to how much investment experience you have.

Part V: Heading into Retirement

Your retirement savings may have to support you for 30 years or more, so this is one investment area you need to get right. In this part, you discover how to prepare for surprises such as needing long-term healthcare or having to assist aging parents or adult children. You examine employer retirement plans, Social Security, and other potential sources of retirement income. You also take a look at asset allocation and gauge whether you're on track to have enough money during retirement.

Part VI: Living on Your Investment Earnings and Drawing Down Your Assets

This part takes you into retirement, helping you maximize pension and/or Social Security benefits and reduce your taxes as you decide which retirement accounts to use first. It also helps you develop a strategy for tapping into your assets and continuing to invest them so they offer you a steady stream of income while minimizing the risk that you'll run out of money during your golden years.

Part VII: The Part of Tens

The Part of Tens is a classic *For Dummies* part consisting of top-ten lists. In this part, you find ten tips for building a solid financial foundation and ten ways to minimize risk.

Icons Used in This Book

As you flip through this book, you can see a few different icons that draw your attention to specific issues or examples. Check them out:

If you're looking for a time-saving tool or insider suggestion that you can use immediately, the text next to the Tip icon has what you want.

If you don't read anything else, pay attention to the info next to this icon, which points out information that we just had to stress because it's *that* important to your financial well-being.

This icon alerts you to common pitfalls and dangers that you have to be on the lookout for when managing your personal finances.

This icon marks ideas you should pay special attention to when the economy looks shaky or you're really struggling.

Where to Go from Here

This book is organized so you can go directly to the part or strategies that matter to you right now. Worried about debt and your credit score? Flip to Strategies #11 and #12. Need information on diversifying your stock portfolio? Strategies #42 through #45 can help you out.

If you're just beginning to get your financial house in order, we suggest you start with Part I and possibly work through to Part IV. If you're getting closer to retirement, you may want to peruse Parts I and II and skip to Part V. If you're already in retirement, Part VI is specifically for you.

Part I
Laying a Solid Foundation

The 5th Wave   By Rich Tennant

Being Dracula's slave didn't pay much, but Renfield always found extra money to invest.

In this part . . .

Before you make any investment decision, you can benefit by balancing current events with some historical perspective. Life is full of uncertainties, so in this part, you get a thorough review of some personal financial planning strategies that'll help you minimize or avoid many of the financial uncertainties you face.

Keep Your Feet on the Ground

By Derek Lenington, CFP, and Dylan Ross, CFP

Successful investors are grounded. They're logical and disciplined, and they don't let emotions drive investment decisions. Successful investors understand and embrace the idea that the economy is *always* uncertain; it may have seemed more certain in the past, but that's with the benefit of hindsight.

The U.S. economy has cycled between good and bad times, and you can expect that trend to continue (see Strategy #2 for more historical perspective). Unless you think that trend will end and things will always be either good or bad forever, every bad period must be followed by a good period and every good stretch has to be followed by a bad one. The big unknown is how long each period will last.

People often focus on an unanswerable question: When are things going to turn around? When times are good, your investments do well and you hear rumors of bigger bonuses at work this year. The question of when it'll all change seems less important, but the answer still remains uncertain. The question is much more pressing during the bad times, when investments haven't performed well or talk of an economic recession picks up. However, if you embrace the fact that the economy is *always* uncertain, the strategies in this book can help you make better decisions about your investments.

This book is filled with information on the tactics, strategies, and steps you should take with your money. But this strategy is focused on how *you* — the key player in your financial life — need to prepare for and approach your finances. The following guidelines will help you ensure that your attitude, decisions, and behavior truly support your desire to invest successfully during uncertain times.

Invest in Yourself

You are your biggest asset, thanks to your ability to earn money, and you need to protect and develop that asset. This means more than the occasional doctor's visit and a jog around the block. You can let yourself sink into a rut, afraid to move, or you can challenge yourself to move ahead and earn a new degree; seek out a new, potentially more rewarding job; or master new technologies and apply them in your professional and/or personal life.

You may also need to retool your physical plant, so to speak — losing weight, improving your focus and energy level with exercise, or budgeting for additions to your wardrobe so you feel good about the way you look.

No matter your age, show a real interest in being a part of fast-paced change, or risk being considered a dinosaur (remember — they're extinct). Not only do these steps better position you for the uncertainties of life discussed in Part I, but they also help you increase your value:

✔ **Make yourself indispensable at work.** See Strategy #4 for tips about beefing up your networking efforts, sharpening your skills or adding new ones, and going back to school.

✔ **Exercise, eat well, and get enough sleep.** Strength and flexibility, proper nourishment, and a good night's sleep may increase your productivity and help to keep your mind sharp.

✔ **Be creditworthy.** For tips on improving your credit and debt, see Strategies #10 and #11.

✔ **Prioritize, prioritize, prioritize.** Making more money sounds great, but at what expense? Take some time to get your priorities in order and find the balance that works for you. Think about family, sleep, and mental and physical health.

✔ **Talk to someone.** If your finances are causing you mental and/or emotional stress — or distress — get help! A financial professional can help you take control of your finances and map out a plan for you to succeed. If financial concerns are only one of a number of issues causing you to feel overwhelmed, speaking with a counselor or other mental health professional can help lighten that load, which will make everything on your plate more manageable.

Know Your Financial Situation

It's impossible to make the best financial decisions without first understanding your current personal financial situation. You need to assess your strengths and weaknesses as well as the current economic environment. This check-up can produce anxiety — you have areas of relative strength and ones needing improvement — but that's okay. What's not okay is to avoid putting together a plan that improves the areas that need shoring up. (Part I of this book can help you assess your financial health across a range of important categories.)

If you need help with your self assessment or financial review, consider hiring a fee-only financial planner to help. Because fee-only planners don't sell products or receive commission, their advice isn't constrained to certain products and will be in your best interest. Membership organizations such as the National Association of Personal Financial Advisors (www.napfa.org) and the Garrett Planning Network (`www.garrettplanningnetwork.com`) are good resources. You can also check the Certified Financial Planner Board of Standards, Inc., (`www.cfp.net`) to make sure the planner you've selected is a CFP certificant, ensuring a minimum level of training and competency.

Strategies #9 through #15 can help you address areas that are often weak links, and Parts II and III can give you various tools and techniques you can use to make change happen. If you haven't yet thought about retirement in a concrete way, Parts V and VI offer spending and investment strategies to reduce the risk you'll outspend your resources.

Keep Your Emotions in Check

Fear and greed are two powerful emotions that influence your investment decisions for better or worse (usually for worse). Completely ignoring emotions is a tall order for most folks. Remember that although worrying is okay at times, you have to work around these powerful emotions to be a successful investor. Keep these tips in mind when managing your emotions:

- **Acknowledge your emotions.** Admit when you're feeling fearful or greedy. Only by acknowledging your feelings can you guard against their influence on your actions. You can't discount fear as an influence on your decisions until you first admit that you're afraid.

- **Don't wait for the feelings of fear or greed to go away before you act.** They may never completely vanish. This book can help you develop financial plans and strategies to guide your decision making. When your emotions surge, refer to this book to stay on course.

- **Understand how emotions fit into the economic cycle.** You probably feel best about investing when markets have been going up, up, up. The higher the recent increase, the better you may feel about putting you money in. But only people who already had their money in the market, *before* it started going up, got those big, attractive gains. They had their money in the market when it didn't feel best.

- **Remember, everyone's in the same boat.** If the economy is slowing down or contracting, it also impacts your neighbors, co-workers, other consumers, and producers. You're not being left behind while everyone else is passing you by.

- **Avoid people who try to exploit your feelings.** Turn off the financial channels. Their programming is intended to play to your emotions to keep you tuned in. If you have to watch, remember that it'll be sensationalized at times. News editors need to make the news sound exciting, even when it's really not.

- **Don't dwell on things beyond your control.** Instead, focus on what you *can* control. (See the next section.)

Control What You Can

Events that influence your personal financial situation fall into one of two categories: events that you can control and events you can't. It's important to recognize things that are out of your control, but don't dwell on their outcomes. Focus on what you can control. You have no control over the following: inflation, tax increases, stock market returns, interest rates, and what others are doing. But here's what you can control:

- ✔ How much you spend
- ✔ Your level of personal finance and investing knowledge
- ✔ Where you put your hard-earned money (see Part II for detail)
- ✔ How much risk you take (see Part III)
- ✔ How you react to what you can't control

Put Your Goals in Writing

You may have heard the old saying "If it isn't being measured, it probably won't change; and if it does change, you probably won't notice." This holds true for financial goals, too. Part IV is all about setting and achieving goals, from buying a home to raising children and preparing for retirement. Setting realistic goals is important, but it's equally important that you devise a system for tracking your progress. You'll enjoy checking off your progress as you reach your milestones.

You may be tempted to give yourself a bit too much leeway in meeting your targets, so have someone keep you on track. You'll benefit from finding an accountability coach to work with: a spouse, partner, or friend. Coaches don't need to know every intimate detail, but they do need to know the following:

- ✔ Your goal
- ✔ The info you'll be reporting
- ✔ How often you'll give them an update

Offer to do the same in return — keep it fun and get started.

Realize That This Has Happened Before (And Will Happen Again)

By Debbra Dillon, CFP

*U*ncertain economic times come and go. These times can be especially challenging if you aren't prepared for them. No one knows exactly when a major economic event will occur or what it'll look like, but if you're prepared, you stand a good chance of weathering it.

When you're preparing for uncertain economic times, understanding what's happened in the past can help. History provides clues to help you avoid common mistakes made during challenging times. So what kinds of events create uncertain economic times, and what clues do they hold for you today? This strategy takes a look at three types of events that can unexpectedly affect your financial security.

Weathering Major Economic Events

Most major economic events, such as stock market crashes, happen when a normal economic cycle gets out of balance. Have you had the experience of looking forward to an extravagant dinner, and then as soon as dinner arrives, eating until you felt you'd burst? Afterward, you regret indulging and swear you won't do it again, but after a while, you forget the uncomfortable experience and start making plans for another indulgent meal. This is how economic cycles work, too: You see periods of rapid growth often inspired by exciting technological advances. Occasionally, investors overindulge and a bubble develops. Unfortunately, when the bubble bursts, people have to suffer until things even out again.

Stock market bubbles and crashes

One of the most famous bubbles of the last century occurred in the so-called Roaring Twenties, which came to a startling end with the stock market crash of 1929. The overindulgence of credit and spending combined with wild speculation in the stock market led to the Great Depression, which lasted about ten years. Will the U.S. experience another depression like the Great Depression? Who knows, but you can prepare yourself just in case. Here's how to position yourself well:

- ✔ **Steer clear of consumer debt.** In the Great Depression, those in debt got hammered when it came time to pay up.

- ✔ **Pay your mortgage off as soon as possible.** Minimizing your mortgage debt is also a smart thing to do. Having too much debt — of any kind — puts you in jeopardy if times get really tough and you lose your income, run out of savings, and can't borrow more money.

- ✔ **Save for emergencies.** Those with cash set aside are able to roll with the punches.

- ✔ **Take advantage of future investment opportunities.** Some people took advantage of lucrative investment opportunities — believe it or not, some people actually prospered during the Great Depression.

- ✔ **Develop a broad skill set.** Jobs were extremely hard to come by during the Depression, and those with a wide range of skills had an easier time finding employment.

Although depressions are rare, stock market bubbles and ensuing crashes are not. In fact, since the end of World War II, the United States has had 12 occasions in which the stock market lost more than 20 percent of its value. But take heart; over that same period, the market gained 7,079 percent, in spite of the crashes.

Bubbles are surprisingly similar to each other. Take the dot-com bubble of the 1990s that burst in 2000. As in the 1920s, investors believed that easy riches could be had in the stock market. Internet and technology stock prices soared to dizzying heights until the bubble burst in March 2000 and the party ended. The dot-com bust didn't lead to a depression, but it did do a lot of damage to people's investments. Here's how to avoid getting hurt when a stock market bubble bursts:

- ✔ **Maintain a diversified portfolio.** Investors who were seriously injured in the tech wreck had most of their money in dot-com and technology stocks. If you have a diversified portfolio and remain invested for the long term, don't panic when a bubble bursts. Stay the course and let the market work things out.

- ✔ **Avoid the next hot investment.** Resist the urge to get caught up in the irrational exuberance of new technology.

Real estate bubbles and crashes

Bubbles aren't limited to just the stock market. The housing bubble started in 2001 as speculators fled the stock market and set their sights on real estate, sending home values up. When housing prices started to deflate, some homeowners found they owed more on their mortgage than their house was worth. As low introductory interest rates reset to higher rates, many homeowners found themselves unable to pay their mortgages. Foreclosures skyrocketed. When the bubble burst, it left a credit crisis unseen since the Great Depression. You'll know the full effects of the 2007–2008 real estate burst when you read about it in the history books. To protect you from a real estate crash, do the following:

- **Don't rely on your mortgage lender or real estate agent to tell you how much house you can afford.** Work out your budget and make sure you can afford the mortgage payment along with associated housing expenses.

- **Put at least a 10-percent (preferably 20-percent) down payment on the home.** Pass on zero–down payment financing. If you can't afford a down payment, you likely can't afford the home.

- **If you don't plan on being in a house for at least five years, don't buy one.** Rent instead. In most cases, breaking even on a home purchase takes at least five years due to the costs involved in buying and selling a home.

- **Avoid using home equity lines of credit for consumer purchases.** Use home equity lines of credit exclusively for emergency purposes.

- **Don't rely on a home equity line of credit as your sole source of emergency funds.** Keep your emergency funds in cash reserve accounts, like savings accounts or money market mutual funds. If, however, you deplete these accounts in a prolonged emergency, you can then turn to your home equity line of credit.

Rapidly rising commodity prices

Not all economic events are caused by speculative bubbles. The Arab Oil Embargo in 1973 forced gas prices to quadruple from 25 cents to over a dollar per gallon. People waited in line for gasoline for hours. The economy slipped into a recession, which led to a nasty decade of rising unemployment and double-digit inflation. Take these steps to prepare for periods of rapidly rising commodity prices:

- Consider economizing your energy use. Ride your bicycle or drive a fuel-efficient car. Invest in energy-efficient appliances in your home.

- Maintain an emergency fund to cover unexpected price increases.

- Purchase staples in bulk.

Standing Strong During Political Events

Political events are often unanticipated and shocking. Assassinations and terrorist attacks can tempt you to panic. Historically, these types of events have caused only short-term economic uncertainty. Take John F. Kennedy's assassination on November 22, 1963. The market lost 3 percent on November 22 as people panicked and sold their stock. However, on November 26, the market not only recovered that tragic day's losses but was actually up 4.5 percent. It pays to stay invested.

The September 11, 2001, terrorist attacks on the World Trade Center and the Pentagon shocked the U.S. The Dow Jones Industrial Average lost 7.1 percent in one day and by the end of the week had fallen 14.3 percent, its biggest one-week point drop in history. Fortunately, the Dow recovered its lost ground in two months. Here's how to stay safe during an unexpected political event:

- **Don't panic.** Knee-jerk reactions will almost always come back to haunt you.

- **Maintain a diversified portfolio.** This is the single best way to weather economic uncertainty.

Witnessing Global Conflicts

You may think that wars would have a negative impact on the economy, but actually, for the most part, the opposite has occurred. World War II was the most costly war in terms of government expenditures and human lives. Gearing up for and supporting the war actually produced a booming economy. The Korean War and the Persian Gulf War had similar effects, although a recession did follow the Gulf War in 1992.

On the other hand, the Vietnam War and the War on Terror have had relatively negative effects on the economy. The Vietnam War lasted for 16 years, and the average return for the S&P 500 during that time period was a dismal 3.91 percent. Likewise, the average return for the S&P 500 for 2001 through 2007 was a depressing 3.02 percent. Here's how to survive long periods of low market returns:

- Don't depend on high investment returns when planning for your retirement or other financial goals.

- Keep investing periodically throughout these periods.

- Include fixed-income investments, such as government bonds and certificates of deposit, in your portfolio.

Plan for Life's Uncertainties

* *

By Denisa Tova, CLU, ChFC, CFDP, CFP

* *

*I*t's a bright, beautiful morning, and you walk outside, feeling on top of the world. You set your coffee cup on top of the car, and you realize that the cup is slanted. Either the horizon has changed or something's wrong with your car. You look down, and suddenly you're not having such a great day. You have a flat tire.

Or it's a bright, beautiful morning, and your telephone rings. Your real estate agent tells you the property on the lake that you've wanted for years has just been put on the market. Now you're really feeling on top of the world. But a thought crosses your mind: Do you have enough money set aside? It's such short notice!

Life can throw you curves that may be frustrations or opportunities. But life doesn't always pick the best time for whatever's happening in the financial markets. In this strategy, you discover how to make sure your savings are ready — even if the market isn't.

Keep an Eye on What's Going On

For years, the market may grow with gusto and vigor and then suddenly turn south. Likewise, many of the goals that you plan for throughout your life — such as going to college, getting married, buying a house, having children, helping pay for your children's education and weddings, and at long last enjoying your retirement — may suddenly turn out to be more expensive than you thought. Other factors can increase the uncertainty of reaching your goals, too. Consider the following:

- ✔ College costs are growing at nearly twice the current inflation rate.

- ✔ Companies are cutting back on or entirely cutting out their traditional defined benefit pension plans.

- ✔ New retirees may need 70 to 80 percent or more of their current income to maintain their standard of living.

- ✔ Healthcare costs are rising at twice the rate of inflation while the median annual income for a couple drops from $48,551 to $16,770 after retirement.

✔ Social Security and Medicare both face cutting benefits at some point in the future.

✔ Unexpected events around the world can send inflation soaring at the same time the economy is slowing down or in a recession.

Good financial planning involves setting objectives, developing a plan to get from where you are to where you want to go, and then monitoring what's happening and making adjustments when needed. Monitor such things as the national economy, your local economy, your job and your employer, your family situation, and your personal life. Part of your plan should include ways to deal with unexpected situations. Stay aware at all times of how each thing you monitor affects your planning; by doing so, you're able to adjust your plan and keep heading in the right direction.

Motivate Yourself to Save and Develop a Plan

If you haven't planned ahead like you need to, it's never too late. You don't have to become a recluse, take up basket weaving, or try hang gliding to relieve your troubled mind. Nor should you just work as long as you can and hope for the best or buy a lottery ticket each week.

Do yourself a big favor by starting to plan today. Planning means that you protect your future, live comfortably, and know your options.

Practically speaking, that means that you may need to motivate yourself to save money. Think of it this way: If you lost $20 down a drain in the road, would you recover? Would your life continue? Would you starve, or would you just have to buy less ice cream and fewer DVDs? How about $100? That'd be a harder hit, but you should still be able to withstand the blow.

If you haven't thought before about what kinds of uncertainties can sabotage your financial goals or what unexpected opportunities might pop up, now's the time to start thinking about them. And now's the time to start saving your money for future contingencies rather than spending on stuff you can do without. The reality of life is that things like ice cream and DVDs are ways to throw your money down the drain. You know they're fun to have, but think about the overwhelming anxiety that can occur when something bad happens or when you're financially unprepared for a good opportunity. That anxiety far outweighs the benefits of seeing the latest movie or getting your chocolate fix.

If *saving* and *self-restraint* are words that aren't normally part of your vocabulary, you can motivate yourself to start saving and keep saving with these five steps:

1. **Adjust your attitude.**

   When you save money, think of it as buying your future.

2. **Give thought to all the life events that may be possible and decide which ones you want to be a part of your life.**

   Those life events may be starting a business, buying a house or vacation home, traveling, or doing other activities that bring balance to your life.

3. **Create two funds and start to save money for your goals.**

   Make sure you have the following funds:

   • An emergency fund (see Strategy #10 for details on a rainy-day fund)

   • A make-my-life-great fund (see Strategy #13 for more on setting goals)

4. **Build a portfolio, even if you're still in debt.**

   Why? Because you'll do whatever is necessary to keep afloat financially, so you're already motivated to pay those credit card bills. Keep paying them *and* start saving toward your life goals.

5. **Don't let anything intimidate you.**

   It doesn't matter how small the amounts you save seem at first. Remember that they'll grow over time.

 If all the details of planning seem overwhelming, seek professional help. You can find a Certified Financial Planner in your area by searching at www.cfp.net or by going through the Garrett Planning Network at www.garrettplanningnetwork.com.

Finally, remember that putting money aside and into your checking, savings, or money market accounts isn't enough (for more on cash investments, see Strategy #16). These accounts are fine to park cash that you may need in the short-term, say within three to five years, but they're poor choices to fund retirement needs 10, 20, or even 30 years in the future. To make all your financial sacrifices worth the trouble, you need to invest the money you set aside in one or more portfolios (depending on the length of time to each goal). This book discusses investment types and how to build a portfolio in Parts II, III, IV, and V.

Protect Your Ability to Earn Income

By Gwen Gepfert

*I*n today's uncertain economy, job changes are sometimes forced on people when companies go out of business, lay off employees due to cost savings measures, or just downsize due to competitive pressures. Take the following quiz to see whether you're prepared to face the next round of cuts:

- ✔ Have you conducted a recent (and honest!) assessment of your strengths and weaknesses at work?

- ✔ Have you recently reviewed your job description to make sure that you're exceeding in your job responsibilities?

- ✔ Do you hear about jobs that are available in other companies but aren't advertised?

- ✔ When your co-workers leave your company to take a new job, do they recommend you for any open positions in their new company?

- ✔ Have you found easy ways to gain further education or training in your chosen career?

If you didn't answer *yes* to all these questions, perhaps you're not as secure in your current job as you imagine or as well prepared to make a job change. Your career and financial goals are too important to leave in the hands of your employer. Don't let yourself be surprised or unprepared. Instead, concentrate on meeting the recommendations in this strategy.

Make Yourself Indispensible

No one is 100 percent indispensable, but you should strive to become an employee that your company would have difficulty replacing. Not only does this strategy reduce the likelihood of your receiving a layoff notification, but it also puts you in the driver's seat in terms of potential promotions, raises, and other workforce benefits. Here are some ways to become *almost* irreplaceable:

- ✔ **Take initiative.** Take on new responsibilities outside of your current job description. Bring your manager solutions, not new problems. Jump in to help your company when staff vacancies occur.

✔ **Keep your skills up-to-date.** Stay current in your field of knowledge. Read industry magazines and reports, monitor pending legislation and technology advancements, and learn new software that can make you more efficient.

✔ **Develop an impeccable reputation of dependability.** Do your homework and be prepared for meetings and projects. Meet deadlines. Be punctual. Take responsibility for your actions and mistakes to highlight your professional integrity.

✔ **Be a considerate and positive team player.** Maintain a positive attitude and don't keep company with complainers or naysayers. Be nice to your co-workers and support them. Prove yourself to be trustworthy and someone for inexperienced members of your organization to look up to.

It takes a lot of hard work to establish a positive reputation, but it's fairly easy to develop a negative one. Pay attention to how others perceive you and listen openly to performance feedback. Take prompt measures to fix any issues that have resulted in your being viewed as less than a model employee.

Boost Your Networking Skills

One crucial skill during uncertain economic times is your ability to network. Professional relationships can be a great source of referrals to potential job openings. Don't let shyness get in your way of building a strong list of personal contacts. Follow these simple steps:

✔ **Always be open to meeting new people.** Start conversations with strangers, and don't forget to exchange business cards. Join professional organizations and go to meetings to develop a wider range of contacts.

✔ **Keep your contact information organized and easily accessible.** You never know when you may need to ask someone to make an introduction for you into a company. Consider creating a database or special file of contacts. Be sure to keep in touch so you can stay abreast of changes in their career as well as contact information.

✔ **Never burn bridges when you leave a job.** Previous co-workers or supervisors can provide great leads to potential jobs as well as provide informal personal references.

✔ **Write articles for trade or industry periodicals.** Not only is it fun to see your name in print, but you also increase your professional profile within your industry.

✔ **Remember that networking is a two-way street.** Your professional relationships can be a great asset to you throughout your career, but don't drop the ball when someone asks you for help.

✔ **Don't forget to thank your contacts for their help.** A personalized thank-you note goes a long way to show your appreciation for the help you received. Remember that you may need their help again someday.

Many open jobs are filled by word of mouth. Most employers are more comfortable hiring applicants who are recommended by trusted employees or partners versus hiring qualified candidates who just walk in from the street. Make sure your contacts are recommending you for these jobs!

Even if you're content in your job, always keep your eyes open for new and better opportunities. Many of the best career opportunities come when you're least expecting them. In case you want to respond to a sudden opportunity, make sure your resume is up to date and relevant. (*Resumes For Dummies,* 5th Edition, written by Joyce Lain Kennedy and published by Wiley, contains many helpful hints for preparing your resume.)

Broaden Your Skill Set

Today's most effective employees don't allow life's circumstances to get in the way of their full income potential. These individuals embrace the concept of lifelong learning, finding this journey both rewarding and enjoyable. Make a conscious effort to develop your own plan for continuing to learn and grow in your job. These simple steps allow you to be better prepared for your next job opportunity:

✔ **Conduct a personal skill review.** Check your last company performance evaluation and make sure you're actively improving noted areas of weakness. Compare your skills to those required by new jobs you may pursue — the Internet is a great resource for conducting both skill and salary research.

✔ **Develop a career path.** Create a roadmap that can take you from your current job to your dream job. Break it into a series of realistic baby steps. Document the skills required to take you from today's job to tomorrow's.

✔ **Capitalize on your natural skills and interests.** When people do what they love, success becomes a natural byproduct. Build on your strengths by finding ways to improve your skills in your current position.

✔ **Act now, while you're still employed.** Having the right skills and qualifications for any position you apply for is essential, so start developing those new skills or get the training while you're still employed.

↙ **Take advantage of easily accessible training tools.** There are many simple ways to gain additional training; you just need to look for them. They include the following:

- Reading business books and training manuals

- Watching training videos

- Attending industry seminars and conferences

- Researching industry topics on the Internet

- Learning from a mentor

- Attending adult education classes

- Downloading podcasts to your MP3 player and listening to them in your car or while you exercise

Go Back to School

Whether you're going back to school to gain a competitive edge in the job market, obtaining additional education to keep current with changes in your field, or working toward your dream job, have a plan to choose the right school:

1. **Select a certification or degree that's widely recognized.**

2. **Pick an accredited school.**

3. **Decide how you want to attend classes.**

4. **Leave no stone unturned when looking for financial assistance.**

Ask your human resources office whether your company offers a tuition assistance program or whether you'll be reimbursed for all or a portion of your tuition. Visit your school's financial aid officer to see whether you're eligible for any low cost loans, assistanceships, fellowships, scholarships, or grants. Research private grants or scholarships. Depending on your family income level, you may qualify for the Hope Credit or Lifetime Learning Credit (see `www.irs.ustreas.gov/taxtopics/tc605.html`). Also prepare a free application for federal student aid at `www.fafsa.ed.gov`; it can't hurt to give it a try!

#5

Assess Your Medical Insurance

· ·

By Helga Cuthbert, CFP

· ·

C hoosing the right healthcare insurance coverage can be daunting and complex. The many different models all have unique features. To get the coverage you need at the best value, assess your situation, know the jargon of the industry and the plans offered, and then determine what works best for you.

Know the Lingo

Health plan documents are full of jargon, but don't be intimidated. Here are some helpful definitions of terms you may come across:

- **Cap:** The maximum amount the insurance company will pay over a lifetime
- **Claim form:** A form that either you or your healthcare provider must complete and send to the insurance company to receive payment for services rendered
- **Coinsurance:** Percentage of the healthcare bill you have to pay after the deductible
- **Co-payment (or co-pay):** Out-of-pocket charge for a visit to the doctor or hospital
- **Covered expenses:** Those expenses the insurance company agrees to pay for; not all expenses are covered by the plan
- **Customary fee:** The amount most healthcare providers charge for a particular service; sometimes called *usual and customary*
- **Deductible:** Out-of-pocket expenses before the insurance plan begins paying
- **Exclusion:** Services not covered by the insurance company
- **In-network:** The insurance company selects this list of healthcare providers you can choose from to avoid higher costs
- **Maximum out-of-pocket expenses:** The most you have to pay in a year for deductibles and coinsurance

- ✔ **Out-of-network:** Licensed healthcare providers who aren't on the in-network list
- ✔ **Premium:** Annual cost of the insurance coverage
- ✔ **Third-party payer:** Anyone, other than you, who pays for your care

Examine the Types of Healthcare Plans

The two basic types of health insurance plans are traditional care and managed care. The following sections give you the details you need to distinguish between the two.

Traditional care plans

Traditional care insurance is also known as *fee for services* or *indemnity plans.* Traditional plans have the following features:

- ✔ You generally pay higher out-of-pocket expenses at the time of service, including expenses up to a set deductible limit.
- ✔ After meeting deductible limits, you share the bill with the insurance company. For example, you may pay 20 percent while the insurance company pays 80 percent. You continue sharing the bill until you reach your maximum out-of-pocket expenses; then the insurance company pays 100 percent of your expenses up to its cap.
- ✔ You may be responsible for keeping track of expenses and submitting requests for reimbursement from the insurance company.
- ✔ The insurance company pays for only usual and customary expenses. Any additional charges are your responsibility.
- ✔ Not all insurance companies offer wellness or preventative care with this type of plan.
- ✔ The insurance company usually has few restrictions on which medical providers, including specialists, you use.
- ✔ If your plan is considered a catastrophic or high-deductible major medical health plan, it will have lower annual premiums than a plan with a lower deductible.

Traditional plans are becoming increasingly scarce as insurance companies move to the managed care plans outlined in the following section.

Managed care plans

Managed care health plans involve an arrangement between the insurance company and a select network of healthcare providers. These providers are referred to as *in-network* providers. Most of these plans cover wellness care or preventative care — such as well-baby care, doctor visits, and mammograms — at varying levels.

Three basic categories of managed care are *Preferred Provider (PPO), Point of Service (POS),* and *Health Maintenance Organizations (HMO).*

PPO

A PPO allows you the most flexibility to choose your healthcare providers within the managed care options. For that flexibility you or your employer will pay higher costs for insurance than you would with a POS or HMO.

Following are some features of PPO plans:

- ✔ Although your co-pay is usually small, you may have deductibles. If you go outside the network, your co-pay is generally higher and you're likely to pay a larger portion of the bill yourself.

- ✔ You can usually see a specialist without getting preapproval from your primary care physician, as long as your specialist is in-network. Going to a specialist out-of-network raises any co-pay amount and your total costs.

- ✔ If you go out-of-network, you may have to submit claims forms.

POS

POS plans are similar to PPO plans, but you have to choose an in-network primary care physician who manages your care and refers you to a specialist when needed.

Following are some additional features of POS plans:

- ✔ Insurance premiums for POS plans are typically lower than with a PPO and higher than an HMO.

- ✔ If you choose to see a specialist without being referred by your primary care physician, you pay more in out-of-pocket expenses.

- ✔ You may have to file your own claims forms unless you're being treated by your primary care physician.

- ✔ Out-of-network providers can be much more expensive. You'll likely pay 10 percent more out-of-pocket to see an out-of-network provider than you would if you went in-network.

HMO

HMO plans are designed to provide you with quality healthcare at the lowest price. To manage costs, HMOs drastically limit your options for healthcare providers. But they do value preventative healthcare. They realize that prevention is cheaper than treatment. Following are some HMO features:

✔ They usually have the lowest premiums.

✔ These plans are least flexible in the selection of service providers.

✔ Patients must choose an in-network primary care physician who controls referrals. You can't refer yourself to a specialist or go out-of-network without paying the full cost of the service. And think twice before running to the emergency room. If the reason for your visit isn't deemed an emergency by your HMO, you could get stuck with the bill.

Ask Yourself Some Questions

Now that you know the ins and outs of the various plans, here are some questions to ask before choosing a plan for you and your family:

✔ **Do you currently have doctors you want to continue visiting, and do you want the freedom of choosing other doctors if additional care is required?** If so, avoid HMOs altogether. PPO and POS plans can work, but traditional care plans are best because they allow maximum flexibility.

✔ **Are you aware of any upcoming medical events, like surgery or starting a family?** If you're thinking of switching plans, make sure preexisting problems or maternity costs are covered. Find out whether there's a waiting period before coverage begins.

✔ **Do you have children entering college?** Again, HMOs may not be your best option. Check your PPO and POS plans to see whether any physicians and hospitals in the college area are acceptable to the network. Out-of-network expenses can be prohibitive.

✔ **Do you plan on having periodic wellness checkups?** HMOs are your best bet financially because wellness checkups are usually encouraged with no additional co-pays. Traditional care plans often don't cover regular checkups, so all costs must come out-of-pocket until you reach the full deductible. PPO and POS plans usually require a co-payment for regular checkups, flu shots, and blood tests.

✔ **Do you hate filling out claims and keeping receipts?** A managed care plan is probably best for you, assuming that you're willing to stay in-network. Traditional care plans are often reimbursable plans in which you pay costs upfront and then submit paperwork for reimbursement.

#6

Assess Your Disability Insurance

By Neil Vannoy, MBA

Disability insurance (DI) can help alleviate the financial burden by replacing a portion of your income if you become disabled. Be prepared for the uncertain economic times that could result from a disability by taking time to assess your DI coverage.

Disability insurance protects your ability to earn a living. Especially in uncertain economic times, don't underestimate the importance of insuring your paycheck.

The Nuts and Bolts of Disability Insurance

Following is a rundown of what you need to know about disability insurance:

- **What's covered:** Most DI policies cover disabilities that result from accidents, though some also cover disabilities resulting from illness. Because younger people are more likely to become disabled from an accident and older people are more likely to become disabled from an illness, you need to know what kind of coverage your policy provides.

- **How much coverage:** Benefits are usually between 40 and 70 percent of your income. Why don't insurance companies cover a higher percentage of your income? Well, how much incentive would you have to recover and return to work if you could earn the same amount watching TV?

- **Qualifying for payments:** Before you can collect benefits from your DI policy, you have to satisfy the *elimination period,* or waiting period. This is the insurance company's way of making sure you're really disabled before they go through the trouble of sending you money. The elimination period varies with each policy. It also works like a deductible, keeping premiums lower.

✓ **How long payments last:** DI policies can have either a short- or long-term benefit period. *Short-term policies* usually pay benefits for three to six months, although some provide benefits for up to two years. The elimination period for short-term policies generally ranges from 1 to 14 days.

The benefit period for *long-term policies* can range from a few years to the rest of your life. The most popular benefit period for long-term policies is *to age 65.* The elimination period for long-term policies ranges from 30 to 365 days.

Look Under the Hood of a DI Policy

Here are some details to pay attention to — you can find them in the policy itself or as riders (optional amendments added to the policy).

Defining disability

So who decides whether you're disabled? The insurance company, of course, so it's important to know the definition of disability that's in your policy:

✓ **Own occupation:** By this definition, you're disabled if you can't perform the duties of your usual job, even if you could do some other kind of work.

✓ **Any occupation:** You're considered disabled only if you can't work at any job that you're qualified for by education, training, and experience.

✓ **Total disability:** You're disabled only if you're unable to work at any job at all. Yikes! You may be able to operate the timer on a deep fryer at a fast food restaurant, but would you *want* to? Try to get another definition of disability in your DI policy.

Tacking on riders

You may want to consider putting some of these additional provisions on your policy:

✓ **Cost of living adjustment (COLA):** This rider increases your benefit of your policy with inflation up to a maximum that you elect, generally from 4 to 10 percent. The benefit continues to increase every year that you remain disabled. This rider is extremely important, especially when you're younger.

- ✔ **Automatic increase:** This rider usually allows for a total benefit increase of 20 to 25 percent over the first three to five years of the policy. Your premiums go up with the benefit.

- ✔ **Future increase option (FIO):** If you qualify for only a small amount of disability coverage now but expect to be making big bucks later in your career, you can guarantee that you can increase your coverage later, regardless of your health, by selecting the future increase option. This rider allows benefit increases — usually up to age 55 — by providing proof of higher income. You won't have to prove insurability to get the increase!

- ✔ **Social Security offset:** This rider supplements your disability benefit if Social Security doesn't pay the Maximum Family Benefit and if no benefits are payable under a State Disability Insurance program. It also supplements your disability benefit if Social Security pays no benefits and benefits are payable under a State Disability Insurance program.

- ✔ **Waiver of premium:** This rider waives any premiums while you're disabled. There's a three-month elimination period, but premiums that were paid during the elimination period are generally refunded.

- ✔ **Residual benefit (partial disability):** This benefit allows you to return to work part-time while continuing to receive a portion of your benefits. Most policies require a minimum loss in earnings (such as a 20-percent reduction) to qualify for residual benefits.

Choosing renewability provisions

All DI policies contain renewability provisions that explain how your coverage will continue. Most policies are one of the following:

- ✔ **Guaranteed renewable:** The insurance company will continue to renew the policy, but the premiums can be increased for an entire group of policyholders (for instance it may be increased by state or occupational class).

- ✔ **Non-cancelable and guaranteed renewable:** The insurance company can't cancel or raise the premiums.

- ✔ **Conditionally renewable:** Policies can be renewed at the insurer's discretion. Unless you believe your insurance company has a big heart and loves you, you should stay away from these policies!

Purchase Your Policies

Many employers offer group coverage without a medical exam if you sign up during the initial enrollment period. Some preexisting conditions may be excluded from group coverage for up to two years. Group DI is generally less expensive than an individual policy because most employers pay a portion of the premium. Some plans have a *portability option* that allows you to convert your group coverage to an individual policy when you leave your job.

You can purchase individual disability insurance directly from an insurance company or through an insurance broker. Unlike group insurance, you have to go through underwriting to get the policy. One of the greatest benefits of individual DI is that changes in your health, employment, or occupational class don't affect your coverage after the policy is issued. Even if you become uninsurable in the future or switch to a risky occupation, your individual policy remains in force as long as you keep paying the premiums.

The higher the chance you could become disabled and the larger the benefit, the higher the premium. To see all the factors that go into it, check out the following chart:

Factor	*How It Affects the Premium*
Age	Premiums increase with age.
Gender	Women are at greater risk of disability than men, so their premiums are higher.
Occupation	Riskier occupations have higher premiums.
Elimination period	You get your money faster with a shorter elimination period, but you also pay a higher premium.
Benefit amount	The more the potential benefit amount, the higher the premium.
Riders	Adding riders increases the premium.
Definition of disability	Policies with more favorable definitions of disability (for instance, own occupation) have higher premiums than policies with less favorable definitions.
Renewability provision	The more guarantees about renewability, the higher the premium. (For instance, a non-cancelable and guaranteed renewable policy has a higher premium than a conditionally renewable policy.)

Don't forget about taxes! If you pay the premiums for your policy, the benefits you receive are generally tax-free. If your employer paid part or all of the premiums, part or all of the benefits are taxable.

#7

Assess Your Long-Term Care Insurance

By Louise Schroeder, CFP

*I*nsurance policies probably aren't on your list of fun reading material. They're hard to understand, and as a result, very few people read them or know what to expect until they file a claim. But with long-term care (LTC) insurance, understanding the policy terms is critical to help you plan for the uncertainty of your later years.

Understand the Basics: General Policy Information

Check your insurance company's financial rating, not only when you buy but also every year thereafter. Selecting a financially strong insurance company increases the likelihood of benefit payments when you need them, especially during periods of economic uncertainty. Businesses that rate insurance companies include A.M. Best, Moody's, Standard & Poor's, Fitch, and Weiss. Look for a rating that's strong, excellent, or superior.

Also know whether your policy is tax-qualified or non-tax-qualified. Depending on your age each year, the premiums for a tax-qualified policy may be partially or fully deductible as an itemized deduction on your income tax return; also, your benefit payments aren't considered taxable income. Both of these benefits can save you money. Policies sold today are generally tax-qualified, but the IRS hasn't ruled on older, non-tax-qualified policies, so it's uncertain whether their premiums and benefits receive the same treatment.

Likewise, make sure your policy is renewable. Policies sold today are renewable, but if you have an older policy, ask about this.

Also ask what your options are if the insurance company increases your premium and you can no longer afford it. Many companies have increased premiums on one or more existing policies. Although you may purchase a policy from a company that has never raised premiums, you have no guarantee that it won't happen in the future. Ask whether premiums will be waived while you receive benefits.

Consider whether you could afford the premium if it were to increase by 30 percent or more. Also, ask how you'd pay if you encounter financial difficulty. Unless you choose to pay premiums over a shorter period of time, such as ten years or until age 65, you'll pay premiums until you start receiving benefits. Shorter premium payment periods greatly increase the premium paid.

Be clear on where your policy covers care. Most current policies cover care in a skilled nursing facility, an assisted living facility, a home (yours or that of someone you live with), an adult day care facility, a hospice home, or other living arrangements listed in the policy. Continuing care retirement communities include independent living, assisted living, and a skilled nursing unit, so you want a policy that offers comprehensive coverage.

If you plan to remain at home for as long as possible, be familiar with your policy's respite care benefit. Check how many days per year are allowed for your caregiver to take a break, and what your options are for where respite care can be provided. If you do have to move to a care facility, know the number of days your policy will pay for reserving your room if you have to be in a medical facility or if you'll be temporarily absent for other reasons.

Know How You Qualify for Benefits

The age of your LTC insurance policy determines the requirements for receiving benefits. Policies issued after 2000 generally require that you need substantial assistance with at least two of six activities of daily living, which include eating, bathing, dressing, transferring (from a bed to a chair or wheelchair), toileting (using the toilet), and managing incontinence.

Otherwise, you must need substantial supervision due to cognitive impairment. Policies issued earlier than 2000 often have more lenient requirements.

The definitions of *substantial assistance* and *substantial supervision* are important, too. These definitions vary widely in older policies and are much more consistent in newer policies. If these definitions don't appear in your policy, contact the company.

Review Policy Conditions

Know who will write your plan of care. Many policies specify a certified home health practitioner of your choosing. Some policies make a care coordinator available. This person is usually paid directly or indirectly by the insurance company.

Some insurance companies offer incentives, such as a reduced or waived waiting period, if you use their care coordinator. And some companies actually penalize you if you don't use their care coordinator by reducing certain benefits or eliminating a benefit. Be sure to understand the terms of your policy. If incentives are offered, find out what the additional premium would be if they were added as a rider. The insurance company has to make up these costs somewhere.

Select and Purchase Benefits

Your selection of LTC insurance benefits should be a part of a detailed long-term care plan. The amount of the daily (or weekly or monthly) benefit you select should consider what services the policy does or doesn't cover and where you receive those services. Your choice should also factor in other resources you will (or won't) have. See Strategy #63 for more information.

Understand benefit payment

Know how much of your daily benefit will be paid. Here are some common options:

- ✔ **Payment of the full benefit regardless of the actual expenses incurred:** Newer policies may offer this as a rider that increases your premium. The trade-off is less use of your resources in the future.

- ✔ **Payment of actual expenses up to the amount of the benefit:** If actual expenses are less, the difference stays in the policy and may increase the amount of time over which benefits will be paid.

- ✔ **Payment of the going rate for the service being billed:** Find out how the going rate is determined. Is it the rate for the same service within the same care facility? Within the town, city, state, or region? The danger is a benefit less than the actual expense incurred.

The length of time you choose to receive benefits is important. Most policies offer benefit periods ranging from just one year up to as long as lifetime. The longer the time period, the larger the premium. However, the premium difference for a ten-year policy versus a lifetime policy is usually fairly small. Some policies may divide the benefits period into a specified number of years of care at home and a specified number of years in a facility. You have more flexibility with a benefit period that covers unlimited care in all places.

Another important benefit is the *waiting period.* After you need care, this is how many days you wait before expenses are covered by your benefits. It's similar to a deductible on other types of insurance. Waiting periods can run from 0 to 365 days or longer. The longer the period, the lower your premium. The higher inflation rate for long-term care may make a shorter waiting period a wise choice.

To make a more-informed decision, compare extra premium payments over the number of years until you may need long-term care to the cost of 30 or 60 days of care today inflated over the same time period.

Maintain flexibility

For maximum flexibility and control, be sure the benefit amount is the same whether you receive care at home, in an assisted-living residence, or in a skilled-nursing residence. Some policies offer a 100-percent benefit for care in a skilled-nursing home and a reduced amount for care in your home. This factor may force a move to a care facility sooner than necessary.

Some policies have separate waiting periods for care at home, in an assisted-living residence, and at a skilled nursing residence. Be sure you have to meet the waiting period only once during your lifetime. This applies to situations when you may receive care for a while and then not need care for a period of time.

Consider Inflation Protection

Long-term care insurance is something you may not use for many years, so consider inflation protection. Policies generally include this as a rider for an additional premium. Common benefits include the following:

- ✔ **Simple inflation protection:** Your daily benefit and total benefit amounts increase each year by a percentage that's applied to the original amount.

- ✔ **Compound inflation protection:** Your benefit increases by a percentage each year that's applied to the amount of the past year's benefit. That means benefits will rise higher than with single inflation protection.

- ✔ **Additional purchase inflation protection:** You have an option to purchase additional benefit *increments* periodically at prevailing rates for your age. Be sure you understand all conditions related to accepting or not accepting the increase in benefit.

Assess Your Life Insurance

By Neil Vannoy, MBA

*O*ne of the most uncertain times for a family can be after the unexpected death of a loved one — especially someone the family depended on for financial support. Reviewing your life insurance coverage can help ensure your loved ones are protected if something happens to you.

Calculate Needed Coverage

Two simple methods to estimating your life insurance needs are the income replacement approach and the needs approach.

Income replacement approach

The income replacement approach to estimating life insurance needs has you predict how much you'll earn from now until you retire. Here's the formula:

Life insurance needs = annual income × years until retirement

For example, suppose Gail is 35 years old and plans on retiring in 30 years at age 65. She currently earns $65,000 per year. Gail's life insurance needs = $1,950,000 (or $65,000 × 30).

Although the income replacement approach is great for a rough estimate, it doesn't account for raises you may receive or for inflation.

Needs approach

The needs approach, which takes into account the short- and long-term needs of your beneficiaries, is more accurate than the income replacement approach and is the method used by most professionals. Here's the formula:

Life insurance needs = money required for short- and long-term needs − available financial resources

When using this approach, be as accurate as possible. Inflation will affect the future value of your beneficiaries' needs. Consider contacting a fee-only advisor if you want help using the needs approach.

Compare Current Life Insurance Coverage to Your Calculated Need

After you know how much life insurance coverage you need, compare that amount to your current coverage. If you're currently underinsured, you have two options:

✔ **Replace your current life insurance policy (or policies) with a single policy.** Most life insurance policies offer *breakpoints* (discounts) when you purchase large amounts of coverage, usually making it less expensive to have one large policy rather than several small ones.

✔ **Buy an additional policy.** The cost of insurance increases as you age, so in some cases, purchasing an additional policy may be less expensive than replacing an old policy.

If you discover you have too much coverage, consider the following:

✔ **Think about your future needs.** If you foresee new kids, debts, or big raises on the horizon, or if your health has changed, you may want to hang on to what you have.

✔ **If you're sure you don't need all your life insurance, you can usually reduce or simply cancel a policy.** If you have a term policy, contact the agent about reducing the coverage or just stop paying the premium. If you do need part of the coverage, compare the cost of the reduced policy to your options on the market.

✔ **If you have a permanent policy — either whole life or universal life — ask your agent for the net surrender value.** This is the amount of your cash value that you get to keep after surrender charges. If you're reducing coverage, there may still be a charge to your cash value, even though you're keeping the policy. You may find that you're better off keeping the policy, at least until the surrender charges no longer apply.

If you decide to replace an existing life insurance policy, never cancel your existing policy until you've obtained replacement insurance. Additionally, each state requires disclosure forms to anyone replacing existing life insurance, so read them carefully.

Pick the Right Type of Life Insurance for Your Situation

There are two types of life insurance policies: term and permanent. Think *term* for a temporary need and *permanent* for needs that'll last for your lifetime.

Term life insurance

Term life insurance covers a certain period of time, typically 10, 15, 20, or 30 years. Consider matching the term of the policy to specific milestones, such as when children leave home, when college is paid for, or when you retire. You pay for the policy for the entire period. At the end of the term, the policy expires, just like auto or homeowner's insurance. (For a higher premium, some term policies will return all premiums paid if no benefits are paid during the entire term.)

Term coverage costs less than permanent because it's temporary and very few policies actually result in claims (that is, most are cancelled or expire). The lower cost of term insurance makes it a great choice if you have a limited budget and need a lot of coverage, but you don't need permanent coverage.

Because term insurance expires, you may want a policy that allows you to renew the policy for an additional term or to switch to a permanent policy before the policy terminates:

- *Renewable term insurance* allows you to renew the policy at the end of the term without providing proof of insurability, although the premiums will increase because you'll be renewing at a higher age.

- *Non-renewable term insurance* is less expensive than renewable term insurance because it automatically expires at the end of the term.

- *Convertible term insurance* allows you to convert term insurance to a permanent policy before the end of the term. Premiums on the permanent policy are based on your age when you convert. This is a great way to secure low-cost coverage now and have the option to switch to a permanent insurance later.

- *Non-convertible term insurance* is less expensive than convertible term insurance because it doesn't give you the right to convert it to a permanent policy.

Permanent life insurance

Permanent life insurance doesn't expire after a specific term, making it a good choice if you want to leave money to your kids, cover estate taxes, fund a charity, or ensure additional financial security for your loved ones. Permanent policies include an investment portion, referred to as the *cash value.* Premiums on permanent policies are higher than term premiums. A portion of each premium covers the cost of the life insurance and other policy expenses; the rest is credited to the cash value.

The life insurance cost is low at first, so most of the premium will be credited to the cash value in the early years. Less and less of the premium is credited to cash value as the cost of insurance increases with age. In most cases, if you pay enough premiums into your policy over a long time period, the cash value will be large enough to cover future premiums. Table 8-1 shows the three primary types of permanent life insurance policies and compares some of their features.

Table 8-1		Permanent Life Insurance Policies
Policy Type	*Premiums*	*Returns on Investment*
Whole life	Level premiums for life	Similar to long-term bond returns
Universal life (UL)	Can increase, decrease, and even skip premiums	Similar to money market investments or 3- to 5-year U.S. Treasury bonds
Variable universal life (VUL)	Can increase, decrease, and even skip premiums	Feature a separate account in which you choose among subaccounts, similar to mutual funds; returns depend on what you select, though additional fees for subaccount managers make costs in a VUL higher than in other permanent policies

For most permanent policies, you can borrow against the cash value; any loans outstanding at time of death are deducted from the proceeds. UL policies allow you to withdraw from your cash value with no interest charges.

Unlike whole life policies, UL policies are completely transparent, meaning that the cost of insurance, expenses, and investment earnings are disclosed. And you can change the face value. Decreasing the face value is simple, but increasing the policy requires proof of insurability. In addition, you can select between two death benefit options:

> ✔ **Option 1 (or A):** The death benefit remains level.
>
> ✔ **Option 2 (or B):** The death benefit increases with the cash value.

Permanent policies are complex, so be sure to work with an agent who can help you understand the policy type that's best for your situation.

Purchase Your Life Insurance

Calculate the amount of life insurance coverage you need, determine whether to increase your current coverage, and pick the best type of policy for your needs. Now it's time to actually get the coverage. You can choose between an individual or group policy.

Opt into a group policy

Most employers provide group life insurance without *underwriting* (a medical exam to show evidence of insurability). In fact, employers can provide up to $50,000 of life insurance as a tax-free benefit to employees. Group insurance is a great option if you have health problems that would keep you from being approved for an individual policy.

Most group life insurance policies can be converted to individual policies without proof of good health when or if you leave your job, but a converted policy may be more expensive than an individual policy because you don't have to prove insurability.

Go it alone with an individual policy

Individual policies are purchased directly from a life insurance company or through an insurance broker. Unlike group insurance, you can select the insurance company, the policy, and the coverage amount.

One of the greatest benefits of individual policies is portability. You don't have to worry about losing coverage if you change jobs. And changes in your health don't affect your coverage after the policy is issued. Consider an individual policy for the bulk of your life insurance needs to ensure continued coverage regardless of changes in your employment or health. Use employer-provided group life insurance to supplement your coverage.

Take Stock of Your Current Financial Picture

· ·

By Cheryl Krueger

· ·

*F*inding a good path to your destination is difficult if you don't know where you're starting. During uncertain economic times, one of the first steps to meeting your major financial goals is to find out where you are now. A net worth statement is a great tool to find out where you are financially. As soon as you know where you are, you can compare that to where you want to be.

Prepare a Net Worth Statement

You may think of what you own and what you owe as the most important parts of your financial life, but it's the combination of the two that truly matters. If you have $1 million in assets, that sounds like a lot. But what if you also owe $930,000 in mortgages, student loans, and credit card debt? The difference between your assets and your liabilities is your *net worth,* which is what gives you stability in times of financial uncertainty.

You can think of your current net worth statement as the You Are Here sticker on your financial map. Your net worth statement summarizes what you own, what you owe, and what would be left if you paid off everything you owed. *Assets* include money, investments, your house and furniture, your car, other real estate, and anything else you own. *Liabilities* include your mortgage, car loan, other loans, what you owe on your credit cards or other accounts, and any other amounts you owe to others. Here's how to find your net worth:

Net worth = assets – liabilities

To meet many of your financial goals, you need to increase your net worth, either by increasing the amount of assets you have or by reducing your liabilities. A regular review of your net worth statement tells you a lot about how you're progressing. For example, you'll be able to see the following:

✔ If you're increasing your assets through saving or decreasing your assets through spending

✔ Whether your invested assets are growing at the rate you expect

✔ How you're progressing toward eliminating your debt

✔ Whether you're drawing down your assets too quickly during retirement or whether you're able to afford that month-long European cruise after all

Preparing the net worth statement isn't difficult; it just takes a bit of time and access to your financial statements. If you use personal finance software like Quicken or Microsoft Money, much of your net worth statement is available to you already. Figure 9-1 shows a sample net worth statement.

Net Worth Statement

Date: _____

Assets	Balance	Liabilities	Balance
Cash		Credit card _____	_____
Checking Accounts	_____	Credit card _____	_____
Savings Accounts	_____	Credit card _____	_____
Money Market Accounts		Auto Loan(s)	_____
		Student Loan(s)	_____
Investments		Mortgage	_____
CDs	_____	HELOC	_____
Mutual funds	_____	Personal loans you owe	_____
Stocks, bonds, etc.	_____		
Employer savings plans (e.g., 401(k), 403(b), etc.)	_____		
Value of employer pension(s)	_____		
IRAs, Roth IRAs, etc.	_____		
		Total Liabilities	_____
Other assets			
Home	_____		
Personal Property	_____		
Auto	_____		
Life insurance cash value	_____		
Business interest	_____	**Total Net Worth** _____
Total Assets	_____		

Figure 9-1: A sample net worth statement.

Use the Net Worth Statement to Reach Your Goals

Tracking your net worth over a period of time can help you weather the ups and downs of an uncertain economy. By looking at the big picture, you don't get as discouraged when an investment stumbles if other investments are still gaining in value. Knowing that a bump in the road doesn't mean you'll never reach your goal can help get you back on track to meeting your long-term financial goals.

How does this work? Don't simply complete one net worth statement and call it a day. Here's how to look at your net worth:

1. **Commit to how frequently you'll calculate your net worth.**

   This can be quarterly, semiannually, or annually. More frequently than quarterly is overkill; less frequently than annually may put you far off course when you do review your position.

2. **Calculate your initial net worth.**

3. **Calculate your net worth at the next calculation period.**

4. **Compare the changes in assets, liabilities, and overall net worth.**

   Are you getting closer to your goals or farther away from them? Make it a point to understand the general direction of each category. Are your assets lower now because your investments are down with the market? Or are your investments down while the market is up? Are you spending more than you're earning and depleting your assets to cover your living expenses?

5. **Identify where you have control over improving your financial direction.**

6. **Plan actions to increase your net worth before the next review period.**

Tracking your net worth periodically through the ups and downs in the economy can help you to keep from losing sight of the financial progress you're making.

Assess Your Current Location

So where are you on the financial roadmap? Knowing where you are and how you're progressing toward your goals of building assets or paying down debt helps you focus on your financial resources and obligations. Consider each of the following three levels and find out which one best describes your financial situation.

Level 1: Shaky

Are you always feeling off-balance in your financial life? You're at the Shaky level if one or more of these statements apply to you:

✔ Your employment or retirement income sources don't provide regular and sustainable income.

✔ You're unable to save any part of your income.

✔ You need to use credit to provide for regular living expenses (food, rent or house payment, and so on).

✔ You have significant debt payments.

✔ Your net worth is decreasing year to year.

If you're Shaky, it's difficult to weather any financial environment, let alone an uncertain one. Shaky individuals need to either increase their income or decrease their expenses, fast. Sometimes, you may need to take an extreme action to increase your financial stability, such as selling your home to produce a more manageable housing expense; selling a nice but too-expensive car; getting a second job; or going back to work if you've taken time off. Pay particular attention to Strategy #4 and Strategy #11.

Level 2: Stable

Stable individuals feel comfortable about today but may not be prepared for any changes in the future. If you're a Stable individual, many of these statements describe you:

✔ You have regular and sustainable income.

✔ You're able to break even or even save a little every month.

✔ You have auto and homeowner's (or renter's) insurance but no other significant insurance.

✔ You don't have significant amounts of consumer debt.

✔ You don't know how much money you need for retirement.

✔ Your net worth is level or slowly increasing.

If you're a Stable individual, you may be setting yourself up for some tough times if things get turbulent. Because you're not struggling to get from paycheck to paycheck, you feel okay about your current location on the financial map, but a single devastating event can send you off course. It's time to move to the next level, where your net worth is increasing noticeably every year (or if you're retired, continuing to increase or at least stay at a level that'll meet your needs). For now, make sure you read the strategies in Part I of this book.

Level 3: Secure

If you're a Secure individual, you not only live within your means today but also plan for the future. The following statements describe you:

- ✔ You have a cash account with at least three months of expenses to use in case of financial emergency.

- ✔ You know your most significant financial risks and have plans to deal with the unexpected.

- ✔ You save for major purchases, such as automobiles and college education, to reduce or eliminate borrowing for them.

- ✔ You have a growing retirement portfolio (or if retired, you have a plan to invest and spend down your portfolio). You know how much money you'll need for a comfortable retirement.

- ✔ Your net worth is increasing regularly toward your ultimate goals.

Secure individuals have the best ability to weather the ups and downs of an uncertain economy. But even Secure individuals have some areas where they could improve their planning for volatile times. If you're in the Secure category, make sure you read through Parts II and III, and read the strategies from Parts IV through VI that most apply to you now.

#10

Save

By Kim Jones, CFP

*L*ikely lurking somewhere in your past (or present) is a grandmother who nagged you about saving money. Perhaps she didn't nag. But at the very least she probably counseled, advised, suggested, instructed, and just plain told you to save.

For most children, the future is tomorrow morning. But for the savvy saver who listened to grandmother, the future is that rainy day when you need cash but your current income isn't enough to cover the unexpected downpour.

You can be certain a rainy day will arrive; you just can't be certain when.

Just Save It

You can find as many ways to save as you can to spend your money. And no matter how much your paycheck increases, you'll probably have no trouble finding more things to buy with the extra money.

So what's a hard-working gal or guy to do? Follow these two rules:

- ✔ Rule #1: Just do it
- ✔ Rule #2: Pay yourself first

You can't spend what you don't have. That's why you set aside a portion of your paycheck each month and then spend what's left. If you find this concept painful, play a game with yourself. Tell yourself that you'll just try it for a month or two.

Some folks call this strategy, "Set it and forget it." First you set it, and then you forget it. And soon you'll be on your way to feeling smug about that tidy sum in the bank.

Decide Where to Put that Rainy-Day Nest Egg

Common advice from financial gurus is to sock away an emergency reserve of three to six months worth of living expenses in easily accessible savings. That way you won't put yourself in a bind by having to ask Uncle Henry for a loan (yikes!) or by borrowing too much on credit cards when a budget crisis crops up. Even worse would be to liquidate a long-term investment account such as your 401(k) or an IRA (which will cost you not only income tax on the amount withdrawn, but also a 10-percent penalty!).

Your reserve account should be:

- ✔ Readily available on short notice
- ✔ Relatively safe
- ✔ Earning interest or dividends

You could put your dollars in a piggy bank. But a piggy bank doesn't pay interest and, let's face it, those piggy banks are so cute and easy to raid! Instead, put the money in a bank money market account or money market mutual fund. Have your credit union or bank directly debit your paycheck or checking account before you have a chance to spend the money. The bank will be delighted to do it, and you'll get excited seeing your rainy-day fund grow each payday. You'll also be able to heave a sigh of relief (rather than cringe) the next time an unexpected expense comes up.

Make Room for More Savings

Want to know the most important, most brilliant financial tip that exists in the world today? *Spend less than you make.*

If you automate those rainy-day savings (also a good strategy for long-term savings such as your IRA), you spend less than you make without having to think about it.

Suppose you determine that you want to amass a $7,500 nest egg (three months of expenses at $2,500 per month). At 3 percent interest, saving $200 per month will allow you to reach your $7,500 goal in three years.

Perhaps you're still insisting that there's simply no room in your budget for savings. Well, sometimes you just have to eat those Brussels sprouts. Take a look at what you're spending on things that aren't absolutely essential, that don't match your life goals, or that don't give your life pleasure. Keep track of your spending for several weeks. Carry a little log book in your pocket and write down everything you spend. After several weeks, take out the log book and your regular monthly bills. Look at where your money has been going. (It's helpful when doing this exercise to have a glass of wine or your favorite mug of tea by your side.)

What to ponder:

- ✔ Do you need a landline phone *and* a cellphone?
- ✔ Do you need to buy books or is the library a better choice?
- ✔ Do you shop in bulk and waste half of what you buy when buying smaller quantities of just what you need would be more cost-effective? (Buying less can be helpful to the waistline, too.)
- ✔ Can you host a potluck with friends instead of meeting them at a restaurant?
- ✔ Can you (heaven forbid) make your own coffee at home?
- ✔ Could you live in a modest home?
- ✔ Could you buy a gently-used car rather than the latest new model?
- ✔ Do you have subscriptions to magazines you never read or health club memberships you never use?

The idea here is not to feel deprived, but rather to make conscious spending decisions. Looking closely at where you're spending your money can help you make decisions about where to cut so that you can free up those savings for the emergency fund without feeling bereft.

Hey, you may find that the joy of watching your savings grow far exceeds the momentary pleasure of an impulse purchase.

If you need a little boost, here's one to try. The next time you pay something off, whether it's a small credit card balance or a car payment, continue making the payment. Only now, make the payment to that rainy-day account. You likely won't notice anything other than the size of the pay-yourself-first account increasing.

To further inspire yourself, post a bar graph of your goal on your refrigerator. Mark your progress on it so you can congratulate yourself every day.

Manage Your Debt

By Rick DeChaineau, CSA, CRPC, CFP

*T*hink of your lifetime income and earnings as a pipeline that flows from when you start making money to the last day of your life. Along the way, various faucets in the pipeline open and divert money to pay for needs (such as living expenses, a home purchase, furniture, and transportation) and wants (like big-screen TVs, vacations, a fishing boat, and more). For items you buy using debt — mortgages, loans, credit card purchases — the faucet opens wider and runs longer because you're paying not only for the item but also for interest. The result is that you have to either work longer to earn more money to repay the debt or scale back on your goals.

When uncertain economic times occur, the amount of debt you've accumulated can magnify the threat to your financial well-being. After you sign on for a debt, you no longer control that faucet. If something unexpected occurs, you have less cash flow and fewer options. This strategy explains how to close those faucets and keep the pipeline from running dry.

Avoid Bad Debt

The best way to keep your income pipeline filled is by avoiding unnecessary debt. Not only does setting aside money for future expenses save you the cost of debt interest payments, but it can also earn money for you if you invest in an interest-bearing account. As you save, you help fill your pipeline instead of draining it!

Putting off purchases until you've saved enough also gives you an additional reserve beyond your emergency fund (see Strategy #10). For example, if you're saving money for a new barbecue, you can instead use those funds to replace a clothes dryer that tumbled its last towel or any other unexpected expense that exceeds your emergency fund.

But like most people, you can't afford to pay cash for everything. Buying your home most likely required a mortgage. Buying cars, furniture, and appliances may involve financing. When you can't pay cash for high-cost items, you need to borrow at least some of the amount needed for your purchase.

Four criteria determine whether debt is good or bad. Before taking on debt, ask yourself the following questions. If the answer to *all* four questions is yes, you're signing up for good debt:

- **Is it a need?** If dependable transportation is a requirement for your job, buying a car to replace one that's on its last legs is clearly a need. But if you have a working TV and those ads for big-screen flat-panel models are making your mouth water, you're looking at a want — which leads to bad debt.

  Note: Where you live is important for your quality of life, so although you can live in an apartment, you may choose to buy a home to provide a more desirable environment, which would qualify as a *need* on the scorecard.

- **Do you need to buy it before you can save up for it?** Consider the timing. You're looking at good debt if your car is beyond repair and you need dependable transportation as soon as possible. If the big-screen TV is on sale this weekend, you can wait. (Do you think they'll get *more* expensive as time goes on?)

- **Can you afford the payment?** If the payment fits in your budget, you won't have to cut back on other needs. That's good debt. If you can't afford it, you'll have to cut back on some newly defined "extras" — like gas, food, and braces for the kids.

- **Are the financing terms okay?** Check the

  - Rate

  - Terms

  - Prepayment penalties (which should be none)

  With good debt, you may have checked with your bank, credit union, and so on, so you know the interest rate is competitive and the length of the car loan isn't longer than 48 months. You're into bad debt if you use the in-store financing offered by the salesperson to buy the TV, getting saddled with an early-payment penalty.

Saving up for a future expenditure keeps you in control of your money. By signing up for debt, you give away that control. Avoiding bad debt keeps more money in your income pipeline going towards your needs, wants, and other goals.

Dump Debt Sooner

Few things both make you feel good *and* improve your financial situation as much as paying off debt! The sooner you can shut off those debt faucets, the longer your income pipeline will stay filled.

Reduce your rates

Your first step in dealing with existing debt is seeking to reduce your interest rates. Here's how:

- ✔ You may have gotten your home mortgage when rates were much higher — check on the rate you can get by refinancing.
- ✔ Call your credit card companies and ask for a lower rate. Tell them about lower-rate offers you've gotten in the mail. Do this at least once a year.
- ✔ Check with your bank or credit union to see whether you can refinance your car loan at a lower rate. Consider the cost of refinancing and whether it's worth the lower payment you may get.

When checking on lower-rate refinancing, ask the same questions about terms and prepayment penalties that you would when looking for good debt.

Accelerate your payments

As soon as you're paying the lowest rates available, you want to start accelerating debt payments to get out of debt sooner. Whether it's old bad debt you got before reading this book or good debt, the less interest you pay, the better. The order in which you eliminate your debts depends on the type of account and how its interest is calculated.

Here's the usual priority order for paying off debt:

1. Credit cards and other revolving consumer accounts
2. Auto, furniture, and appliance loans
3. Boat and RV loans
4. Home equity loans
5. Home equity lines of credit (HELOC)
6. Student loans
7. Home mortgages

You can most efficiently pay off your debts by applying any extra amount to just one account at a time (usually the one with the highest interest rate and smallest balance). As soon as that first account is paid off, accelerate payments on account number 2 by applying the full amount you'd been paying on account number 1 (basic payment plus the extra amount). As each debt is paid off, keep rolling the full amount being paid to the next debt account.

You can find a free debt-reduction calculator that helps you see how much interest you'll save and helps you pick which debt to pay off first at www. whatsthecost.com — it lets you do calculations in U.S. dollars, euros, or British pounds.

As soon as a credit card account is paid off, don't close it — just cut up the card. Closing an account you've paid off hurts your credit score by reducing the total amount of credit you have available.

Improve Your Credit Score

By Derek Lenington, CFP

Although your credit score is a factor in determining your mortgage rate, your credit score also influences rates you get on credit cards and car loans. It can also have an impact on your homeowner's and car insurance rates, and it may even be considered when you apply for a job! Here are some tips on improving your score.

Get a Free Credit Report

Your credit score is only as good as your credit report, and getting a copy is both easy and free. The Federal Fair Credit Reporting Act (FCRA) requires each of the three major credit reporting companies, Equifax, Experian, and TransUnion, to provide you an annual report at no cost. You can request it in one of three ways:

- ✔ Online at www.annualcreditreport.com
- ✔ By telephone at 877-322-8228
- ✔ By mail at Annual Credit Report Service, P.O. Box 105281, Atlanta, GA 30348-5281

Reports are limited to once from each company every 12 months. Otherwise, you pay a fee of $10 per report.

In addition to your name, address, Social Security number, and date of birth, be prepared to provide previous addresses if you've moved in the last two years as well as at least one piece of personal information only you would know, such as a regular monthly payment amount on a mortgage or auto loan.

AnnualCreditReport.com is set up by the three major credit reporting companies, and it's the only authorized Web site that exists. Other sites may offer a similar service but do so in an attempt to sell you unnecessary services or collect personal information. The official site will never solicit you or sell your name or information.

Understand Your Credit History

After you have your report, focus on the five main components that comprise your credit history:

✔ **Personal information:** This includes your name (as well as former names), current and past addresses, Social Security information, and employment history, often with salary information. This information is collected from previous credit applications and is often incomplete or inaccurate.

   Whether you're single, married, divorced, or separated, your credit history should include information only about *you.* Spousal information should be included only when you're both legally obligated to pay on a listed debt or if you're both permitted to use a particular account.

   Your personal information doesn't contain information about your religious preference, age, net worth, race, political affiliation, medical history, criminal record, or any other personal information not directly related to credit.

✔ **Monthly account information:** This section includes information from financial institutions including major credit card issuers, major department stores, and other creditors you pay on a monthly basis. The information includes credit limit, current balance, maximum amount ever borrowed, payment history (whether you pay on time or take 30, 60, 90, or more days to make a payment), date opened, and any write-offs or collection actions ever taken.

✔ **Account information reported only when delinquent or in default:** Creditors such as utilities, insurance companies, doctors and lawyers and other professionals, smaller retailers, and some property management companies report only when an account is past due or collection proceedings have begun. For this info to be included in your report, the creditor must report this information within 90 days of taking collection action. This date is then used to start the seven-year clock, during which this very negative information can remain on your report.

✔ **Public records:** All three credit reporting companies pay data collection companies to pull information from governmental agencies. This is information anyone can obtain through public records such as court filings (lawsuits, divorces, judgments, and liens), foreclosures, and bankruptcies. More recently, it also includes child support enforcement delinquencies.

✔ **Inquiries:** Inquiries may be soft or hard. *Soft inquiries* aren't reported or of concern to potential creditors. This category includes

   • Requests you make of your own report

- Inquiries that are part of unsolicited, preapproved credit card offers

- Periodic reviews of your credit history conducted by current creditors

The second type, *hard inquiries,* includes inquiries made when you apply for credit of any sort. These inquiries can negatively impact your credit history. Too many hard inquiries makes it look as if you're applying for credit wherever and whenever you can, so obtaining credit becomes more difficult.

Minimize hard inquiries by not signing any form that allows a creditor to look at your credit if you're just casually shopping for a car or to refinance your mortgage.

Keep the Good, Fix the Bad

After you read and understand what's on your credit report, your next steps are to build on the existing good information and to minimize or eliminate the negative.

Fix all errors and omissions

You have the right to dispute the accuracy or completeness of any item in your report. The credit reporting companies are required to update the status, or delete unverifiable information, within 30 days of receiving your request. Use the Request for Reinvestigation form that's provided with your credit report. If not provided, you may obtain one from the agency's Web site. Using these forms speeds up the process. Enclose copies of documents that support your claim.

When sending supporting evidence with your Request for Reinvestigation form, never send the original documents, and always track your submissions by using certified mail with return receipt requested or a similar service.

If you don't receive a satisfactory or timely response, contact the creditor directly and demand that your claim be investigated, copying the credit reporting agency. Here's the contact information for the three main credit reporting agencies:

Equifax
Phone 800-685-1111
Web site www.equifax.com

Experian
Phone 888-397-3742
Web site www.experian.com

TransUnion
Phone 877-322-8228
Web site www.transunion.com

You may also want to contact the Federal Trade Commission (FTC) if you're still not satisfied, so make sure to keep copies of all correspondence to and from the credit reporting companies and creditors. You may file a complaint against a credit agency directly with the FTC online at www.ftc.gov/ftc/bcppriv.htm — or call the FTC at 877-382-4357.

Avoid credit repair clinics. At best, they don't do anything you can't do yourself. At worst, these firms charge outrageous fees and suggest potentially illegal practices.

You're allowed a brief statement (100 words or less) explaining any disputed information in your report, but your statement can't just explain factually correct but negative information; you can use this statement only to dispute errors. However, statements to the credit reporting companies are rarely effective. It's usually best to explain negative information directly to a potential creditor.

Add good information to your report

Yes, you can request that each of the three agencies add information to your file. Although they're not required to do so, they often do if the info can be verified. Focus on missing positive account histories, even if the account is closed. Also add information that explains or corrects potentially negative information.

Creditors care most about demonstrated payment responsibility. Account diversity also matters, as does the extent of historical credit, so an old credit card payment history is well worth the effort to add to your report.

Add missing information

Often, you find an account's positive credit history missing on only one or two of the three credit reporting companies. Send a copy of the correct report from the agency with the complete information to the agencies missing it. Include a brief cover letter explaining your request. Copies of monthly statements from the missing creditor make it more likely the information will be added.

Missing or incomplete information on current and prior employers or residences can make it difficult for potential creditors to verify information or obtain a sufficient profile to make a favorable determination. This is particularly important if the job or address change has happened in the last two to three years.

Don't assume the information you've corrected or added will be permanently changed on your report. Sometimes your corrections inadvertently disappear. Review your report at least annually and more frequently if you know you'll be applying for a large amount of credit sooner than that.

Keep a good mix of accounts

Don't close all your old accounts. A variety of accounts over a long period of time and with proven patterns of borrowing and full repayment creates a favorable credit profile. Closing unused credit accounts decreases your *utilization:* your ratio of total debt outstanding to available debt. Potential creditors like to see low utilization.

Opening a bunch of new accounts solely to improve this ratio, however, is also a bad idea. The mix of newer and older accounts helps determine your overall creditworthiness. A number of new accounts opened over a short period of time negatively impacts your file.

#13

Set and Prioritize Financial Goals

By Abigail Pons, MBA, CFP

*I*f you don't take time to set financial goals, you tend to deal with issues haphazardly, addressing whatever happens to bubble up at the time. For example, without a plan, a leaky roof can easily cause vacation prospects to slip away; however, proper goal-setting can allow you to visit Niagara Falls without ending up with your own personal waterfall in the living room.

Consider the following reasons to invest some time in setting financial goals:

- ✔ You achieve financial peace of mind.
- ✔ You gain the power of living within your means.
- ✔ Time is your friend, allowing you to put away less money over longer periods of time.
- ✔ Your goals are free to change over time.

This section helps you put your goals in place and start working toward them.

Get Started

Although setting personal financial goals doesn't require an advanced degree, it does take some consideration (and maybe a cup of coffee). Most people have limited resources and have to be honest about what's most important in life. Become your own Personal Finance Project Manager, and start by getting it all down on paper:

1. **Make a list of all your goals.**

   Write it *all* down — new refrigerator, new roof, new car, vacations and travel, retirement, college funding, and so on. Don't forget the goals that you take for granted. For instance, if you have a five-year loan for your car, you committed to the goal of owning the car at the end of five years by taking out that loan. Take the time you need to make sure your list is complete.

2. **Attach a price tag to each goal.**

You need to know how much each goal costs in light of your budget and other goals. Do this before prioritizing, because sometimes the cost of a goal becomes a deciding factor in setting those priorities.

Short-term goals are easier to address because the costs are much more predictable. For example, if you're hoping to buy a new car outright in two years, you can be pretty sure that the current cost of the vehicle, plus a reasonable adjustment for two years of inflation, will be a realistic estimate.

For longer-term goals, such as retirement and college savings, setting a price tag can be tricky. Check out the college cost calculator at saving-forcollege.com and see Strategy #54 and Strategy #55 for good information about accumulating adequate funds for retirement.

3. **Prioritize your goals.**

When you have a good feel for the cost of your goals, list them in order of importance to you. Prioritizing brings a great deal of perspective to the process. You may find that some goals become unimportant enough that you remove them altogether. Or you may make some important lifestyle decisions, such as buying a used car instead of a new one, in order to achieve a goal more meaningful to you. Don't be discouraged by cost (for example, the cost of retirement) — just realize that it's important to get planning now so you can consistently chip away at it over time.

4. **Assign a tentative timetable to your goals and visualize how much they'll cost at various points in your life.**

Consider the scale of a big, long-term goal, such as retirement, against smaller goals, such as vehicle purchases and travel. And don't forget the effect of inflation over time.

Compare Short-Term and Long-Term Goals

There are some big differences in how you handle and invest for short-term and long-term goals. This section lays them out for you.

Short-term goals

Generally, you want to achieve *short-term goals* in the next five years. They may include the following:

- ✔ Saving for a down payment on a new home
- ✔ Paying off credit card debt
- ✔ Buying a car
- ✔ Taking a vacation

Keep your savings for short-term goals in liquid investments. *Liquid investments* can quickly and easily be converted to cash; examples include

- ✔ Savings accounts
- ✔ Money market accounts or mutual funds
- ✔ Short-term CDs with staggered maturities

You don't want to invest in anything that may significantly drop in value, such as an individual stock, leaving you with less cash at the very time you need it.

Leave some money in your emergency cash reserves. The money you're directing toward short-term goals should be in addition to your rainy-day fund, an in-case-of-emergency account that can support you for three to six months. Like savings for short-term goals, your emergency cash reserves should be invested in highly liquid, easily accessible investments. (See Strategy #9 to make sure you're covered.)

Long-term goals

Long-term goals are usually more than five years away. Most people have just a few long-term goals, such as retirement, college education funding, or starting their own business in ten years.

Several factors make long-term goal planning tricky:

- ✔ **Inflation:** It'll certainly occur, but you can't possibly know at what rate.
- ✔ **Investment returns:** You can't be certain how much your investments will make over long periods of time.
- ✔ **Taxes:** They can go up or down.
- ✔ **Changing costs of your goal:** Many factors can affect the cost of your long-term goals, making the price tag a moving target. Will you have Social Security or a pension payment during retirement? What will medical expenses look like?

There's simply no way to know these things, so you have to make reasonable assumptions about them with current information. Generally, with long-term goals, it's best to err on the conservative side — assume that inflation and taxes will be higher, that investment returns will be lower than those in the last few decades, and that you'll face larger medical costs in retirement.

The good news? Because your long-term goals are far into the future, you can take more risk in pursuit of higher return with your investments for long-term goals. And here's even better news: Uncertain economic environments can present long-term investment opportunities. The important thing is to stay the course with your investment plan.

Put Your Plans in Motion

After you set your goals and know what you want to do with your money, actually putting that money to work toward your goals is the essential next step. Here are some tips:

- ✔ **Pay yourself first.** You've no doubt heard it before, but it's good, reliable wisdom: You have to pay yourself first, or your money will find someplace else to go, without fail. If you want to achieve a financial goal, you have to make a payment toward that goal.

- ✔ **Keep the money separate from spendable funds.** One of the added benefits of retirement accounts is that they're set aside from your everyday household funds. Accessing your retirement accounts is a hassle, and if you do it too early, you may pay a penalty. For other goals, keeping money mentally separate from your disposable funds may be harder. Consider keeping funds for other goals in a separate earmarked account to make it less tempting to raid.

- ✔ **Automate.** One of the great things about the modern, high-tech financial world is the ability to automate money transfers. Not only is it easier to pay your mortgage and credit card payments on time, but you can also set up automatic monthly transfers to your savings or investment accounts. This is important because it removes the decision-making process from the picture and enables you to pay the most important person first — yourself!

After you define your goals and have a plan to achieve them, continue to revisit and reevaluate them on a regular basis. Give special attention to those moving-target long-term goals. If your current spending on short-term goals is maxing out your budget, you may be sabotaging progress toward your long-term goals. Make sure you review your priorities regularly.

Don't Let Your Money Beliefs Sabotage Your Goals

By Diane Blackwelder, CFP

Self-knowledge is power. To avoid sabotaging your financial goals, particularly in rough times, self-awareness and flexibility are essential. You're not likely to change your money personality, but by acknowledging your strengths and weaknesses, you can change your tactics and achieve financial success.

Know Your Money Personality (And the Weaknesses That Come with It)

Some finance professionals may say, "Who needs a financial plan? All you need to do is spend less than you make and invest the rest." Sounds simple, right? So why is it so difficult to execute? Most of us know how to get ahead financially, but we're handicapped by our own counterproductive ideas.

Everyone has a belief system surrounding money. Some people mirror the beliefs of their parents, while others adopt completely opposite attitudes. Identifying your money personality is the first step in understanding how your beliefs may be affecting your bottom line.

Here are three basic money personality types:

- Spenders
- Savers
- Procrastinators

Don't worry — no money personality is better than the others. Most people have a little of each. But when facing uncertain times, idiosyncrasies can raise their ugly heads.

Spenders

You've likely heard the saying, "Keeping up with the Joneses." Well, spenders are the Joneses. They live in the right house, live in the right neighborhood, drive a shiny new car, and are most likely buried under a mountain of debt.

Spenders live by the mantra, "I deserve it." They live in the moment and consider money a measure of success. Ironically, spenders feel frustrated because they have no money in the bank. And during uncertain times, spenders may feel a crunch from their overexuberance.

Do you often reward yourself by buying new shoes or a new toy? Is there more month left than paycheck? Do you vow each year to start a savings plan?

Everyone splurges once in a while. But when spending undermines your financial security, today or in the future, it's time to get a grip. Consider the following tactics:

- ✔ **Freeze your credit cards — literally.** Take your credit cards and freeze them in a cup of water. It may sound silly, but waiting for your credit card to thaw will take the spontaneity out of splurging. If you prefer a less extreme measure, adopt a cooling-off policy; don't allow yourself to purchase a single item over a preset limit, say $50, without waiting 24 hours.

- ✔ **Think about tomorrow.** Preparing a financial to-do list will help prioritize spending. Suppose your goal is to have $5,000 in the bank by year-end. Set up automatic drafts from your checking to savings, and invest in yourself. Before you make an expensive purchase, ask yourself, "Will this purchase mean something to me in a year?"

Savers

The term *penny pincher* comes to mind when describing a saver. Savers clip coupons, live on strict budgets, feel guilty when making major purchases, and find great joy in watching their bank accounts grow.

Savers, unlike spenders, have a hard time living in the moment. A saver often refrains from taking a vacation or replacing his 10-year-old car. The saver's motto is, "Safety is king." A saver would rather bury his money in the backyard than risk losing a penny. Negative economic news is particularly worrisome to the saver.

Would friends and family describe you as cheap? Do you feel you'll never have enough money? Has it been years since you bought a new suit or gown (after all, '80's fashions are coming back!)?

As far as financial security goes, there are worse things than being a saver. However, in all things there must be moderation. If you're a saver, try to remember the following:

- **Risk is not a four letter word.** Take more risk with your money in exchange for greater rewards. Investing your money in a diversified portfolio will make your money work as hard as you do. Investing is a long-term proposition. Don't let hiccups in the market distract you from your goals.

- **Relax.** Review your financial goals. After you establish your needs and find ways to make your money work harder for you, give yourself permission to enjoy the rest. Instead of researching bargain prices on toilet paper, spend your time planning a much-deserved vacation.

Procrastinators

Spenders and savers are on the extreme ends of the money personality spectrum. Procrastinators, on the other hand, live with their heads in the sand. Walk into a procrastinator's house and you're likely to find stacks of unopened mail. Procrastinators are overwhelmed by financial matters and will do almost anything to avoid them.

Procrastinators spend a fair amount of time worrying about money, but they seem unable to act. They put off paying bills, enrolling in their company's retirement plan, setting goals, and even filing their taxes. During uncertain times a procrastinator will justify putting off any financial decision.

Do you file an extension for your taxes every year? Do you wait until a collection agency calls before you pay your doctor's bill? Would you rather have a root canal than balance your checkbook?

Many people put off today what they can do tomorrow. When it comes to money, procrastinating can harm not only your credit, but also your financial security. If you find yourself trending this way, take the following actions:

- **Install safety nets.** Automate as much of your financial affairs as possible. Setting up automatic bill payment and regular transfers to your investment accounts will ensure that you get it done.

- **Feather your nest.** Make an effort to learn more about financial planning. Enroll in a personal finance class at a local community college or read personal finance books. By investing in yourself and building knowledge, you'll be better prepared to weather financial storms.

Work to Improve Yourself

After you know what kind of money personality you have, and you understand where that type of personality may fall short, you can begin to make improvements. In addition to addressing the specific personality-related shortcomings mentioned previously, try the following:

- ✔ **Find an accountability partner.** Share the responsibilities of managing your money with your spouse, significant other, or a professional. Having an accountability partner will keep your weaknesses in check and build on your strengths.

- ✔ **Think small.** Don't expect an overnight reversal of your belief system. Start with small steps, like taking a class or preparing a to-do list. Minor changes often bring big results.

#15

Avoid Common Mistakes in a Down Market

By Warren McIntyre, CFP, and Richard Weimert, MBA, CFP

*U*nfortunately, investment markets don't always go up. As a matter of fact, the U.S. stock market has declined about one-third of the time since 1926. Seeing the value of your investments go down can often be emotional, but the markets have produced consistent increases in value over very long periods and through all kinds of challenges. Here are some things to focus on when the inevitable down periods occur.

Keep Cool

Don't let a market slump make you do something you'll regret later or derail your investment program. When the going gets tough, the urge to bail out of stocks can be strong. But panicking can wreck an investment plan faster than anything. Being out of the market won't allow you to keep up with rising costs of living. In addition, repurchasing later may result in a cycle of buying high and selling low. If you haven't developed a long-term investment plan, do it now. If you have, review it to make sure it still reflects your financial goals (see Strategy #13).

Here are some things to consider when markets are rocky:

- ✔ **Communicate with your financial advisor, if you have one.** Financial advisors earn their keep in turbulent times, and a good one will be able to walk you through the holdings in your portfolio and reaffirm your investment strategy.

- ✔ **Do nothing.** Sometimes doing nothing is preferable to action. Try leaving your account statements unopened for a while. When you look at them every three months or so, you may find the account values are higher than you thought, especially if you're adding to them on a regular basis.

✔ **Don't watch, listen to, or read too much commentary.** During a downturn, the news media has plenty of disheartening stories. The talking heads and bloggers are there for *infotainment,* not to make you money.

✔ **Act less like a day trader and more like legendary investors Warren Buffet and John Bogle.** They see market madness as normal and transitory and take advantage of opportunities in the hard times. Check your stomach for risk. If a big dip invokes too much anxiety, consider putting a larger proportion of your portfolio in less risky assets, like bonds and even cash. But be sure that doing so doesn't jeopardize your long-term goals.

Stick to the Basics

Market turmoil causes investors to question their own judgment and seek different approaches, but the only thing investors really need to do is follow some fundamental principles. Consider the following:

✔ **Invest in securities and use strategies you can easily understand and that have withstood the test of time.** The subprime mortgage crisis and the collapse of Enron are examples of strategies that failed because some very smart people couldn't control their complex schemes. Be sure you understand your investments, including risks, fees, and other costs.

✔ **Make sure you're well-diversified globally.** The U.S. isn't the only market in the world, and every day we become more dependent on a global economy. See Strategies #39 through #46 for strategies and asset allocations that will make your portfolio less risky.

✔ **Use mutual funds and exchange-traded funds.** Unless you have at least $500,000 to invest and the time and expertise to monitor individual securities closely, you'll be better off with well-chosen mutual funds or exchange-traded funds (ETFs). (See Strategies #20 and #22 for the ins and outs of these investment vehicles.) The value of an individual stock or bond can go to zero, but a mutual fund is usually so diversified that losses are temporary. To reduce risk, limit any single stock or bond to no more than 10 percent of the portfolio. Be conscious of too much overlap in individual securities or in styles of funds in your portfolio. Your advisor or online tools can help you analyze the portfolio.

The 10-percent rule especially applies to employer stock. High concentration in employer stock is one of the most common mistakes made by 401(k) participants. Be aware of how much company stock you hold in all your various portfolios. With your employment and potential retirement benefits already aligned with the fortunes of your company, limiting personal exposure in your company's stock is best.

✔ **Keep costs in mind.** High costs are magnified when returns are low. Self-directed investors can minimize costs by using index funds and ETFs. If you need or want an advisor, don't be afraid to ask how the advisor is compensated and about the expenses of the products used.

Uncertain economies and markets make adjusting your portfolio even more important. Many proprietary products handcuff investors by imposing heavy surrender charges or exit fees. Annuities are the most common offenders, but other illiquid investments, such as limited partnerships, can keep you from making the necessary changes.

Be Savvy

Beyond the basics, a smart investor can employ a variety of strategies to cope with adverse market conditions. Give some of these strategies a try:

✔ **Pay down debt.** The return on investment by paying off a loan is equal to the interest rate charged — but unlike other investments, the return is guaranteed. Even paying down a mortgage (often considered good debt) may be the best investment you can make in a down market.

✔ **Invest for *total return* (the combination of growth and income), not just income.** Down markets often coincide with sluggish economic conditions. Income investors feel the squeeze when rates on CDs and other income investments drift lower and lower. Invest for the highest total return consistent with your risk tolerance and then take distributions as needed.

✔ **Continue to invest the same amount of money on a consistent basis, be it weekly, monthly, or quarterly.** By sticking with the program in good times and bad, and increasing the amounts of your contributions when you can, you can build wealth regardless of market conditions.

✔ **Automate your savings program.** Participants in 401(k) plans enjoy both automatic investing and dollar-cost averaging, but most financial institutions will arrange similar systematic investing in other types of accounts.

✔ **Use target maturity and life-cycle funds.** These *funds-of-funds* provide a complete portfolio rebalanced automatically, ensuring broad diversification and effortless investing.

Take Advantage of the Turmoil

You can't control what happens in the markets, but you can turn market turbulence into opportunities. Consider actions like these during market declines:

- ✔ **Buy more.** A decline in prices means investments are on sale. If you're saving and adding to your accounts, you should be delighted with a down market. You want the value of your holdings to be higher when you retire or when you need them — it doesn't matter so much what they're worth now.

- ✔ **Rebalance your portfolio at least annually.** Market declines can cause your allocations to stray far from your target. To get your portfolio back in line, you buy what's gone down and sell what's gone up. Buy low, sell high.

- ✔ **Harvest your tax losses.** *Tax-loss harvesting* (selling assets in which you have a taxable loss and replacing them with other nearly identical securities) is a great and legal way to take advantage of the tax code. Just be careful to avoid *wash sales* — basically, the IRS will disallow your loss if you buy back the same security within 30 days of selling it. This includes mutual funds. You can, however, buy similar mutual funds; for example, if you sell a large cap value fund, you can buy another large value fund immediately, as long as it isn't the same fund you just sold.

- ✔ **Convert traditional IRAs to Roth IRAs.** When you convert from a traditional IRA to a Roth IRA you must pay the income taxes now. But you won't owe taxes later. If converting to a Roth is beneficial for you, it makes sense to do it when the account balance is lower because your immediate tax bill will be lower.

Don't fixate on income taxes. Fear of paying taxes has prevented more people from taking necessary actions than just about any other reason. If your analysis suggests that selling is required, don't let the tax consequences stand in the way. Besides, with special rates for long-term capital gains, the tax bill may be lower than you think.

#16

Use Non-Investment Options to Improve Your Finances

By Will Humphrey

*E*very day the media bombards you with information about the stock market, leading economic indicators, and other financial news. Although all this info may be important to somebody somewhere, you want to make the most of the money you have that's *not* invested in the market. Your checkbook, not the Dow or NASDAQ, is the bottom line you deal with every day. By focusing on your checkbook, you can improve your bottom line. Moreover, gaining control of your personal finances can ensure that you have money to invest in the first place.

 Devoting time and effort to organizing and prioritizing your spending gives you better control of your money, helps you reach your goals, and provides peace of mind during uncertain times: You know where your money is going and you stay in control.

Keep Track of Your Money

If you're like most people, you don't know where all your money goes. You have a lot of ways to buy things these days, from debit cards and credit cards to paper checks and cash. With online access to your bank account, you may not even balance your checkbook!

Having all these ways to spend makes it hard to keep track of your spending each month. But if you're going to take charge of your finances, you need to know. Money that disappears is lost forever and can't be saved or invested or used to help make the car payment.

You have plenty of options for tracking your money, ranging from low-tech to high-tech. Whatever option you choose, you need to track your spending for a full month. Don't try to recreate all your spending from a previous month because you won't recall everything you spent.

Write it all down

One option to keep track of your spending is to use good old 3-x-5-inch index cards to record spending:

- ✔ List all your monthly automatic drafts from your bank account on card 1 (mortgage payment, car payment, and so on)

- ✔ List all your regular monthly checks on card 2 (utilities, cable, phone, and so on)

- ✔ List all your other spending on card 3, including purchases at the grocery store, restaurant meals, gasoline, a jolt of caffeine from the coffee shop, all those items from big box stores and warehouse clubs, and so on. Purchases made without even thinking about them are the ones that really add up.

Both you and your spouse or partner must track purchases if you're going to get a real handle on your spending.

Many online tools can also help you track your spending. You can find examples of these tools at www.mint.com and www.mvelopes.com. Quicken and Microsoft Money have software that you can use for this same purpose.

Categorize and discuss your results

At the end of the month, take your index cards (or spreadsheets) and sort your purchases into categories. You can choose to have a few or many categories, but the more specific you are, the better you'll be able to tell where your money is going. You'll likely be surprised at the totals you see for some categories.

You can make sorting your expenses pay off more easily by dividing items into wants and needs. Keeping your priorities in mind can help you resist the siren song of around-the-clock advertising.

Now that you can see where the money is going, you and your spouse or partner can decide whether your spending is in line with your priorities. This may well require a heart-to-heart conversation about what's truly important. You both have to recognize that your spending (and saving) should be brought in line with your goals. This conversation may not be easy, but focus on the long-term benefit of the exercise, keeping in mind the positive impact it'll have on your financial well-being.

Use Automatic Payments to Take Control of Your Money

You can employ some of the same services that make it easier to spend (electronic payments, online bill-pay, and so on) to ensure your spending and savings stay in line with your priorities. The following steps take advantage of automated payments to get you started. Because most people budget by bank balance rather than on an item-by-item budget, you and your spouse or partner will have to adjust your spending to avoid emptying your everyday account:

1. **Choose a primary bank or credit union account where your paycheck will be deposited.**

2. **Establish at least one savings account to save for your emergency fund and important goals.**

3. **Open another checking account for everyday spending.**

   Using cash, debit cards, or checks, here's where all the spending that you have at least some control over — such as food, gas, coffee, dining out, and entertainment — will come from.

4. **From your primary account, set up automatic payments.**

   Automatic payments should go to the following:

   • Needs, including rent or mortgage, utilities, and insurance

   • Contributions to your savings account for your emergency fund and important goals

   • Contributions to your everyday spending account; the amount transferred to this account each payday is the balance after first covering your needs and savings

Although you can fine-tune this system (for instance, by having an additional separate account to pay for gas), you can see the intent from this example.

Turn to Financial Professionals for Guidance and Accountability

You're obviously someone who's ready to take charge of your finances or are looking for reassurance that you're making solid financial decisions in uncertain economic times. Consider taking the next step, which is to engage financial professionals to provide additional guidance to ensure your financial well-being. If you haven't already done so, give serious thought to developing a professional relationship with these professionals. The fees they charge will likely be money well-spent because their advice can save you money both in the short term (immediately in some instances) and in the long term. Here's how you may benefit from their services:

- ✔ **Certified Financial Planner:** Studies have shown that individuals with a financial plan in place have more success in growing their net worth and meeting financial goals compared to those lacking a plan. Simply stated, if you don't have goals that you're aiming for with big-ticket items (retirement funding, primary residence purchase, buying a vacation home, college funding, inheritance planning, and the like), you're leaving things to chance. You can think of a financial planner as a fiscal fitness coach.

- ✔ **Certified public accountant:** By engaging a CPA to complete tax planning and tax returns for you, you'll likely reduce the money you shell out to the local, state, and federal governments at tax time.

- ✔ **Estate planning attorney:** A will is only one of several documents necessary to protect you, your spouse or partner, and other loved ones in the event of your death or incapacity. A competent attorney can help you develop a plan and create the legal instruments needed should bad things happen.

If you need help choosing a good financial advisor, check out *Personal Finance Workbook For Dummies,* by Sheryl Garrett (Wiley).

Part II
Using Investment Vehicles and Accounts throughout the Economic Cycle

The 5th Wave   By Rich Tennant

In this part . . .

The investment marketplace is overflowing with choices. On top of that, you can find even more "expert" opinions on how to use these options to best meet your needs. In this part, you get an overview of the types of investments and accounts that are available to you as well as an explanation of each investment vehicle or account and when it may be appropriate for you.

Include Cash Reserves: Savings, CDs, and Money Market Accounts

By Paul Dolce, MBA, CFP

*Y*ou may think of cash as the comfort food of investing. When things get dicey, you feel like pulling your money out of investments and moving it to where it'll be safe. Maybe you simply can't stand the thought of watching your investments decrease in value, a frequent problem in times of economic uncertainty. Having an investment strategy that holds up in good times and bad can help overcome those concerns. And cash is one component of every good investment strategy.

You can use cash for a variety of things, including the following:

✔ **Your emergency fund:** Use emergency funds to cover unexpected expenses.

✔ **Short-term goals:** These include goals that are less than five years away, such as saving for a car or a down payment on a house.

✔ **Investment stability:** Include cash investments in your investment strategy as a *core investment* (primary holding) and to reduce *volatility* (a measure of how rapidly the value of your portfolio goes up and down).

✔ **Temporary component:** You can also use cash as a temporary component of portfolios meant for long-term goals. You may hold cash in these portfolios for a variety of reasons, including the following:

- You've sold an investment and a suitable replacement isn't immediately available.

- You want available cash so you can take advantage of an anticipated investment opportunity.

- You need to take income from your account, so you have to keep a portion of it in cash for safety. You don't want to have to sell an investment at an inopportune time so you can take income out of your portfolio.

Your Cash-Equivalent Savings Options

Savings accounts, CDs, and money market accounts are three vehicles that you can employ to ensure that your cash is working for you. Generically called *cash equivalents,* each of these investments has been designed with safety in mind — in other words, their value remains relatively stable.

Savings accounts

Savings accounts offered by banking and thrift institutions are safe, very safe. The Federal Deposit Insurance Corporation (FDIC) insures savings accounts at member institutions up to $100,000 per depositor. And certain retirement savings accounts, such as IRAs, are insured up $250,000.

Savings accounts are liquid, too. This means you can pull your money out whenever you need it without having to worry about early withdrawal fees, gains, losses, or other complications that often come with other investments.

Savings accounts also have a downside: They pay low interest rates. When interest rates in the general economy decline, interest rates paid on savings accounts can be downright pathetic and may not even keep up with inflation. If inflation is increasing the cost of the things you buy by 3 percent each year and your savings account is paying you only 1 percent in interest, the purchasing power of the money in your savings account is actually declining by 2 percent per year. It actually costs you money to keep your funds in a safe account.

Online savings accounts, such as ING Direct (www.ingdirect.com) and HSBC Direct (www.hsbcdirect.com), offer FDIC-insured savings that typically yield a bit more interest than regular bank savings accounts. Because these institutions don't have physical branch buildings and staff and because all activity is conducted online, their expenses can be lower. To use them, simply open an account at their Web site and then fund the account by initiating an online electronic transfer from your regular savings institution to your new account. You can transfer money back whenever you want to in the same manner. You can also pay many of your bills electronically from these online savings accounts. This can even save you money in postage!

Keep money in savings accounts only for your ultra short-term needs, such as your emergency fund or that down payment you're making next month. You have better options available for your longer-term investments.

Certificates of deposit

Certificates of deposits, or CDs, are offered by the same institutions that offer savings accounts. CDs are FDIC-insured, so they're safe like savings accounts. However, they generally pay slightly higher interest rates than savings accounts.

CDs can offer both safety and higher rates because they aren't as liquid as savings accounts. CDs have predetermined maturity terms, typically ranging anywhere from six months to two years or longer. When you buy a CD, you should plan to keep it until the end of its term. If you redeem your CD before it matures, you may have to pay an early withdrawal penalty or forfeit a portion of the interest you earned.

A bank's CD rates may be negotiable. Banks often offer special rates to attract funds from investors like you. Shop around on the Internet or by phone to find the best rates in your area. If they're better than your bank's rates, talk to an investment specialist at your bank and ask her to match the better rate — it can't hurt to ask. Just like any other business, banks don't like to lose customers, and they'll sometimes do what it takes to keep you from taking your money elsewhere.

Money market accounts

Although they aren't FDIC-insured, money market accounts combine some of the best features of savings accounts and CDs.

Like savings accounts, money market accounts are liquid. You can write checks on them and take your cash out anytime you want; you don't have a waiting period like you do with CDs. Restrictions, however, may include minimum check size, how many checks you can write per month, or minimum account balances you have to maintain to get the best rates and/or avoid monthly fees.

Money market accounts offer better interest rates than savings accounts. Sometimes the rates aren't quite as attractive as those for CDs, but you have access to your money anytime you want; you don't get that with a CD.

You can open a money market account at most banks and institutions that offer savings accounts and CDs. Many mutual fund companies also offer money market accounts. Money market mutual funds frequently offer even better rates than bank money market accounts, so be sure to do some checking before you invest.

An added feature of money market mutual funds is that they invest your money in a variety of investments. For example, you can purchase municipal money market mutual funds (also called *munis*) in which your earnings will be exempt from federal and possibly even state taxes. Or you can choose a U.S. Treasury money market fund that invests only in rock-solid government securities. Be sure to read the fine print in the brochure or prospectus.

So Which One Is Right for You?

When you're choosing the type of cash accounts to use, consider the following:

- ✔ Your investment strategy
- ✔ When you may need your money
- ✔ The current rate of inflation and whether the interest rate will keep up with inflation
- ✔ Your comfort with using Internet institutions versus your local bank
- ✔ Your familiarity with mutual fund companies
- ✔ How easily you can access your money
- ✔ What restrictions and limitations are associated with each type of cash account

When times are tough and markets are going down, keep your short-term cash needs in mind. If you know you're going to need cold, hard cash sometime in the next couple of years, keep that amount in a nice, safe cash option. Keeping short-term money in long-term securities like stocks and bonds is flirting with disaster.

Government Bonds: Should You Loan Uncle Sam Your Money?

By Michael Oswalt, CPA

*T*hroughout U.S. history, individuals have had the opportunity to "invest in America" through the purchase of U.S. government securities. U.S. Treasury securities are simply IOUs from good ol' Uncle Sam. When you buy a Treasury security, you're lending money to the federal government for a specified period of time. Uncle Sam borrows money in a number of ways; the most common are savings bonds, Treasury bills, Treasury notes, Treasury bonds, and agency bonds.

The best way to purchase the securities outlined in this chapter is directly from the U.S. Department of Treasury's Web site (`www.treasurydirect.gov`). You have no fees and no commissions when you buy or sell direct. You can also purchase the marketable securities through your broker, but be prepared to pay a minimal fee for the transaction.

During uncertain economic times, part of your portfolio should be striving for predictability, safety, and liquidity. For these objectives, government securities historically have reached the mark. Read on.

U.S. Savings Bonds: Tried-and-True

Savings bonds are *nonmarketable* securities, which means that when you purchase the bonds, they're registered to you and you can't sell them to another investor through the financial markets. Uncle Sam offers two types of these bonds, Series EE and Series I, which are backed by the full faith and credit of the U.S. government and are considered the safest of all investments. Here's more info on each type:

   ✔ **Series EE bonds:** These bonds earn a fixed rate of return set by the U.S. Treasury. They're *accrual bonds,* which means the interest accumulates and is compounded semiannually (rather than being paid to the owner as it's earned each month). If you hold one of these bonds, you receive the interest when you redeem the bonds.

✔ **Series I bonds:** The interest you earn from I bonds comes in two parts:

- A fixed-rate component established when you purchase the bond

- A second component that's equal to the rate of inflation, adjusted semiannually (based on the consumer price index for March and September)

Although the fixed-rate interest component for Series I bonds is low, these bonds help protect you against inflation. If inflation goes up, so does the interest rate you earn because the variable-rate portion is adjusted every six months; for example, when the fixed-rate component is 2 percent and the inflation adjustment is 5 percent, an investment in a Series I bond is guaranteed to return 7 percent. But remember, the total interest rate can also go down as the inflation adjustment decreases.

For both bonds, the purchase limit is $5,000 per Social Security number for each calendar year. You can easily purchase and redeem the bonds in electronic format through the Department of the Treasury's Web site (www. treasurydirect.gov). If you purchase the bonds electronically, you can get any denomination of $25 or more, including penny increments. The purchase price is equal to the face value.

You can also purchase the bonds in paper form through various financial institutions and payroll savings plans. Paper I bonds are offered in denominations of $50, $75, $100, $200, $500, $1000, and $5,000; they're purchased for their face value. However, you can get paper versions of EE bonds at half their face value; they'll be worth face value at maturity. Paper EE bonds are offered in denominations of $50, $75, $100, $200, $500, $1000, $5,000, and $10,000.

The interest on both bonds compounds semiannually for 30 years, but you don't have to hold the bonds for that long. You can redeem the bonds after 12 months, but you pay a three-month interest penalty if you redeem the bonds within five years of the purchase date.

As for tax treatment, U.S. savings bonds are exempt from state and local income tax. Federal income tax on interest earned can be deferred until redemption or final maturity, whichever occurs first. Tax benefits are available when you use the bonds for education purposes.

Gimme a "T!" Treasury Securities

Most of Uncle Sam's debt is made up of *marketable* (tradable) securities: Treasury bills, Treasury notes, Treasury bonds, and TIPS. Like savings bonds, each of these securities is backed by the full faith and credit of the government:

- ✔ **Treasury bills (T-bills):** T-bills are short-term, highly liquid securities that mature in one year or less. They're similar to a savings account or a money market fund. You can buy them at less than face value and receive the full face amount when the bill matures.

- ✔ **Treasury notes (T-notes):** T-notes are intermediate-term investments with maturities of more than one year but less than ten years. You can probably expect to earn a somewhat higher interest rate on T-notes than on T-bills. The notes pay interest every six months. They're the most popular Treasury securities because they offer a good mix of the safety of short-term investments and the higher yields of long-term bonds. Investors often use them to fund specific future expenses, such as college or retirement income.

- ✔ **Treasury bonds (T-bonds):** T-bonds are long-term investments with terms between 10 and 30 years; they pay interest every six months. Because they're long-term issues (and investors assume more risk with a fixed-income, long-term investment), they typically pay a higher interest rate than T-notes or T-bills.

- ✔ **Treasury Inflation Protected Securities (TIPS):** TIPS are government-issued bonds whose principal amount adjusts to the rate of inflation. Both the interest payment and the principal face value of TIPS are affected by changes in the consumer price index (CPI). Because the principal is indexed to the CPI, if the index rises during periods of inflation, your principal and interest are guaranteed to increase; therefore, the real purchasing power of the investment keeps pace with the rate of inflation. If *deflation* (a reduction in the general level of prices) occurs, TIPS are guaranteed to pay at maturity the greater of the original face value of the bond or the inflation-adjusted value. So what's the downside? Because of their built-in inflation protection feature, the interest rate on TIPS tends to be lower than on other Treasury notes or bonds.

When you invest in TIPS, you pay taxes on the income generated *and* the principal that accrues with inflation. A way to avoid paying income tax before you receive any income is to hold TIPS in an IRA.

Government-Sponsored Enterprises and Agency Bonds

A number of U.S. government agencies and various government-sponsored enterprises (GSEs) issue debt securities. Technically, these securities aren't backed by the full faith and credit of the U.S. government; they rank one notch below U.S. Treasury issues in terms of safety. But because these government agencies play such a valuable role in the U.S. economy, the government isn't likely to allow one of its agencies to default on these debt obligations. GSEs and federal agencies issue securities that, due to their lack of explicit guarantees, generally provide higher yields than Treasury securities do. Pick up a copy of *Bond Investing For Dummies,* by Russell Wild, for greater detail on agency bonds.

Bond investments, in general, don't move in tandem with stock investments, so including a mix of bonds in an investment portfolio gives you a powerful tool in an uncertain economy: diversification. A mix of intermediate- or long-term Treasury and agency bonds can provide a steady stream of essentially credit risk–free income.

Does Uncle Sam Equal Risk-Free?

Because Treasuries are backed by the full faith and credit of the U.S government, they're considered to have essentially no credit risk. Only a monumental event or combination of events — such as war, government scandal, or a collapse of the economy — would prevent the U.S. government from repaying its debts. If these events occur, the government has the power to increase taxes and print additional money if the need arises. So you have almost no credit risk, but you do have other types of risks, just as you would with any type of fixed-rate security. Here are the major risks:

- ✔ **Interest-rate risk:** This is the risk that a bond's value will fall when interest rates go up. If you keep your bond until it matures, you'll receive all the principal and interest you expected. However, if you need to sell your security before it matures and interest rates have gone up, you'll probably have to sell it for less than you paid for it.

- ✔ **Inflation risk:** This is the risk that a bond's return won't keep up with inflation. This risk is a special concern for government bond holders; the longer the term of the bond, the greater the risk. Because lending Uncle Sam money involves no credit risk, the return is lower than it would be on higher-risk investments. If the U.S. economy is experiencing a period of inflation, the purchasing power of the dollar declines and so does the real value of your bond. TIPS and I bonds provide unique inflation adjustment features that help reduce this inflation risk.

Decide Whether Fixed Annuities Are Right for You

By Buz Livingston, CFP

Does an income stream that lasts a lifetime sound appealing? Adding a fixed annuity to your investment mix guarantees you won't outlive your nest egg during uncertain times. An *annuity* is a promise from an insurance company to send you, the *annuitant,* payments for the rest of your life. If you live a long time, you win; a premature death means the insurance company wins.

Annuities come in two distinct flavors: fixed and variable. *Fixed annuity* payments remain constant. With a *variable annuity,* the payment changes as the annuity's underlying value fluctuates. This strategy covers fixed annuities; for the lowdown on variable annuities, turn to Strategy #22.

Weigh the Pros and Cons

A fixed annuity isn't suitable for everyone. Like other investment options, fixed annuities have their fair share of pros and cons.

Good reasons to buy a fixed annuity

The perfect candidate for a fixed annuity is an older investor in good health who has a family history of longevity and who is more interested in spending his or her money than passing it to heirs. If you want to spend the last dime, an annuity is just the ticket. Following are some other reasons to buy a fixed annuity:

✔ **Generating income:** One of the best reasons to buy a fixed annuity is having more money to spend. In some instances, an annuity can generate more income than a bond portfolio. For instance, a $100,000 bond portfolio at 4.5 percent interest may give a single, 70-year-old female an annual income of $4,500. But if she instead opts for a $100,000 immediate annuity, she may rake in $8191.56, over 82 percent more a year. (However, if this individual dies with the $100,000 bond portfolio, $100,000 goes to her heirs. If she dies with this immediate annuity, the income stops and there's nothing to leave to the heirs.)

✔ **Building your pension:** With the demise of traditional, defined benefit pension plans, you may find the security of lifetime income attractive.

✔ **Freeing money for other investment:** Retirees can use fixed annuity payments to cover basic living expenses, allowing the stock portion of their portfolios to be invested more aggressively.

✔ **Paycheck replacement:** Consider a fixed annuity as a way to replace your paycheck.

✔ **Deferring taxes:** If you're not eligible for a Roth IRA contribution or are making the maximum contributions to your retirement account, a fixed annuity is an option for tax-deferred growth.

✔ **Protecting Medicaid benefits:** In some states, annuities aren't subject to creditor claims or considered assets for Medicaid qualification purposes. Discuss asset protection and Medicaid planning with an attorney to determine whether a fixed annuity is appropriate for you.

✔ **Replacing a life insurance policy you no longer need:** If you own a life insurance policy with cash value, consider a tax-deferred 1035 exchange to get a fixed annuity contract without immediate tax ramifications.

✔ **Replacing an underperforming annuity:** You can replace an existing, poorly performing annuity by initiating a 1035 exchange for a new and improved version. But be wary. Unscrupulous salespeople often encourage 1035 exchanges but gloss over additional surrender charges on the new annuity. Make sure you understand the implications of any new surrender charges resulting from a 1035 exchange.

Never put all your assets into a fixed annuity. Make sure you're buying an annuity from a highly rated insurance company, and always buy a no-load annuity with low annual expenses and zero to low surrender charges.

Reasons not to buy a fixed annuity

High commissions can inspire zealous salespeople to tout the benefits of fixed annuities while glossing over the limitations. Many states require suitability disclosures. Here are some of the risks:

- ✔ **Conservative returns:** Fixed annuities are conservative investments. Be suspicious when someone touts an above-average return.

- ✔ **Relatively young age:** Fixed annuities generally work better for older folks; you should be in or near retirement. The older you are, the higher your payment will be.

- ✔ **Heirs:** Buying an annuity leaves less for your heirs to inherit unless you purchase a rider, but the rider results in a lower monthly payment. Your heirs also don't receive the benefit of a step up in basis should you die before you begin annuity payments. They may be subject to substantial income taxes.

- ✔ **Inflation risks:** Purchasing an annuity means you're locking in for the rest of your life, so unless you purchase an inflation rider, which will reduce your payments, the payments from a fixed annuity remain the same. Many years of high inflation can erode your purchasing power.

- ✔ **Health:** If you're in poor health, a fixed annuity is a bad idea. Remember, an annuity is "living insurance" because it pays more the longer you live. If you die shortly after buying an annuity, the insurance company wins.

- ✔ **Withdrawal penalties:** Withdrawals before you reach age $59\frac{1}{2}$ trigger a penalty. Also, annuities often charge a fee for any redemption during the beginning of the contract (called the *surrender period*). Don't buy an annuity unless you're absolutely certain you won't need the funds as a lump sum for something like medical expenses.

  Make sure you understand how surrender charges are calculated. Generally, surrender fees decline the longer you own the annuity. For example, a five-year surrender charge may levy a 5 percent penalty in year one, 4 percent in year two, and so on.

An *equity-indexed annuity* (EIA) is a fixed annuity guaranteeing a minimum rate of return tied to an equity index such as the S&P 500. This is an illusory sales pitch. High fees, exaggerated returns, and long surrender periods make EIAs uniformly inappropriate. The Securities and Exchange Commission (SEC) has issued a special alert regarding equity indexed annuities (www.sec.gov).

Choose a Payment Schedule

In terms of payment schedules, you can choose from two types of fixed annuities:

- ✔ **Immediate:** Payments can start anytime within 13 months. You can transfer a lump sum of money into an immediate annuity and turn on the tap to start receiving guaranteed income for life.

> ✔ **Deferred:** The payment start date depends on your contract. The longer you delay, the greater the payment. Deferred annuities are inappropriate for most investors. The only reason to have a deferred annuity is to shelter income taxes, and you can do that in many less expensive ways. However, if you're planning to annuitize soon but not quite yet, a deferred annuity may make sense.

Select Any Riders for Your Contract

As with any insurance policy, riders are available on fixed annuities during the payout phase. They're set terms added to the basic contract. Popular riders include the following:

> ✔ **Return of premium or installment refund:** Gives your beneficiary up to the full amount invested should you die before receiving payments equaling your initial investment
>
> ✔ **Specific term guarantee (term certain):** Locks in a number of years that the annuity will pay the annuitant or beneficiary
>
> ✔ **Spousal benefit:** Lets the surviving spouse receive the benefit; a 50 percent spousal benefit is a popular option, but surviving spouses often find this amount is insufficient
>
> ✔ **Inflation protection:** Increases the monthly payment every year; the annuitant can select the level of inflation protection, from 1 to 3 percent

If you invest primarily in fixed income instruments such as bonds or CDs, consider an inflation-protected annuity. Otherwise, a diversified stock portfolio offers a better choice for inflation protection.

Insurance companies aren't charities, so riders on annuities aren't free. All riders reduce your payments. For example, a 20-year guarantee offers a lower payment than a 10-year guarantee. And if you choose a 2 percent inflation rider, your monthly payment will be lower than with a 1 percent rider.

Simplify with Target-Date Funds

By Derek Kennedy, CFP

*W*hen your employer asks you to pick the investments in your retire-ment account, you may feel you're in for a tough decision — almost as if you had to choose only one kind of ice cream for the rest of your life. The usual reaction to the ice cream question is to respond with your favorite flavor. But like the clever kid who chooses Neapolitan — chocolate, vanilla, and strawberry in a single carton — you can choose a fund that's the Neapolitan of the investment world, allowing you many flavors of funds within a single package.

Target-date funds — also known as *life-cycle funds, target retirement funds, target maturity funds,* and *age-based funds* — are mutual funds whose assets change based on your age. Because a target-date fund invests in other mutual funds, it's known as a *fund of funds.* These funds are a big hit with defined contribution retirement plans like 401(k)s. Employers and employees both love their simplicity, ease of use, and built-in variety.

One-Stop Shopping for a Diversified Retirement Portfolio

Target-date funds typically invest in a mix of other mutual funds to create an asset allocation consistent with the length of time an investor has until retirement, as designated by the date in the fund's name, such as XYZ Target 2030 Fund.

These funds are generally offered by large mutual fund families who manage the underlying funds, including Vanguard, Fidelity, and T. Rowe Price. Managers automatically rebalance the mix of funds over time so the asset allocation continues to reflect your proximity to retirement. The mix of funds within the target-date fund is more aggressive for younger investors and becomes more conservative for older investors.

Don't confuse a life-cycle fund with a *lifestyle fund,* also known as a *target-risk fund* or *risk-based fund.* These funds are also typically fund of funds, but they offer a static asset allocation. Although automatic rebalancing does occur, the asset mix doesn't change as you get closer to retirement. Target-risk funds usually come in three varieties: aggressive, moderate, and conservative. They're intended to correspond with an individual's risk tolerance.

The Upside of Target-Date Funds

Target-date funds can be beneficial in uncertain times, even if you're an experienced investor and even if you don't intend to use them as your core retirement savings. For instance, with small accounts, the automatic rebalancing feature may help save on the trading fees you'd pay on individual funds if you were to rebalance them yourself. These fees can be a significant drag on performance in accounts with small balances. Also, because most mutual funds require minimum initial investments, target-date funds give you the benefits of diversification in accounts not large enough to fund the investment minimums of multiple individual mutual funds.

Target-date funds can be an important investment tool in uncertain economic times because they keep you focused on saving rather than worrying about investment choices. They allocate and maintain your investment with your retirement date in mind. The ability to maintain an appropriate asset allocation and avoid emotional reactions to market conditions and uncertainty may be the single most important thing that you can do for your investment portfolio over the long haul.

Great Isn't Necessarily Perfect: The Downside of Target-Date Funds

Like any investment, target-date funds have tradeoffs and issues relating to personal situations and preferences. Here are some to be aware of:

- ✔ Target-date funds aren't personalized. The asset allocations are designed to be generally appropriate for people of a certain age or distance from retirement. That allocation may not be consistent with your own risk tolerance or financial situation. If you expect to retire in 2032, should you select the target 2030 fund or the target 2035 fund? Most target-date funds target age 65 for your retirement, but what if you plan to work longer than that? What if, due to other sources of retirement income, you don't intend to start accessing the money in your 401(k) for many years beyond your retirement date?

- ✔ Funds with the same target dates offered by different companies often have different initial allocations, may change allocations over time differently, and may have different allocations after they reach their target at retirement.

✔ Target-date funds can be difficult to integrate with other parts of your investment portfolio.

Target-date funds are already diversified. Investors are often tempted to add other investments to their account because they know that diversification is important and having just one mutual fund feels wrong. Don't give in to the lure. Doing so can undermine your asset allocation and defeat the purpose you have for using a target-date fund.

✔ The underlying funds may not include exposure to as much of an asset class or as many asset classes as you may like.

However, for ease of use and the potential to get it mostly right, target-date funds can be a fantastic option.

Evaluate Your Options

A target-date fund may be a one-stop-shop, but it's not a one-time decision. Here are some ideas to keep in mind when evaluating which fund is right for you:

✔ Consider whether the internal asset allocation and progression is consistent with your needs, and compare allocations among various fund managers.

✔ Consider the fees. Target-date fund fees are based on the fees of their underlying assets, and though not typical, some managers may charge an additional management fee on top of those.

✔ Consider the track record and performance of the underlying funds. Some target-date funds are based on a mix of index funds, and others rely on actively managed mutual funds. Which type of funds suits you best?

No matter which fund you choose, monitor the fund's asset allocation and compare it to your own evolving preferences over time. And as with any investment, you should continue to monitor the fees and performance of the underlying funds at least annually to make sure that everything is on track.

#21

Invest in Mutual Funds

· ·

By Bruce Sneed, MBA, CFP

· ·

Mutual funds are an established way to invest in an uncertain economy. At their core, *mutual funds* are merely a collection of shares of individual companies' stock, possibly corporate or government bonds, and maybe some cash. By owning shares in a mutual fund, you actually own a few shares in dozens or possibly hundreds of different stocks or bonds.

Reap the Benefits of Mutual Fund Investment

People invest in mutual funds for four fundamental reasons: professional management, diversification, convenience, and marketability. The following sections outline these benefits, which make mutual funds most attractive when capital markets are unusually volatile.

Professional management

Mutual funds offer professional management of your money. These managers have the training and resources to keep abreast of and adjust to market changes. Unfortunately, fund managers don't have a crystal ball giving them the ability to foresee the future; don't expect your manager to keep you completely out of harm's way.

Fund managers are required by law to select and manage fund holdings in accordance with the fund's investment objectives and policies, as described in the fund's prospectus. These objectives may be designed to minimize your risk exposure.

Diversification: Spreading out the risk

Mutual funds help eliminate some of the risk involved in investing in individual stocks and bonds by giving you shares in many different assets. Remember Enron or MCI? How did that work out for employees who based their futures on company stock? Mutual funds also reduce your cost of diversifying by sharing transaction costs with other shareholders.

Although every mutual fund buys many securities, the funds themselves come in a wide variety of styles and classifications. Some mutual funds specialize in growth, some in value. Some invest in U.S. markets, others in foreign markets. Some invest only in bonds, others in a blend of stocks and bonds. A well diversified portfolio invests across many styles and types of mutual funds. See Strategies #39 through #46 for information about asset allocation and diversifying your overall holdings.

Read the prospectus summary and annual report. Sometimes the titles of mutual funds can be misleading. A fund with the word *growth* in its title doesn't have to be fully invested in growth stocks. Also, your mutual fund manager's investment style can drift, especially in turbulent markets.

Convenience

The convenience of mutual funds begins with the initial purchase and continues with investments, withdrawals, reinvestment of dividends and capital gains, record-keeping, and tax reporting. Mutual funds make it easy and inexpensive to *dollar-cost average* (invest regular amounts of money at regular intervals). This strategy is especially beneficial when markets are highly volatile — you end up buying more shares when costs are low. You can usually find everything you need to read, see, or do at a fund's Web site; otherwise, call the fund company.

Marketability

Marketability means you can easily buy or sell mutual fund shares. Unlike owning a house, you may be able to quickly exchange shares in a mutual fund for another investment or cash. Marketability gives you the flexibility to create and maintain a diversified portfolio.

Choose from Types of Funds

There are two major types of funds:

> ✔ **Open-end funds:** These are the most common type of mutual funds. You purchase and redeem the shares of open-end investment companies each day at their current *net asset values* (NAV) plus sales charges or minus redemption fees, if any. The NAV is calculated at the end of each day based on the value of the fund's underlying securities (stocks and/ or bonds). There's no limit to the number of shares that can be issued.

✔ **Closed-end funds:** Like open-end funds, closed-end funds buy many different stocks or bonds. But these make an initial public offering (IPO) of a *specific number of shares* and then trade on the stock exchange — similar to common stocks — at either a premium or discount to their NAV. Their market price fluctuates throughout the day based on supply and demand. Closed-end funds can be more volatile because they may have less trading volume then a similar open-ended fund.

Because the initial offering price of a closed-end fund includes a sales commission, the shares are issued at a premium over the invested assets. However after the IPO is completed, closed-end funds often trade at a discount. Therefore, it makes sense to forego purchasing new offerings of closed-end funds. Instead, you should consider purchasing shares when they become available on the stock exchange at a discount from their net asset value. Table 21-1 summarizes the differences between closed-end and open-end funds.

Table 21-1	Comparing Open-End and Closed-End Mutual Funds	
Feature	*Closed-end Funds*	*Open-end Funds*
Shares sold	At IPO	Continuously
Shares sold to/bought from	Stock exchange	Fund company
Share price	Market price	NAV
Share price changes	Continuously	End of day
Transaction costs	Commissions	Sales/redemption charges

Choose the Level of Management: Trying to Meet or Beat the Market

Mutual funds may be either index funds or managed funds. *Index funds* buy a set collection of securities and mostly leave the portfolio alone, earning you investment returns as the underlying values of the stocks or bonds you hold appreciate. *Active fund* managers select securities in an attempt to beat the market or achieve a better risk-adjusted return than the market. However, they put a dent in your earnings by charging higher annual management fees.

Index funds

Index funds are popular because they're inexpensive, easy to understand, and give you a return similar to the market your index fund is designed to track. Because of their popularity, mutual fund companies continue to bring several varieties of index funds to market. Funds are indexed to all types of assets and subsequently have all kinds of investment styles, expected returns, risk, and expenses.

Stock index mutual funds invest in a particular segment of the financial market, such as the S&P 500 Stock Index, or in the entire market, such as the Wilshire 5000 Total Stock Market Index. Their objective is to simply match the market returns of that index by investing in the securities in the index. Index funds typically have very low expenses.

Common stock index funds can take you on a rough ride in a volatile market. Because the fund is usually fully invested and doesn't maintain substantial cash reserves, it's fully exposed to market ups and downs. However, over the long term, stock indexing is a sensible investment strategy.

Bond index funds work a little differently, but the basic objectives are the same: Try to match market returns and keep expenses low. Bonds aren't as liquid as stocks, so transaction costs are a bit higher and it's harder to match the benchmark. The standard benchmark is the Lehman Brothers Aggregate Bond Index, which comprises all investment grade bonds. You may find it suitable to invest in a fund targeting this index if you have an intermediate-term investment horizon.

Actively managed funds

Actively managed funds attempt to deliver returns greater than that of the overall market or aim for lower returns with less volatility. Fund managers use a myriad of factors to analyze the economy, industry sectors, and specific companies. Some managers consistently outperform the market on a risk-adjusted basis, but studies show that the majority don't. Managed funds tend to be higher cost than index funds because of the cost of maintaining a research staff and because of more frequent trading.

Some managed funds have low correlation to the market (maybe because they have substantial cash) and therefore hold up pretty well in a downturn but don't do so well when the market rebounds. Others use leverage to magnify the volatility both on the upside and the downside. Most actively managed funds fall somewhere in the middle.

Pick the Funds That Meet Your Needs

After you decide to invest in mutual funds, check out these tips on selecting the right funds for your situation:

- ✓ **Understand your investment objectives, time horizon, and tolerance for risk.** If you're investing for retirement or college more than ten years away, you want to use common stock funds, which can outpace inflation. For shorter-term objectives, less volatile short-term bond funds or money market mutual funds are more appropriate. Regardless, never assume more risk than is necessary to meet your objectives. See Strategy #40.

- ✓ **Decide whether you want to be an active or passive fund investor (or both).** There are thousands of fund choices and many variables to consider, including the fund company, portfolio manager, portfolio characteristics, cost of ownership, and past performance relative to peer groups. If looking at all these variables seems like too much work, then passive investing through common stock index funds may be for you.

- ✓ **Be sure you want to buy bond funds, not individual bonds.** A bond fund has a substantially fixed maturity, so you're always exposed to a certain level of principal risk no matter how long you hold the fund; the maturity of a bond, however, declines steadily, and your principal risk declines each year you hold the bond. Here's how to decide what's right for you:

    - If you want to maintain a fixed stream of interest income payments, buy individual bonds.

    - If you don't have enough assets to buy a diversified portfolio of bonds (Strategy #27), you're best off with a bond mutual fund.

    - If you don't want to analyze bond fund criteria, select a bond index mutual fund.

- ✓ **Pay attention to the fund fees.** Some funds have upfront fees, called *front-loads,* which are really commissions that go to the sales force or companies. Others have redemption fees, called *rear-end loads,* charged when you sell your fund. Still others nick you for a small percentage every year that you own the fund as an additional load.

Hedge Your Bets with Variable Annuities

By Cheryl Krueger

*T*ake a fixed annuity, add control over investment options, sprinkle in some guarantees, and what do you have? A variable annuity. Variable annuities have many of the same characteristics of fixed annuities (see Strategy #19), including tax deferral and the potential for lifetime income. But unlike fixed annuities, variable annuities allow the policyholder to choose the investments that determine the return instead of relying on an insurer's interest return.

Because the variable annuity is an insurance product, it can provide guarantees that aren't available in mutual funds, making this product attractive in uncertain times. Many of these guarantee features appeal to clients looking to benefit from market returns while limiting their risk of losing money.

Understand the Basic Variable Annuity

Like fixed annuities, variable annuities come in two forms: deferred and immediate. (Refer to "Get Assured Income in Retirement" later in this strategy for more information on immediate annuities.) A *deferred variable annuity* essentially looks like a mutual fund account.

When you buy a variable annuity, you select from a limited list of investment funds provided by the company. Your variable annuity account value reflects both gains and losses of the selected investment funds, so you can end up with losses in your variable annuity account. All variable annuities have the following characteristics:

  ✔ Tax deferral on the amount left in accumulation

  ✔ No federal limits on contributions

✔ Funds that are kept separate from the insurer's other assets, so they're not subject to the claims of the company's creditors or other customers of the variable annuity company

✔ Earnings subject to a 10-percent penalty tax if withdrawn prior to age 59$\frac{1}{2}$

Be aware of the various expenses that a variable annuity charges:

✔ **Surrender charges:** If you withdraw from your annuity within the first several years of your payment, the company may keep a certain percentage of the initial premium as a surrender charge. These charges generally start at around 7 percent and decrease by 1 percent per year.

✔ **Fund management fees:** These fees, which go to the investment manager, are a percentage of the account balance. They may vary from 0.25 percent to over 1.00 percent per year, depending on your choice of investment funds.

✔ **Mortality and expense charge:** The insurer charges this fee to cover its expenses and to provide any insurance benefits such as death benefit guarantees and guaranteed withdrawal benefits. These charges can vary from 0.50 percent to over 1.00 percent annually.

✔ **Policy fees:** Insurers may charge a flat fee per contract, typically around $30.

Look into Riders Designed to Reduce Risk

Variable annuities can provide guarantees that mutual funds can't. Twenty years ago, the typical variable deferred annuity had a simple guarantee: the return of your premium to your heirs if you died. But now, you can find many different options to choose from. If you want protection from declines in the markets, these riders may appeal to you.

Use your annuity for retirement income

Annuities are retirement investments, so it's not surprising that insurers have started to enhance variable annuities to provide protection against declines. Here are some of the more common riders:

✔ **Guaranteed minimum income benefit:** With this benefit, your retirement income is based on the value of your annuity account or on your initial premium accumulated at some interest rate (usually 4 to 6 percent), whichever is greater. The benefit applies only if you

- Keep your deferred annuity for a period of time (five to ten years).

- Use the annuity for retirement income benefits, or *annuitization* (receiving regular payments at regular intervals for either a lifetime or a specific period of time).

Many insurers cap the growth at 2.5 to 3 times the original premium.

✔ **Guaranteed lifetime withdrawal benefits:** If you have this rider, you can withdraw a percentage of your account value every year and not outlive your withdrawals. This rider is an alternative to annuitization, and it provides protection against decreasing account values during your retirement.

These guarantees are designed to appeal to investors who are loss averse, and variations appear continuously. Unfortunately, they're an expensive addition to an annuity contract. Keep in mind that with any of these riders, you're buying insurance — and there's a good chance you won't collect just as you won't collect on your auto insurance if you're a good driver. Rather than fully benefiting from increasing markets, you're paying an annual fee to get a floor on your losses.

If you have money to invest, don't get sold on the appeal of annuity guarantees alone. If you do buy, be prepared to have your money invested for at least ten years. Never put all your savings into an annuity contract. In most cases, you should keep IRA and other retirement plan money out of annuities. Read your contract and prospectus, and remember that you have ten days after you get your contract to change your mind.

Finally, note that the insurance company provides the guarantees, even though your assets are in a separate account of the insurance company. Make sure you're dealing with a highly rated company. For insurance company ratings, go to www.ambest.com; make sure your insurer is rated excellent or higher.

Pass your annuity on to heirs

If you're going to pass your annuity on to heirs, the guaranteed minimum death benefit (GMDB) should appeal to you. This rider is still available in its original "return of premium" form; as a matter of fact, most annuities continue to include the cost of this benefit in their basic mortality and expense charge. For an additional cost, you can buy guarantees that lock in death benefits at a higher rate. Different policies have different ways of determining the amount of the guarantee, and charges vary.

The tax benefits of annuities make them more attractive as a retirement vehicle than as a way to transfer money to your heirs. Annuities don't get a step up in basis on death, so your heirs will owe income tax on all your deferred earnings. If you want to use your annuity money during your lifetime, don't pay for an accelerating death benefit guarantee.

Make sure you get your annuity money back

The guaranteed minimum accumulation benefit (GMAB) promises that you'll get your money back if you keep the annuity for a certain number of years, usually ten. If you're not comfortable with downside investment risk and you're a good candidate for an annuity purchase, you may find this feature attractive. The typical annual cost is 0.20 to 0.30 percent.

Get Assured Income in Retirement

You may wonder how long your retirement nest egg will last. An *immediate annuity* (so named because payments start immediately) guarantees that you won't outlive your income. With a *fixed* immediate annuity, payments generally remain level, which means that after a few years, inflation eats away at your income. A *variable* immediate annuity uses market investment returns to (hopefully) provide an increasing benefit stream.

With a variable annuity, benefits are initially based on an assumed interest rate (AIR). This rate is usually in the range of 3 to 6 percent. You may get a choice of rates, or the insurer may have a single rate available. The higher the AIR, the higher the initial benefit. If your selected portfolio yields more than the AIR, your benefit will increase. If your yield is less, your benefit will decrease.

Look for variable annuities with low fees. Select a lower AIR so you'll have more upside potential. And see whether your company offers a *leveling* benefit so your payments change only annually rather than every month.

Manage Your Variable Annuity

When you bought your variable annuity, did you decide to just let it accumulate and not look at the balance? You need to review a variable annuity periodically, just like any investment. A variable annuity account value fluctuates in the same way the market fluctuates. Here are some tips for managing your existing variable annuity:

✔ **Don't forget to include your variable annuity as you consider your portfolio allocation.** When you allocate your investments, pick the best funds available in your variable annuity and then see how they fit within your overall portfolio. Make sure your financial planner knows what investments you have inside your annuity so he or she can consider them in the overall allocation.

✔ **Know your annuity expenses.** If you've had your annuity contract for more than a few years, you may be paying too much in mortality and expense charges. Today, you can buy a variable annuity with Vanguard, Fidelity, or other low-cost providers that have total fees as low as 0.58 percent annually, rather than the 2.37-percent average annual fee. If you're beyond the surrender charge period, you can roll your existing annuity into a new annuity without taxes by using a 1035 exchange.

✔ **Beware of salespeople who tell you your annuity has matured.** If you have a variable annuity with high expenses, transfer those funds to a new annuity only after you've reviewed the expenses, surrender charges, and funds available in the new product. Call your insurance company directly if you have questions about the maturity (or any other) provisions in your current variable annuity contract.

✔ **If you're not rebalancing your variable annuity to keep your allocations in line, check whether your insurer offers an automatic rebalancing program.** These programs are usually free — you just sign up and choose whether to rebalance quarterly, semiannually, or annually.

#23

Invest in Exchange-Traded Funds (ETFs)

By Charles Levin, CPA

Exchange-traded funds, also known as ETFs, have been around since 1993, but their popularity has mushroomed in the last several years. An *ETF* is simply a basket of stocks or bonds that you purchase just like shares of stock. However, with a single investment in an ETF, you own a piece of dozens if not hundreds of different stocks (or bonds). Unlike index mutual funds, ETFs trade on a stock exchange, so you can buy and sell them just like you buy and sell stocks.

The oldest and most popular ETFs track very broad, well-known indexes such as the S&P 500 Stock Index. However, a wide variety of methodologies has emerged for creating new indexes that are tracked by ETFs, ranging from the straightforward to the very complex.

During uncertain economic times, when financial markets tend to exhibit much greater volatility, maintaining discipline takes on even greater importance. ETFs can make it easy for you to implement and maintain this restraint. But you need to know enough about the universe of ETFs to use them wisely. (Part II has several strategies to help you understand risks associated with investing, assess your risk tolerance, and allocate your assets to minimize risk.)

ETFs versus Index Funds: Which Should You Buy?

Index mutual funds and ETFs, especially those ETFs that track broad indexes, have many similarities. However, their structural differences — where they're traded, how they're priced, and so on — can mean that one or the other is a better choice for investors in different situations. (See Strategy #21 for more on index funds.)

Table 23-1 lists the key structural features of ETFs and index funds.

Table 23-1	Exchange-Traded Funds and Index Funds	
Category	*ETFs*	*Index Funds*
Where bought and sold	Traded on the stock exchange	Bought and sold directly from the mutual fund company
Basis of pricing	Based on supply and demand; may be higher or lower than the actual value of the securities held in the fund, though over time they should follow closely to the index they're tracking	Based on the prices of the securities held inside the fund (equal to the fund's net asset value, or NAV)
Timing of pricing	Trading and price quotes are available throughout the day	Priced once per day at the close of trading; you place your order before market close at a price that isn't known until the end of the trading day
Commissions	Paid on each trade based on the commission rate your broker charges	Commission-free if purchased directly from a mutual fund company; can be charged if purchased through a brokerage account

So should you invest in ETFs or index funds? Here are some guidelines:

- ✔ If you're going to be making smaller, periodic investments, such as when you have an amount regularly withdrawn from your bank account or withheld from your paycheck for your company's 401(k) plan, you're likely better off using an index fund purchased directly from a mutual fund company to avoid paying commissions every time.

- ✔ If you're going to be making a single or occasional investment, then the impact of the commissions won't matter much over time. The next priority is then to compare the fees being charged by ETFs and index funds following the same index. ETFs often have lower fees, which can mean a great deal over time and is especially important during uncertain economic times.

In the end, the decision can come down to how often you'll be adding to or withdrawing from your investment.

Evaluate ETFs

You definitely need to do some research before investing in ETFs. A great resource is *Exchange-Traded Funds For Dummies.* You can also find a great deal of information about ETFs on the Internet. Here are some useful sites:

- ✔ **Morningstar.com:** `www.morningstar.com/Cover/ETF.html`
- ✔ **Yahoo! Finance:** `finance.yahoo.com/etf`
- ✔ **The American Stock Exchange:** `amex.com`

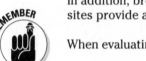

In addition, brokerage firm Web sites and many mutual fund company Web sites provide a wealth of information on ETFs.

When evaluating ETFs, you should focus on these areas:

- ✔ **The index the ETF tracks:** Understand what the index consists of and the rules it follows in selecting and weighting the securities it holds.

- ✔ **How long the ETF and/or its underlying index have been in existence:** You want to buy an ETF that has a track record. If possible, you should also review how the index has performed in good times and bad.

- ✔ **The company that manages the ETF:** Review how long the company has been managing ETFs in general and how long it's been managing the particular ETF you're looking at.

- ✔ **How accurately the ETF has tracked its underlying index:** You can find reports that show the performance of the ETF over various time periods versus its index. If the ETF has been run effectively, the only difference between the performance of the ETF and the underlying index should be the fees charged by the ETF.

- ✔ **The ETF's expense ratios:** The greater the ETF's assets, the more straightforward its investing strategy, and the more prominent and well-known its underlying index, the lower the expenses are likely to be. You should also compare the expense ratios of ETFs that follow the same index. Some have lower fees than others.

Develop an ETF Strategy

Especially in difficult economic times, you need to stick to the basics when investing. Develop an asset allocation that makes sense based on your financial goals, your time horizon for investing, and your capacity for risk. Using ETFs that track broad market indexes gives you wide diversification. Include indexes such as the following, which are all widely used, highly diversified indexes that have been in existence for a long time:

- ✔ **S&P 500:** Large company U.S. stocks
- ✔ **Wilshire 5000:** All U.S. stocks
- ✔ **Russell 2000:** Small company U.S. stocks
- ✔ **MSCI EAFE:** Foreign stocks of countries with developed financial markets
- ✔ **MSCI Emerging Markets Index:** Foreign stocks of countries whose markets are less developed
- ✔ **Lehman Brothers Aggregate Bond Index:** U.S. bonds

Some newer ETFs are much riskier than index funds and ETFs that invest in broad market indexes. The following types of ETFs are too risky to be sensibly used by the vast majority of investors, especially in these uncertain times:

- ✔ A number of the newer ETFs follow much narrower indexes that, for example, may track the stocks of a single country, industry, or commodity (such as the price of oil). These ETFs tend to have much higher fees than those that track broad indexes, and these fees can greatly reduce the value of your portfolio over time. In addition, the more narrowly focused ETFs are often trying to capitalize on what's been most recently the hot segment of the market, and you just may find yourself investing at exactly the wrong time.

- ✔ Some ETFs magnify the positive and negative returns of an index. For example, one ETF uses *leverage,* or borrowing, in order to generate twice the yield of the S&P 500. When the market is going up, this ETF greatly increases your gain. But if the market is down, your losses are magnified as well. If you choose to invest in one of the leveraged ETFs, be prepared for a wild ride through the ups and downs of its performance. Although the gains can be huge, so can the losses.

- ✔ You can also find ETFs that are structured to generate a gain equal to the amount the market or a specific market segment has *lost.*

Only the most sophisticated investors should short-sell ETFs. *Short-selling,* or *shorting,* is borrowing shares from a broker and then immediately selling them with the idea that you'll buy the shares back at a lower price. You're betting that the market is going to decline.

#24

Diversify with Real Estate Investment Trusts

. . . .

By Brian R. Smith, PhD

. . . .

You don't have to be a real estate tycoon or an investor with a high net worth to benefit from real estate. Many people first experience real estate investing when buying their first home. For some, a next step may be the purchase of another residential property or house.

But managing tenants, property, and cash flow can be burdensome. In addition, you have to be savvy when choosing location and negotiating terms and conditions. Furthermore, the cost and complexity of commercial real estate make it out of reach for most investors. If investing in real estate sounds daunting , real estate investment trusts (REITs) may be right for you. REITs are also a common asset class in many diversified portfolios.

Get to Know REITs

REITs are corporations that invest in real estate and pay out at least 90 percent of their income in dividends. Some offer the potential for large dividends and trade on the public stock exchange. REITs are more liquid than traditional real estate investments in which you're the landlord. In addition, investors don't need to worry about negotiating, repairing, advertising, pricing, or selling.

Here are the three types of REITs:

✔ **Equity:** These REITs own and operate income-producing properties — such as apartment buildings, offices, shopping centers, self-storage facilities, and industrial warehouses — and they engage in a wide range of real estate activities, including leasing, development, and management. They're the largest and most widely known type of REIT.

✔ **Mortgage:** These REITs lend money directly to real estate owners and operators or extend credit indirectly through the acquisition of loans or mortgage-backed securities.

Changes in interest rates and the possibility of defaults make mortgage REITs more volatile than equity REITs.

✔ **Hybrid:** These REITs both own properties and make loans to real estate owners and operators.

Table 24-1 describes the characteristics of publicly traded REITs.

Table 24-1	How Publicly Traded REITs Measure Up
Characteristic	*Description*
Performance	The dividends are generally competitive when compared to those of investment-grade corporate bonds, Treasury bonds, and stocks. REITs can provide strong capital appreciation.
Taxation	Dividends are taxed as ordinary income; capital appreciation, as capital gains.
Liquidity	REITs trade like stocks on public exchanges. Transaction costs can be low when you use discount brokers.
Diversification	REITs have low correlation to other asset classes. You can purchase them in mutual funds of REITs, indexes, or as focused exchange-traded funds (ETFs) in particular sectors. Geographic diversity is an additional advantage.
Transparency	Reporting is done in compliance with SEC requirements for publicly listed securities.
Leverage	You can buy REITs, ETF REITs, or mutual fund REITs on margin in taxable brokerage accounts.

See Strategy #23 for more on exchange-traded funds (ETFs).

When REITs aren't offered through public exchanges, investors may be restricted from selling shares (or units) in accordance with specified terms and conditions. These privately held REITs may offer higher dividends and the possibility of significant capital appreciation, but they may require high minimum investments, lack transparency, and have diversification risks that are more difficult to understand.

Fit REITs into Your Portfolio

REITs — which aren't strongly correlated with other asset classes, such as stocks or bonds — should comprise 3 to 10 percent of your total portfolio. Be aware that you may already own REITs in your stock portfolio. For example, the S&P 500 has approximately 2 percent in REITs.

For greater diversification, use mutual funds that own several different REITs. Some good no-load REIT funds include Fidelity Real Estate, Vanguard REIT Index, ProLogis, and Cohen & Steers Realty Shares.

REITs also offer an advantage that traditional rental real estate doesn't: You can readily include REITs in your retirement account (for example, an IRA or Keogh).

So how do you value a REIT? Look at its net asset value (NAV), adjusted funds from operations (AFFO), and cash available for distribution (CAD). If you want to compare REITs to stocks, the price divided by the AFFO is roughly equivalent to the P/E ratio for a stock (refer to Strategy #43 for more on P/E ratios):

REIT value = price ÷ adjusted funds from operations

For more information, contact the National Association of Real Estate Investment Trusts (www.nareit.com).

Consider a Separately Managed Account

By Thomas Arconti, CFP

For most investors, a well diversified portfolio of mutual funds and/ or exchange-traded funds (ETFs) serves them well throughout their lifetimes. However, you may have reason to want a professionally tailored portfolio.

Many studies show that low-cost, passive investing outperforms active investment management over the long haul. But in periods of uncertain economic times, you may want to engage in a specific investment strategy that you believe will perform better under current conditions. Or you may simply take greater comfort in having a professional money manager at the helm. In that case, separately managed accounts (SMAs) may provide an alternative or complement to mutual-fund investing. Read on to discover more about these customized accounts.

Understand What SMAs Are

A *separately managed account* (SMA) is an investment portfolio that one or more professional money managers control on behalf of an individual or institution. Most often, large financial firms like banks, full-service brokerage houses, or fund companies are the ones who offer SMAs.

The account manager provides model portfolios based on selected investment criteria (such as large cap value, small company growth, and so on), but you can get a portfolio that's customized to meet your particular needs, such as minimizing taxable distributions and generating income. An SMA can be comprised of stocks, bonds, cash, or other types of securities, and the account manager has discretion — the ability to buy or sell securities on your behalf — as long as the investment choices conform to the stated investment strategy.

Similar to hiring other professionals (such as an attorney or CPA), you hire an account manager to oversee and manage, on a day-to-day basis, either a portion of or your entire investment portfolio. You may confer with the account manager about your investment account, and at times you may direct the manager to take certain actions; but generally, you hire the manager for his or her particular expertise, and you expect the manager to call the shots regarding investment decisions related to the managed account.

Weigh the Pros and Cons of SMAs

Like any type of investment product or service, SMAs have advantages and disadvantages. On the plus side, here's what you get:

- ✔ **Tax efficiency:** Individual cost basis allows you to harvest capital gains and losses to minimize your capital gains tax liability. In other words, the SMA manager minimizes your taxable gains. With other taxable investments, you'd have to do it yourself.

- ✔ **Professional management:** Professional money managers conduct the research and analysis to make informed decisions on your behalf.

- ✔ **Manager access:** You can discuss the details of your investments and express any concerns or constraints you have with the account managers.

- ✔ **Transparency:** You always know what you're invested in because your account statements list each individual holding, with number of shares, cost basis, and current values.

- ✔ **Customization:** You can include or exclude certain securities or entire sectors. For instance, if you've accumulated a concentrated position in your employer's company stock, such as Intel, you can exclude Intel and similar technology stocks from your holdings.

- ✔ **Liquidity:** You can buy and sell individual securities as needed, as opposed to trading shares of a single fund (as is the case with mutual funds or ETFs).

Here are some of the disadvantages:

- ✔ **High fees and minimum investments:** SMAs typically come with high fees in order to provide the personalized service. The fees are usually charged as a percentage of assets under management (AUM) and can range from 1.0 to 3.0 percent. A minimum investment is generally required as well.

- ✔ **Manager options:** Upwards of 25,000 asset managers are in the marketplace. You have to narrow the field and select the manager(s) who can provide a good fit for you and offer the best chance to achieve your financial goals.

> ✔ **Need for ongoing monitoring:** You have to continually monitor the performance of your manager(s) to determine relative performance to the market: Are the managers worth their fees? Are they staying true to their philosophy and approach? Is there style drift, such as buying growth companies in a value portfolio? What's their trading frequency? Their compliance history?

Compare SMAs to Mutual Funds

The primary difference between a separately managed account and a mutual fund is that in an SMA, you actually own shares of the individual stocks in the portfolio. With mutual funds, you don't individually own any of the underlying shares that comprise that fund. Instead, the mutual fund company owns the shares and the investors share the benefits in common.

Table 25-1 provides a side-by-side comparison of the key features of SMAs and mutual funds.

Table 25-1	Features of SMAs and Mutual Funds	
Features	*Separately Managed Accounts*	*Mutual Funds*
Access to professional managers	Individual investors may have direct access to the account manager.	Individual investors have no direct access to fund managers.
Portfolio structure	Individuals can have a portfolio customized to meet their specific needs and desires.	The portfolio is structured to meet the fund's written investment strategy. No customization is allowed.
Full investment capability	Investors can fully invest the account for maximum potential gain. The manager isn't required to hold cash in the account.	Mutual funds usually hold cash to meet redemption requirements. If short on cash, managers may be forced to sell holdings to meet the redemption demand.
Taxation	Can be tax efficient; by choosing when to buy or sell individual securities in the account, investors can harvest tax losses	Generally not tax efficient for individual investors because buying and selling decisions are made on a global basis (**Note:** Some funds are designed and marketed as tax-managed funds. Others, such as index funds, tend to be inherently tax efficient.)

Features	Separately Managed Accounts	Mutual Funds
Minimum investment requirements	SMAs have much higher minimum investment requirements than mutual funds. Minimums vary but usually begin at $100,000.	Most mutual funds have low minimums. They vary from as low as $50 to $10,000 or more on the high end.
Fees	Management fees vary but are usually significantly higher than those of mutual funds. Total fees include the management fee, brokerage costs, and account service fee. These can range from 1.5% to 3% per year.	Management fees can range from as low as 0.2% for no-load index funds to around 2% for actively managed funds. Brokerage fees and other costs must also be included. These additional fees can result in total costs of about 0.3% to 3% per year.

Exchange-traded funds (ETFs) have many of the same features as mutual funds, except ETFs are fully invested. They offer great tax efficiency and liquidity, with no minimum investment requirements and at a much lower cost than SMAs. For more on ETFs, see Strategy #23.

Examine the Types of SMAs

Just like mutual funds and ETFs, you can obtain separately managed accounts in many flavors. You may want a narrowly focused SMA that specializes in one investment style (such as international growth or large cap value). Or you can employ a strategy mixing small, mid, and large cap equities (an All-Cap Core Equity strategy) that'll meet your needs for a diversified portfolio. Here are examples of how you may use each type of SMA:

✔ **Single-style SMAs:** Suppose you've accumulated a good core portfolio through your 401(k) at work. You also have a sizable taxable investment account. After reviewing your overall asset allocation, you realize you're overweighted in growth company funds and have little exposure to large cap value companies. You'd like the ability to manage capital gains and losses in your taxable account and also believe that in this market environment, an experienced asset manager could probably find good investment opportunities in the value arena. You research separate account managers who specialize in large cap value portfolios and choose one to manage this account for you.

✔ **Multiple-style SMAs:** You're a detail-oriented person who prefers a more hands-on approach to investing and likes the ongoing personal service offered by SMAs. You decide to put your full portfolio in the hands of experts with whom you can confer. To get a diversified, balanced portfolio, you need a multiple-style SMA. Here are two approaches:

- You hire an account manager who serves as the general contractor and then hires subaccount managers, each with his or her own style and sector expertise. This type of multiple-style managed account often requires higher minimum investments (perhaps in the $250,000 category) to achieve proper diversification.

- You find a single account manager who offers a broad-based, diversified portfolio of varying asset classes.

Invest in SMAs Wisely

If you think SMAs may be a viable investment option, do the following:

✔ Define your investment goals and guidelines (see Strategy #13).

✔ Compare SMA investing to ETF or mutual fund investing to make sure SMAs are the right choice for you. (In other words, do you need a custom tailored suit, or will off-the-rack suit you fine?)

✔ Conduct due diligence to find the right managers for you. Be sure to review Form ADV Schedule H. This form, which is required for all managed accounts, describes the SMAs objectives and expenses.

If you search hard, you can find lower cost alternatives to traditional SMAs by hiring asset managers that use very low cost, no-load mutual funds and/or ETFs in the portfolio instead of individual stocks. These managers may charge a fee of 0.25 to 0.50 percent for their services. When combined with the expense ratios of the individual holdings in the portfolio, the total overall management fee could still remain well under 1.0 percent.

✔ Regularly monitor the performance of your investment managers to confirm they're continuing to meet your objectives and are providing benefits in excess of their fees.

Although you can direct the account manger to make changes to your SMA, second guessing or micromanaging the investment decisions isn't a good idea. After all, you're paying for the managers' expertise with the assumption that they can produce better results than you. Agree on the investment strategy upfront and indentify any constraints you have. Then let the account manager make future decisions within those parameters.

Invest in Individual Stocks

• •

By Herb Montgomery, CFP

• •

*I*nvesting in individual stocks can be fun and profitable, but it's not a walk in the park. It also exposes you to higher risks. Start out small, don't invest more than you can lose, and research!

Do Some Serious Soul-Searching

If you're going to take the plunge and begin investing in individual stocks, a question-and-answer period with yourself is in order. Write down the questions as well as the answers to avoid any finger-pointing if things don't go as planned.

Are you willing to be an investor rather than a trader?

An *investor* purchases shares in a company that he or she knows something about and plans to hold these shares to reap the benefits of a successful company. An investor expects both long-term growth in share value as well as the payment of dividends along the way. A *trader* buys shares of stock in a company, expecting the price of the stock to rise rapidly so he or she can cash out with a quick gain.

Historically, investors are more successful than traders over long periods of time. An investor isn't hit with short-term capital gains, trading commissions, and most importantly, the inability to successfully time the market. Investing on a whim or a hot tip isn't investing; it's gambling. Save the gambling for casinos, not your brokerage account.

Investors also need discipline, which includes a systematic approach to taking profits and realizing losses. Don't get caught up in the emotion of the moment. Don't fall so in love with a stock on the rise that you refuse to sell when it starts to drop. Be willing to admit your mistakes and sell a loser before it becomes next to worthless. Remember some of the darling stocks of the past that plunged rapidly while their investors stubbornly held on to them.

How much money are you willing to lose?

Yes, it's possible to lose every cent you put into the stock market! If you have a certain amount of cash that you're willing to risk losing completely, identify the amount, write it down, and don't exceed it.

Also remember the importance of diversification. One argument for investing through mutual funds is that mutual funds can pool money and purchase a wide variety of stocks or bonds. You need to invest in a wide variety of stocks as well. Avoid having more than 10 percent of your total portfolio in any one stock. Also avoid buying too many similar stocks. If you own only technology stocks, for example, and technology goes through a rough patch, like it did in 2001 and 2002, you could lose most of your investment. If you can't diversify sufficiently, consider mutual funds. See Strategies #41 through #46 for more on diversification.

How much time and money can you commit to research?

A full-time job, spouse, children, elderly parent, house, and yard may all compete for your time. Because the time spent researching companies directly affects your success in the stock market, be sure you realize that time spent researching is time taken from your other activities.

If you think you can pick a winning stock, good luck. People choose good stocks all the time, but the good choices are usually the result of good, thorough research. Note that even full-time professionals choose stinkers — think Enron, Lucent, and MCI. The stinkers are often impulse buys or just changing markets.

Research Before and After You Invest

If you're still convinced that buying individual stocks is for you, here's how to approach the work required. Assuming you have the time to do all the research, this section guides you in choosing companies and stocks to invest in and then managing those investments.

Spend some time with annual reports

You need to think about the following characteristics of the companies you're interested in:

✔ **Free cash flow:** What's left after the bills are paid

✔ **Returns on equity:** How much the company made on the money invested in it

✔ **Returns on assets:** How much the company made by using the assets it owns

✔ **Net margins:** How much the company made from every dollar of sales

Each of these items is readily available in the *financial results* section of the company's annual report. Of course, this type of research isn't for the faint of heart or the easily distracted. Never attempt to read an annual report while driving or operating heavy machinery!

These days, annual and quarterly reports are available on every company Web site. Or you can call a company's headquarters and someone there will be happy to mail you an annual report. But don't get carried away by the pretty pictures. Look closely at the financials. Identifying trends is important. Have the returns on equity been growing for the past few years? Are net margins consistently growing? Be sure to check the footnotes to make sure a growth spurt (or loss) wasn't caused by a one-time factor. *Note:* One year of great financials following several years of poor financials isn't necessarily a trend.

Follow some general research advice

Here are rules to consider when doing your own research:

✔ Use an *independent research firm,* someone with absolutely no financial interest in any of the companies under consideration for investment.

✔ Look at the competition. Who's growing faster? Who has better financials? Who has more new products in the pipeline?

✔ Calculate how much the company is worth. Buy a stock only if you can get it at discount to its fair value; you need some wiggle room if the stock price begins to slide.

✔ Pick companies for the long term. Remember that you're an investor, not a trader. Look for companies with solid financials and good growth prospects for the next five to ten years. Traders are hoping for that one big inning. Investors are looking for a championship.

✔ Sell at the right time. The right time depends on the company. If the fundamentals have changed and you probably wouldn't purchase the stock presently, it's time to sell. Perhaps the stock has performed well, but its price is now too high to justify further growth. Or maybe there's been a change in the economy and the company's products aren't as desirable as they once were, or maybe competition has stepped in. Any of these factors could trigger a sale. However, if all the reasons you purchased the stock in the first place still apply, keep it. Sometimes even the best companies experience temporary setbacks.

Don't let any one stock position grow to more than 10 to 12 percent of your entire portfolio.

Know where to find good information

There are numerous free and paid services that can be useful when you're trying to decide whether a company is suitable to invest in at a given point in time. Are these sources always right? No, but if you're not willing or lack the time to do the research, their picks will undoubtedly be better than just shooting from the hip. Here are some sources:

- ✔ Your brokerage account, whether it's with a wire house or discount broker, has several offerings, either paid services or free with your account. Many have stock screens where you enter your criteria and eliminate companies that don't interest you.

- ✔ Yahoo! Finance (`finance.yahoo.com`) has mountains of information about companies — and best of all, it's free.

- ✔ Standard & Poor's (`www.standardandpoors.com`) is one of the major independent research firms that provides accurate, unbiased information to the public. Many good brokerage firms provide S&P's analyst reports to compare opinions with the brokerage's own analysts.

- ✔ Morningstar (`www.morningstar.com`) is a favorite research site for professionals as well as do-it-yourselfers. Their free site is a good place to start, though the Premium Membership (which is quite reasonable) gets you into the screens and more in-depth analysis. They also have several different newsletters both in print and online.

"Expert stock pickers" also put out paid newsletters. Some of them have pretty good track records; some are legends only in their own minds. Most of them probably generate more income from selling newsletters then they do from picking successful stocks. (If they're so good at picking stocks, why do they need to sell newsletters?)

The Five Rules For Successful Stock Investing, by Pat Dorsey, Director of Stock Analysis at Morningstar (Wiley), and *The Ultimate Dividend Playbook,* by Josh Peters, CFA Editor of Morningstar Dividend Investor (Wiley), may be helpful in both your research and your individual stock selection.

Invest in Individual Bonds

By John Vyge, CFP

*I*n uncertain times, reducing the volatility of your investment portfolio should be your top priority. Adding individual bonds to your portfolio is a great way to minimize volatility. Although stocks and stock mutual funds can fluctuate wildly every time a TV commentator announces "what's going to happen next," individual bonds can be your portfolio's Rock of Gibraltar.

Understand Bond Basics

A *bond* is a debt obligation from an issuer, usually a government or corporation. Governments and corporations issue bonds to raise money to build bridges, schools, hospitals, and new factories. They're borrowing money from you, the bond investor. If you hold an individual bond until it matures, you'll receive the face value of the bond along with fixed interest payments — as long as the issuer doesn't default.

The less likely the borrower is to default on payments to you, the less risky the bond; and the less risky the bond, the lower the interest rate the borrower is willing to pay you. In the case of corporate bonds, usually the riskiest of all bonds, bond holders still have priority over the shareholders of the company. In other words, if a company goes out of business, any assets of the company are used up in the following order:

1. Creditors
2. Bond holders
3. Preferred stock holders
4. Common stock holders

Bond types

Bonds are issues by local, state, and federal governments; government agencies; and corporations. You can typically invest in the types of bonds shown in Table 27-1. (See Strategy #18 for more about Treasury and agency bonds.)

Table 27-1		Bond Types and Risks
Bond Type	*Issuer*	*Risk/Interest*
Treasury	U.S. government	They pay interest semiannually and are considered to be credit-risk free.
Agency	Government-sponsored entities such as FNMA, GNMA, and FHLM	They pay a slightly higher return than Treasuries because they're not quite as secure and may fluctuate more in value.
Municipal ($5,000 minimum investment)	State and local governments	They pay lower interest rates but are generally tax-exempt, so the after-tax return is attractive to many investors. The two main types are *general obligation bonds* and *revenue bonds;* general obligation bonds are safer than revenue bonds but often pay a lower interest rate.
Corporate ($1,000 minimum investment)	Corporations, to pay for corporate projects	They attract investors who seek the higher yields in exchange for a higher risk of default.

Some corporate, municipal, and government agency bonds offer additional risk in that they can be *called,* or redeemed, by the issuer at full face value prior to the due date. You therefore miss out on some interest payments.

So how do you decide which type of bond to hold? In a nutshell, if you're looking for the highest level of security, Treasury bonds are for you. Need a tax break? Municipal bonds are exempt from federal tax and can be exempt from state and local tax if you reside where the bonds are issued. Looking for the highest income? Corporate bonds are usually your best bet.

Your return on investment: Yields, yields, and more yields

Why buy a bond when you can just put your money into a savings account or money market account? Well, savings account interest can fluctuate up and down, but bond interest is fixed. Here are four ways of looking at the return you get from a bond:

- ✔ **Coupon interest:** Bonds pay you a stream of periodic interest payments, called *coupons,* semiannually.

- ✔ **Current yield:** The return you get paid annually, in the form of coupons, based on the initial price you paid for the bond, is called the *current yield.*

- ✔ **Face value:** Face value, or *par,* is the dollar amount that'll be returned to you when your bond matures. Most bonds are issued with a face value of $1,000. However, you may purchase a bond for more or less than its face value. The bond matures at face value, so any extra premium you paid reduces your yield to maturity; but if you purchased the bond at a discount, your yield to maturity is higher than the coupon rate.

- ✔ **Yield to maturity (YTM):** YTM is the actual rate of return you receive on a bond investment, if you hold the bond until it matures.

You need to be earning a yield that's higher than inflation. To combat inflation, the Treasury now offers ten-year *Treasury inflation-protected securities* (TIPS). In exchange for a lower coupon interest payment, the face value of a TIPS bond gets adjusted semiannually to reflect inflation. Indirectly, this adjustment actually increases your coupon payment because the coupon itself is based on the inflation-adjusted face value.

Tax treatment

Tax treatment varies, depending on the type of bond:

- ✔ Treasury and agency bond interest is subject to ordinary federal income tax but is exempt from state and local taxes.

- ✔ Municipal bond interest is generally exempt from federal tax, though certain types of municipal bonds, such as *passive activity bonds,* can trigger the dreaded alternative minimum tax.

- ✔ Residents of the state where the bond is issued can avoid state and local taxes. Check your state for specific tax implications.

- ✔ Income from corporate bonds is taxed as ordinary income.

Pay attention to taxes when choosing bonds. Municipal bonds should never be in an IRA because they're already tax exempt; instead, use corporate bonds because of their higher taxable yield. If you're in a very high tax bracket, arrange the overall portfolio so that most of the corporate bonds and other high-yielding securities are inside tax-sheltered accounts, such as employer sponsored retirement plans and IRAs, while keeping municipal bonds and stocks in the taxable accounts.

Comparing yields: A not-so-taxing endeavor

When you buy a municipal bond, the promised yield is often lower than that of other types of bonds. That's because in exchange for a lower yield, you don't have to pay federal tax on the interest you receive. So how can you compare the yield on a municipal bond to that of another bond? You have to calculate something called the *tax equivalent yield* (TEY):

(***Note:*** Check your tax return for your marginal tax rate.) The result in this formula is a number that you can use to compare municipal bonds to other bonds that are subject to federal taxes, such as Treasury, agency, and corporate bonds.

TEY = municipal yield ÷ (1 − your marginal tax rate)

Climb the Bond Ladder in Uncertain Times

When interest rates rise, bond prices fall; and when interest rates fall, bond prices rise. Longer term bonds are more sensitive to interest rate changes, but as a bond maturity date gets closer, it fluctuates less in price.

Changes in interest rates can wreak havoc on the value of your bonds. Furthermore, tying your money up for long periods of time at one interest rate means you may miss out on higher interest rates in a rising interest rate environment. One strategy to combat this problem is to use a *bond ladder,* which consists of short-term, intermediate-term, and long-term bonds. As each individual bond matures, you invest the cash you receive from the maturing bond into new long-term bonds or the highest-yielding bonds available at the time.

Buying bonds

Bonds are available individually through discount brokers, full service brokers, and *bond brokers* (companies that specialize in individual bonds). Each of these providers can design an individual bond portfolio to meet your needs. Just call their fixed income department.

To build a diversified bond portfolio, you should probably have at least $50,000 to start. Otherwise, stick with a low-cost bond fund from a discount broker. For more on building a diversified bond portfolio, see Strategy #46.

For commission-free trades, you can purchase U.S. Treasury bonds directly from the government (www.treasurydirect.gov).

Reviewing bond ratings

Just as you get a personal credit rating, municipal and corporate bonds are rated, too. Bond rating services, such as S&P and Moody's, analyze and rate the financial security of the issuing company or agency. Even though bond ratings can be wrong (even some of Enron's bond ratings were investment grade in the months leading up to its collapse), they're a starting point. Choose from two categories of bonds:

- ✔ **Investment grade bonds:** Bonds rated at this level have a relatively low risk of default. S&P rates investment grade bonds at BBB or higher, and Moody's uses Baa or higher.

- ✔ **Speculative grade bonds:** Bonds rated at this level have a relatively high risk of default. They're also called junk bonds. S&P uses BB or lower, and Moody's uses Ba or lower.

Treasury bonds aren't rated (they're assumed to have no risk of default), and agencies generally receive the highest rating available.

If a bond's rating is changed for the worse due to the profitability or credit rating of the company, the bond's market value may go down. This doesn't change the amount you'll receive if you hold the bond to maturity or the amount of interest you're paid because these amounts are based on the face value of the bond, but it can be a problem if you need to sell the bond prematurely.

Hedge with Options

By Gigi Turbow Marx, MBA

*H*ow many times have you heard the mantra that stocks outperform all other assets in the long term? Unfortunately, many retiree wannabes are finding out the hard way that the long term can be *really* long.

The most important reason to hedge is that waiting for the long term isn't always an option. Investment success comes from careful risk management, which means minimizing losses, not from being a genius stock picker. Broad diversification among asset classes should be your first line of risk management defense (see Strategy #40). But hedging provides you with a Plan B, and having a back-up plan is definitely the best plan in uncertain times! The strategy explains how to use options to hedge.

Know the Options Basics

Options are a *derivative* product. Very simply, that means their value is derived from something else. If you buy or sell options on an asset such as a stock or exchange-traded fund (defined as the *underlying* asset), the price of the option is going to move with that stock or index in a fairly well-defined relationship. That relationship allows you to use options to track price changes in the underlying asset for a fraction of the cost.

Understand how options work

Here are some useful options-related terms you should be familiar with:

- **Premium:** The premium is the price of the option.
- **Strike (exercise) price:** This is price at which you agree to buy or sell the underlying asset if the option is exercised.
- **Expiration:** The date on which the option ceases to exist; all rights and obligations conferred by the option contract terminate when the option expires.
- **Contract size:** One contract is equal to 100 shares of the underlying asset.

Any options contract gives rights to the buyer and commits the seller to obligations. Options also come in two varieties, calls and puts, depending on whether the buyer wants the right to purchase or sell the underlying asset. Table 28-1 shows how these rights and obligations break down.

Table 28-1	Rights and Obligations of Options Contracts	
Buyer or Seller of the Option	*Calls*	*Puts*
Option holder (buyer)	By buying a call option, the holder purchases the right to buy the underlying asset at the strike price.	By buying a put option, the holder purchases the right to sell the underlying asset at the strike price.
Option writer (seller)	By selling a call option, the writer commits to selling the underlying asset at the strike price.	By selling a put option, the writer commits to buying the underlying asset at the strike price.

Perhaps the single most important concept for you to master about options is the following one: Options have a limited life.

Unlike your core portfolio holdings, options expire, and when they do, they no longer have value and no longer exist. That may actually be your goal. If it's not, you can liquidate an option position or roll it over to another strike price or another time period. The important point is that you must do it *before* the expiration. This underscores the point that hedging requires an economic point of view and active oversight.

Look at how you can use options to hedge

You can use options for the following reasons:

- To protect your portfolio
- To generate additional income
- For speculation/leverage

A 2008 Charles Schwab study of options trading found that, contrary to popular perception, only one in four traders surveyed indicated market speculation was their leading reason to trade options. Three-quarters of the respondents used options with the goal of generating income or hedging for risk management.

Okay, but how do you actually use this stuff? In this limited space, I can barely scratch the surface of useful ways to apply options, but the following example may give you some ideas. Consider the unpleasant situation in which one of your ETFs has fallen 20 percent over the past year. In theory, you know that you should try to buy more to reduce your average cost and rebalance your holdings. In reality, you have little cash and even less stomach for further losses.

If you have only $5,000, you could use the whole amount to buy 50 shares of your now-$100 stock today. Alternatively, you could purchase call options — the right to buy that stock — for less money and buy yourself some time to see whether the situation worsens or improves before you commit to buying more stock.

Say you already own 400 shares. You decide to buy four call contracts at a $95 strike price to reduce your cost basis more effectively. You see that you can buy options that expire in four months for a premium cost of $7 a share, costing a total of $2,800 ($7 per share × 100 shares per contract × 4 contracts).

If your analysis is correct and the stock recovers to $105, you've locked in the right to buy up to 400 shares at a cost of the strike price ($95) plus the premium ($7), or $102 per share in total — $3 less than market price.

But what if you really want to add only 50 shares to your position? By selling 350 shares in the stock market at $105 and exercising your contracts to buy 400 shares, you'll get your 50 shares. You'll also get a $1,050 gain on the stock you don't want to keep ($3 × 350)! That's a gain you can use to replenish your cash account or to repair another investment. (And *that's* why they call them *options*, Virginia!)

What if your analysis is wrong and the stock keeps dropping? Again, the value of your options will move in tandem with the underlying asset — that is, down. But you've limited the potential loss on your investment strategy because you can't lose more than the ($2,800) premium you paid, and you've still got some cash left to consider a new strategy.

Do Your Homework

Options trading is a game of strategy similar to competitive chess or sports. It's versatile but complex, so make sure you do your homework and research the risks and returns of any strategy you want to pursue.

Start with the Options Industry Council (OIC) Web site (www.888options.com): The council is comprised of all the U.S. options exchanges plus the Options Clearing Corporation. It has a vested interest in protecting the good reputation of its market, and that means it has a vested interest in protecting you, the investor.

You've probably seen those car ads where they warn "Professional driver on a closed track: Do not attempt." If you're an aspiring do-it-yourselfer, use the Options Industry Council's (OIC's) version of a closed track (www.888options.com) — they offer a virtual trading tool that allows you to practice with electronic money before you put real money at risk!

One visit to the OIC Web site should convince you that you don't need to pay lots of money for an options newsletter. The resources available through the OIC are comprehensive, approved by regulated compliance departments, and free of charge.

Newsletter vendors, whether covering options or any other investment, aren't regulated. They can consequently make all sorts of ungrounded claims about potential investment returns without fear of scrutiny or sanctions. Until you know enough to evaluate which newsletters are reputable, stick with the OIC for education and a registered investment advisor or SEC-regulated broker dealer for implementation.

Take Your First Steps

You may be shocked to discover that you can't just decide that you'd like to try a little options trading one day and go place an order. You first have to apply to your brokerage firm for trading authorization. There are multiple levels of authorization, and you have to graduate through the ranks. Demonstrate financial capacity and reasonable care at conservative strategies, and they'll approve you for more complex strategies. Believe me — they're doing you a favor because they've seen the roadkill. Here are some other important rules of the road for novices:

- **Start with the asset or market you understand best.** Options trading is complex, so make sure you're familiar with the underlying assets.

- **Start small.** Just because you have $5,000 doesn't mean you should spend it all in one place! Options provide a lot of leverage for a wee bit of cash, but it works in both directions — gains *and* losses.

Invest in Commodities

By Robert Friedland, PhD

*A*ny resource whose quality is easily measured can be, and most likely is, a *commodity.* Common commodities include the following:

- Nonrenewable energy such as oil or natural gas
- Agricultural products such as cocoa, coffee, corn, cotton, orange juice, soybeans, sugar, and wheat
- Livestock such as cattle or hogs
- Timber
- Metals such as copper, gold, nickel, platinum, silver, and zinc

Commodity values have cycles different from those of stocks and bonds. They also provide protection from inflation, particularly unexpected inflation. Unexpected or accelerating inflation tends to reduce the value of stocks and bonds. But when the primary source of this inflation is the cost of raw inputs — that is, commodities — the value of commodities also rises.

Although commodities themselves are traded in both local and global markets, the global trading of commodity derivatives plays a huge role in commodity pricing. *Derivative* is a fancy name for a contract that derives its value from something tangible. Common types of derivatives are futures contracts, forwards contracts, options contracts (see Strategy #28), and swaps. (For more information on derivatives, see the latest edition of *Investing For Dummies,* by Eric Tyson [Wiley].) Although handling a contract is less smelly than handling a pork belly, the real purpose of derivatives is to reduce business risk.

When you buy stock, you're buying part of a company. When you buy a bond, you're buying part of the debt issued by that company or government. When you buy a commodity, you're buying the raw input into the production of everything that's produced. Including commodities in your portfolio enables you to diversify your risks in a unique way. You can share in the growth of the global economy and hedge against inflation.

Lock in a Price with Commodities Futures

Commodities markets are essential for those who grow, raise, or extract commodities and for businesses that use these resources in their production. For instance, a farmer decides which crops and/or livestock to raise, in part, by comparing anticipated costs to expected market prices. Although the farmer can reasonably estimate production costs in advance, he or she has no way of knowing what the sale price of the crop will be at harvest. Buying a futures contract allows the farmer to get someone to commit to a purchase price well ahead of time.

How do commodities futures work?

A *futures contract* is an obligation to either sell or buy a particular commodity at a specific price on a specific day. For instance, a farmer can go to the commodities exchange and purchase a contract to sell wheat at a specific price and date in the future. This contract reflects both the farmer's willingness to deliver the wheat at a specific price and the willingness of a buyer to pay that price. A likely buyer is a company that mills wheat into flour. The company needs to plan its production and market the flour to its customers, such as bakeries, so the company wants to lock in the price it'll pay for the wheat it'll need in the future.

If, by the time the crop comes to harvest, the market price (spot price) is lower than the contractual price, the farmer will be glad he or she entered into this contract. The miller, however, won't be so happy, because that company will be obligated to buy the wheat for more than the market price.

This contract eliminates some risks to each business, but the derivatives market helps further. If the miller can anticipate a drop in the wheat price below the contractual price, it'll try to sell its contract ahead of time. If, on the other hand, the market price for this crop turns out to be higher than the contractual price, the tables turn and now the farmer may try to sell the contract in advance. However, the miller and the farmer wouldn't be able to find buyers without a larger marketplace. This is where investors like you come in.

Most commodity investors aren't interested in or capable of taking possession of or delivering the commodity. After all, where would you store 20 tons of frozen trimmed pork bellies or 1,000 barrels of crude oil or 25,000 pounds of copper? Investors are, however, interested in making a profit, and they consider a variety of factors when deciding how much to pay the farmer or miller for the contract. The investor makes judgments concerning weather, infectious disease, accidents, fire, supply, political changes (such as nationalization, revolution, or democratization), currency exchange rates, and the actions of other buyers and sellers. Successful commodity investors have to make buy/sell decisions based on all these factors and perhaps more.

Why invest in commodities?

Assume that a barrel of sweet grade light crude oil is $150. What if you purchased a contract six months ago for $25,000, allowing you to buy 1,000 barrels of oil for $50 per barrel today? You could use this contract to purchase the oil for $50,000 and turn around and sell it for $150,000, pocketing $75,000 ($100,000 minus the contract price of $25,000 — before taxes, shipping, handling, and storage charges). Moreover, if you were savvy enough to have used your margin account, you may have used only $12,500 of your own money to increase your wealth by $75,000 for just one contract. Not bad!

You probably don't want to take delivery of the oil, but someone in the market does, and that person would be willing to pay you for your contract to get the better oil price. The closer you get to the contract date, the more likely someone will be willing to pay close to $100,000 for your contract.

How to Invest in Commodities

You can invest in commodities in multiple ways:

- **Purchase or sell futures contracts.** This is the purest way to gain exposure but volatility can be high. (See the preceding sections for details on futures contracts.) Some investors try to mitigate some of this volatility by buying and selling commodity futures indexes, which bundle related commodities.

- **Buy shares in royalty trusts, which are special trusts that receive income or profits from the commodity.** These trusts can pay high dividends, particularly because the trusts don't pay corporate income taxes. The trust also offers tax advantages by distributing proportionate shares of its depreciation and depletion allowances.

- **Buy commodities through mutual funds and exchange-traded funds (ETFs).** These funds often have different investment strategies, so be sure to read and understand the prospectus before investing. Using a mutual fund (see Strategy #21) gives you professional investment managers, dramatically increases your diversification for a small price, and gives you the convenience of one mutual fund purchase rather than an array of futures contracts.

ETFs (see Strategy #23) have similar advantages but are more likely to simply mirror a particular index of commodity futures. As a result, the ETF's management costs may be less than those of a mutual fund. ETFs, however, can be traded just like stocks.

✔ **Buy traditional stocks or bonds of companies in the business of growing, raising, or extracting a commodity.** A popular approach is to purchase shares in a mutual fund or ETF — often called a *specialty fund* — that focuses on companies that fit a particular commodities theme. But holding the stock of a group of companies in a specialty fund isn't the same as purchasing the commodity. Odds are the company stock will move in concert with the rest of the stock market and, depending on what else the company does or owns, won't be a strong hedge against inflation.

Although you want exposure to commodities, this exposure — either pure or indirect — should be a relatively small share of your investment portfolio. Don't invest in commodity futures, or index-commodity futures, unless you're willing to invest the time and effort to study and follow that specific commodity market closely.

Consider Short-Selling

By Neil Vannoy, MBA

As of this writing, General Motors stock has fallen to levels not seen since the mid-1950s. More than half of the company's value was lost in the first six months of 2008 alone. What does this mean to you? It means that if you hold GM stock, you've probably lost money — even if you've held the stock for 50 years!

Maybe you saw it coming, so you sold all your GM stock. Selling would have kept you from losing money, but what if you wanted to make money instead of just protecting yourself from losses? After all, what happened to GM could happen to another company, especially during difficult economic times. *Short-selling* is a strategy that can help you make money when a company, or the economy as a whole, faces uncertain economic times.

Sell High and Buy Low for Fun and Profit

Short-selling involves selling a stock you don't actually own in order to profit from a decline in price. So when you short a stock, you want the value to drop.

When you short a stock, you borrow shares from your broker through a margin account and immediately sell them on the open market. The proceeds are then deposited into your account.

Eventually you repurchase the shares and return them to your broker to close out the short position. Your goal is to pay less to buy back the shares than you received from selling them. If you do, you get to keep the difference! Here's an example:

1. XYZ stock is trading at $25 per share. You think the true value is around $15 per share. You decide to speculate that the price of XYZ will decline, so you sell short 100 shares of XYZ stock at $25 per share.

2. Your broker loans you 100 shares, you sell them on the open market, and the $2,500 in proceeds is deposited into your account. (100 shares × $25 per share = $2,500).

3. Two weeks later, XYZ stock declines to $19 per share. You purchase 100 shares to return to your broker at $19 per share.

Your profit from the transaction is $600. ($2,500 from the sale of XYZ – $1,900 to repurchase XYZ).

This example doesn't account for the commissions and fees that apply in the real world!

You don't necessarily need to master short-selling yourself to incorporate a short-selling strategy in your portfolio. Some mutual funds, called long-short funds, use short-selling as a part of their active strategy. Walk carefully with these funds though. Make sure you understand and are comfortable with both the strategy and fees.

Now for the Bad News: It's Not So Easy

Sounds easy, right? Well, before you start short-selling your way to untold fortunes, there are a few things you should know.

Short-selling is a speculative strategy with significant risks and may not be appropriate for most investors.

History shows that stocks appreciate

Using history as a guide, the long-term trend for stocks is positive. Although the market drops or trades *sideways* (moves up and down within a limited range) at times, stocks have appreciated more than any other asset classes over long time periods. Although you have no guarantee that this trend will continue, be aware that short-selling involves going against this powerful trend!

You risk unlimited loss for a limited gain

The potential gain from short-selling is limited to the cash you receive from selling the stock, while the potential loss is unlimited. Recall the $2,500 you received from selling XYZ in the example earlier in this strategy. The most you could make from the transaction is $2,500, but XYZ would have to go bankrupt for you to be able to keep the entire amount.

But what happens if the price of XYZ stock begins to skyrocket after you sell the shares short? You're responsible for purchasing the 100 shares of XYZ stock to close the short position no matter what the price!

Although an unlimited loss is really possible only in theory, be aware that the price could easily *double* or *triple* before you have the chance to repurchase the shares. This is especially true for stocks of small companies, or stocks that are *thinly traded* (which means they don't have a high volume of shares that are regularly traded).

In this scenario, if the price of XYZ stock doubles after you sell short, you have to buy back 100 shares at $50 per share. You spend $5,000 to buy the same stock you sold for $2,500. You lose $2,500 and that's before you add in commission fees and the interest you have to pay for the period of time until you close the short position.

You pay interest on losses

A margin account is required for short-selling (see Strategy #31 for more information about margin accounts). If you sell a stock short, and the price of that stock begins to increase, your broker will move money from the cash balance of your account to cover the losses. A margin balance will be created if you don't have sufficient cash to cover the position, and you'll begin to accrue interest charges on the margin balance. So you could not only suffer a loss from your short position, but also end up paying interest for the privilege of losing money!

Learn the Lingo

This section covers the lingo you'll need to know if you dabble in short-selling or if you just want to impress your friends at cocktail parties!

Selling, shorting, selling short, going short, short

These terms are used somewhat interchangeably to describe an investor who's engaged in short-selling. *Selling, shorting, selling short,* and *going short* are used before an investment position is established, and *short* is used to describe the position after the fact. (Note that *buying, going long,* and *long* are the opposite of these terms.)

Again, assume you think XYZ is overvalued. You could say you're considering "selling XYZ," "shorting XYZ," "selling XYZ short," or "going short XYZ." After you establish a short position in XYZ, you simply say you're "short XYZ."

Bull and bear markets

The terms *bull market* and *bear market* are most commonly used to describe the stock market, but they can be used to describe any investment market (such as the bond market, commodity market, or currency market). Security prices in bull markets are increasing or expected to increase; prices are falling or expected to fall in bear markets. Likewise, a *bull* is an investor who thinks a market will rise. A *bear* is an investor who thinks a market will fall. Short-sellers are considered *bearish* because they expect the price of the security to fall.

Short interest

Short interest refers to a specific security's total number of shares that have been sold short. When short interest increases, many investors believe it's a bearish indicator. For example, if the short interest in XYZ stock increases from 2 percent to 6 percent of outstanding shares, it would appear that more investors are expecting the price of XYZ to fall.

Covering

Investors who sell a security short eventually have to *cover*, or buy back, their position. For example, if you short 100 shares of XYZ stock, you later cover the position by purchasing 100 shares.

Short squeeze

No, this has nothing to do with getting pinched on a crowded subway! A *short squeeze* occurs when a rapid increase in the price of a stock leads short-sellers to cover their positions. This increased demand, combined with a lack of supply, causes the price of the stock to continue upward, compelling more and more short-sellers to cover their positions.

Days to cover (short interest ratio)

Days to cover (also known as *short interest ratio*) gives you an idea of the future buying pressure on a stock from short-sellers who will eventually have to cover their positions. This ratio measures the short interest in a stock relative to its *average daily volume* (the average number of shares that exchange hands in a day). The longer the days to cover for a security, the greater the chance of a short squeeze. The formula for days to cover is:

Days to cover = current short interest ÷ average daily share volume

Called away

A short position is established by using borrowed shares of a security, and your broker retains the right to redeem these shares at any time. If the original owner redeems the shares, and your broker can't find replacement shares, you may have the shares *called away* from you. This means you have to cover your position immediately, regardless of market price.

Use Caution When Buying on Margin

By Neil Vannoy, MBA

Buying on margin is similar to buying a home. In home-buying, borrowing money increases your purchasing power and allows you to buy a larger home than you could otherwise afford. *Margin* is basically a loan from your brokerage firm, and buying on margin allows you to purchase more of a security — such as a stock or a bond — than you could on your own.

Know How It Works: Everything's Bigger with Margin

Investors buy on margin to increase their returns. Because margin gives you the ability to buy more stock with less money, an increase in the price of the stock leads to a larger gain than if you hadn't used margin. Here's an example: Assume you pay cash for stock worth $5,000 and that stock appreciates to $5,500. That represents a 10-percent return on your $5,000 investment. Not bad. Now assume you make the same investment by using $2,500 of your money and $2,500 that you borrow from your brokerage firm. The same $500 appreciation would be a 20-percent return on your $2,500 investment ($500 gain ÷ $2,500 investment = 20 percent). Much better! But keep in mind that you have to pay interest to your brokerage firm for the privilege of borrowing its money.

Be aware that margin is a double-edged sword. Buying stocks on margin is great when prices go up, but remember that stocks don't always appreciate. Any loss on a stock purchased on margin is magnified just like gains are magnified. Buying on margin in a volatile market is risky!

Understand the Details

To buy securities with borrowed money, you need a *margin account* at your brokerage firm.

Minimum and initial margin

Before trading on margin, you have to meet margin requirements set by the Federal Reserve Board (the Fed), the Financial Industry Regulatory Authority (FINRA), and your brokerage company. The Fed and FINRA establish the minimums, but your brokerage company can have stricter requirements.

Minimum margin is the minimum deposit required to open a margin account, and it's the lesser of $2,000 or 100 percent of the purchase price. *Initial margin* is the maximum amount your brokerage firm can lend to you to purchase securities, and it's currently 50 percent of the purchase price. You can meet the minimum and initial margin requirements by depositing cash or securities into your margin account.

For example, assume you want to purchase $3,600 of ABC stock on margin. You're required to deposit $2,000 into the account, and your brokerage firm loans you $1,600 ($3,600 purchase price – $2,000 minimum margin = $1,600 margin loan).

Maintenance margin

After you purchase a security, the Fed, FINRA, and your brokerage firm require you to keep a minimum amount of equity in your account. This is called the *maintenance margin.* The minimum maintenance margin is 25 percent of the total value of the securities in your margin account, but your brokerage firm may have higher minimums, especially for risky securities. You can meet the maintenance margin requirement by depositing cash or securities into your margin account.

For example, assume you purchase $10,000 of XYZ stock on margin by depositing $5,000 in cash into your account and borrowing $5,000 on margin. Your equity in the account is $5,000 ($10,000 market value of XYZ – $5,000 margin loan = $5,000 equity). If the value of XYZ falls to $8,000, the equity in your account falls to $3,000 ($8,000 market value of XYZ – $5,000 margin loan = $3,000 equity). If your firm has a 25-percent maintenance margin requirement ($2,000 in this example), your account would still be in good standing. However, if your firm has a 40-percent maintenance margin requirement ($3,200 in this example), you wouldn't have enough equity in your account and would need to deposit more cash or securities to increase the equity up to or above the maintenance margin.

Margin call

You may receive a *margin call* from your brokerage firm asking you to deposit more cash or securities if the equity in your margin account falls below the maintenance requirement. If you don't meet the call, your firm will sell enough securities in your account to increase the equity up to the maintenance requirement. Be aware that your broker isn't required to notify you that your account has fallen below the maintenance requirement or to contact you before selling your securities!

Margin rate

The *margin rate* is the interest rate you pay to purchase securities on margin. Margin rates are based on the broker's call rate, which is the interest rate that brokerage firms pay to banks for financing margin loans. The margin rate will likely be quoted as the broker's call rate (or base rate) plus or minus a margin (for example, "base rate less 0.50%" or "broker's call plus 1.00%"). Be aware that margin rates are variable, so they can change at any time!

Recognize the Risks

Here's a summary of the issues you should consider before buying on margin:

- ✔ **Stocks don't always increase in value.** Buying on margin will magnify your loss if a stock declines in value.

- ✔ **You can lose more money than you deposit.** If the securities you purchase on margin decline in value, you may be required to deposit additional funds or sell some of your securities.

- ✔ **Your brokerage firm can force the sale of securities in your account.** If you can't deposit more money to meet a margin call, your brokerage firm can force you to sell securities to meet the maintenance margin.

- ✔ **Your brokerage firm can sell your securities without contacting you.** Your brokerage firm has the right to sell your securities to meet the maintenance margin without contacting you first. And you may not get a chance to decide which securities are sold.

- ✔ **You're not entitled to more time to meet a margin call.** Your firm *may* extend the time to meet a margin call under certain circumstances.

- ✔ **Your brokerage firm can increase the maintenance margin at any time.** Changes in the maintenance margin take effect immediately and may cause a margin call if you don't meet the new requirements.

- ✔ **You'll pay interest even if you lose money.** Interest is charged on your margin balance whether or not you make or lose money on the trade.

#32

Get the Most Out of Your Taxable Accounts

By Kevin Sale, ChFC, CFP

A *taxable account* is simply any account whose use doesn't give you a tax advantage. It can be a savings account, checking account, brokerage account, mutual fund account, or many others. The key is that income and gains generated by the investments held within the account are taxed.

Most people use taxable accounts almost daily for one main reason: they're flexible. Generally, there are no restrictions or penalties to their use. Any restrictions or penalties that do exist are tied to your investment choice, not your account.

 Taxable accounts are good bets for everyday use or as a temporary holding spot while you determine your approach. They may also make sense as a part of a more complex tax strategy because taxable accounts may provide tax diversification for your portfolio.

Diversify Your Holdings

Social Security and Medicare projections are grim, yet income tax rates are at historic lows. Change may be on the horizon. Then again, income tax rates could remain stable for some time. Much depends on the outcome of political races. The only thing that's clear is that your future income tax rate is uncertain.

As you choose your taxable accounts, the solution is to tax diversify. Different types of accounts have different tax consequences, and because your future tax rate is uncertain, it makes sense to have at least some of your assets in each of the three major tax buckets:

> ✔ **Pre-tax — 401(k) and traditional IRA:** Here you're betting your tax rate in retirement will be less than your tax rate now. In retirement, the ideal time to draw funds is in years where your income need is lower or you have deductions that reduce your taxable income.

✔ **Post-tax — Roth 401(k) and Roth IRA:** With Roth accounts, you make the opposite bet: Your tax rate now is less than it'll be in retirement. When withdrawals from your tax-deferred account will place you into a higher tax bracket, you can pull money from your Roth account instead for tax-free income, keeping yourself in a lower tax bracket.

✔ **Taxable — long-term capital gains:** Taxable accounts aren't a gamble on income tax rates, but they provide flexibility in drawing cash in retirement. Under current law, gains are taxed at just 15 percent when realized after one year, and unrealized gains aren't taxed at all. You should use taxable accounts to generate growth with unrealized capital gains. (A gain is *realized* when you sell an investment at a profit; if the investment has gained value but hasn't been sold, then the gain is *unrealized.*)

Taxable accounts can potentially provide "tax-free" income in retirement. In years with capital losses, you can offset your realized gains with those losses and take the cash tax-free. You may even be able to deduct up to $3,000 of losses against your income.

Using taxable accounts to tax diversify your holdings makes the most sense when you've already contributed the maximum to tax-advantaged vehicles. The added flexibility of a taxable account is unlikely to outweigh tax-advantaged growth for a long-term investment.

Know the Different Types of Taxable Accounts

You can invest in three basic types of taxable accounts:

✔ **Individual:** An account established for one person

✔ **Joint:** Any account owned by two or more people

✔ **Custodial:** An account created for the benefit of a minor

Going solo with individual accounts

If you're not married, the individual account will likely be the type of account you use. With an individual account, you're the sole owner and have complete decision-making authority. In the event of your death, the proceeds from an individual account pass to your estate.

Getting together with joint accounts

Married couples or related persons typically use joint accounts for convenient access so they can manage their financial affairs together. You don't have to be married or related, however, to use a joint account. Table 32-1 shows the two most common types of joint accounts.

Table 32-1		Joint Accounts
Category	*Joint Tenancy in Common*	*Joint Tenancy with Right of Survivorship*
Owners	Two or more unrelated parties	Two or more unrelated parties
Division of ownership	Unequal ownership is permitted.	Ownership must be equal.
Transferring one's stake	Each owner can sell, will, or gift his or her stake to another.	At death, the decedent's share of the account passes to the surviving owners equally.

Taking care with custodial accounts

Custodial accounts are accounts established for the benefit of a minor and are generally opened under the Uniform Gift to Minors Act (UGMA) or the Uniform Transfer to Minors Act (UTMA). The minor is considered the owner of the account, but a custodian must be in place to manage the account.

All funds transferred to the account are considered irrevocable gifts and must be used for the minor's benefit. When the minor reaches the age of majority, the recipient can do what he or she wants with the funds.

Custodial accounts provide irrevocable gifts to a minor. If you act as custodian, you'll manage the funds for the minor's benefit until the minor reaches the age of majority and receives full authority over the funds.

Invest in Individual Retirement Accounts (IRAs)

By Kevin Sale, ChFC, CFP

*I*nvesting in IRAs can be a great way to save in a tax-advantaged manner. They're often used to complement or replace retirement savings at work, and Roth IRAs provide a means to tax-diversify your portfolio. Read on to discover how to use IRAs to increase your savings and fortify your nest egg.

Types of Individual IRAs

IRAs come in two main types:

- **Traditional:** In a traditional IRA, you don't pay any taxes on the income and gains you generate until you withdraw them; all withdrawals will be taxed at your ordinary income tax rate. Annual contributions may or may not be tax-deductible, depending on your circumstances.

- **Roth:** With the Roth IRA, you make contributions on an *after-tax basis*. The income and gains you generate are never taxed; you can make withdrawals tax-free as long as you're over 59½ and the account has been open for more than five years.

    Because you've already paid taxes, you can also remove your contributions or basis tax-free at any time. But if you convert money from a traditional (or SEP or SIMPLE) IRA to your Roth, you have to wait five years before withdrawing those converted funds tax-free.

Contribution Limits

Here are the 2008 IRA contribution limits for both Roth and traditional IRAs:

- Regular contribution: $5,000
- Catch-up contribution (for those 50 and older): $1,000

Table 33-1 presents the income limits for Roth IRAs for 2008. Note that if your AGI is within the phase-out range, you may make a partial contribution (for example, if you're halfway, you can make half the contribution).

Table 33-1	Income Limits for Roth Contributions
Filing Status	*AGI Phase-Out Range for Roth IRA Contributions**
Single or head of household	$101,000–$116,000
Married filing jointly	$159,000–$169,000
Married filing separately	$0–$10,000

* The annual income limit for determining ability to convert traditional IRA to Roth IRA for all filers is $100,000.

Table 33-2 shows 2008 deduction limits for traditional IRAs based on filing status and income if you aren't covered by a retirement plan at work.

Table 33-2	Income Limits for a Traditional IRA If Not Covered by a Retirement Plan	
Filing Status	*MAGI Phase-Out Range*	*Deduction*
Single or head of household	Any amount	Full deduction
Married filing jointly (neither spouse covered by a retirement plan at work)	Any amount	Full deduction
Married filing jointly (one spouse is covered)	$159,000 or less $159,001–$169,000 $169,000 or more	Full deduction Partial deduction No deduction
Married filing separately	$0–$10,000	Full deduction

And Table 33-3 tells you 2008 deduction limits for traditional IRAs based on filing status and income if you *are* covered by a retirement plan at work.

Table 33-3   2008 Income Limits for a Traditional IRA If Covered by a Retirement Plan

Filing Status	MAGI Phase-Out Range	Deduction
Single or head of household	$53,000 or less	Full deduction
	$53,001–$63,000	Partial deduction
	$63,001 or more	No deduction
Married filing jointly	$85,000 or less	Full deduction
	$85,001–$105,000	Partial deduction
	$105,001 or more	No deduction
Married filing separately	$0–$10,000	Partial deduction
	$10,001 or more	No deduction

To Roth or Not to Roth

When you run the numbers using the same assumptions for each type of account, traditional and Roth IRAs are mathematically equal. In other words, if your income tax rate remains the same, you end up with the same amount of after-tax dollars in retirement — regardless of whether you take taxes out before or after you put your money in the IRA.

For example, assume you're in the 15-percent tax bracket and you have $5,000 to contribute. Whether you put the $5,000 into a traditional IRA and pay 15 percent in taxes on a withdrawal or you put the after-tax equivalent of $4,250 ($5,000 – 15 percent = $750) into a Roth IRA, you'll have the same amount of after-tax dollars in retirement.

You do get a built-in advantage with a Roth IRA in terms of contribution limits. The maximum contribution for both Roth and traditional IRAs is the same; however, because you can withdraw the Roth dollars tax-free, the dollars you put into to a Roth are worth more than the dollars you put into a traditional IRA. On an after-tax basis, you can save more money with a Roth than with a traditional IRA.

So what's all the fuss about? Just go with the Roth, right? Unfortunately, it's not that simple. Yes, assuming all things are equal, the Roth is a slightly better option only because you can save more on an after-tax basis. However, the Roth or traditional IRA decision comes down to a question of taxation: Do you expect your current income tax rate to be higher or lower than your income tax rate when you withdraw the money?

- ✔ Generally, if you expect to be in a lower tax bracket in retirement than when you make your contribution, the traditional IRA is the better option. You effectively defer your taxes until they're at a lower rate.

- ✔ If you expect to be in a higher tax bracket when you withdraw the money, the Roth IRA is the better deal. Here, you lock in your lower tax rate and avoid paying taxes at your future higher tax rate.

This decision may seem straightforward, but determining whether your tax rate at withdrawal will be higher or lower than today may be harder than you think. Consider these factors:

- ✔ **Changing tax rates:** Most people make the mistake of assuming that today's tax rates are the same tax rates they'll have in retirement. But considering that income tax rates are at an historical low, you may find yourself with a lower income but an equal or higher tax rate.

- ✔ **Career path:** Although you don't always anticipate it, many career paths are filled with twists and turns. Are you sure about your future income?

- ✔ **Size of your nest egg:** If you're a super-saver, you may live on a higher income in retirement. On the other hand, a small nest egg may fund only a portion of the income you take home today.

- ✔ **A murky future outlook:** Much can change, and making accurate assumptions about the next 20 to 30 years is difficult.

Because the future is uncertain, it's impossible to know whether a Roth or a traditional IRA will be better for you. You may be better off hedging your bets and saving in both tax-deferred (traditional IRA) and after-tax (Roth IRA) vehicles. This strategy is often described as *tax diversification*.

Don't forget that you may already be saving in a tax-deferred manner through your 401(k) or other retirement plan at work. So after looking at all the options, a Roth IRA may trump a traditional IRA if for no other reason than it's the only available option for saving on an after-tax basis — assuming your employer doesn't offer a Roth 401(k) option.

If cash is tight and you feel uncomfortable locking away your money in a retirement vehicle with hefty penalties for early withdrawal, a Roth IRA may be for you; you can still save in a tax-advantaged manner, but you can withdraw your contributions (not your gains) at any time penalty- and tax-free.

Converting to Roth

If your adjusted gross income (regardless of filing status) is below $100,000, you can convert traditional IRA assets to Roth IRA assets without penalty.

Unfortunately, you still have to pay income tax on the assets converted, but you would've done that eventually, anyway. Converting now can help you tax diversify.

If your adjusted gross income is above $100,000, don't worry. In 2010, the income limit for conversions is lifted. Anyone can convert traditional IRA assets to Roth assets (although it may not make sense tax-wise).

Even better, the changes going into effect in 2010 provide two additional perks:

- **Taxes are deferred to 2011 and 2012.** Converting a large balance to a Roth IRA will generate a sizeable tax bill, but Congress lessened the burden by allowing the income tax you must pay to be split between 2011 and 2012. If you expect your 2010 tax bracket to be lower than your future bracket, you can still recognize all the income in 2010.

- **You can sidestep the income limit.** Although an income limit on Roth contributions will still technically exist before and after 2010, you can easily sidestep that limit. You can contribute to a nondeductible IRA (see the next section) and then convert it to a Roth. Before going this route, make sure you understand the tax rules, especially if you have IRAs funded with both deductible and nondeductible contributions, because income tax will be due on the proportionate share of deductible contributions (for all your IRAs, not just your nondeductible IRAs).

Nondeductible IRAs

A *nondeductible IRA* is a bit of a misnomer because it really describes contributions to a traditional IRA that aren't tax-deductible. You lose the tax-deduction either because you've exceeded the annual limit for contributions or because your income exceeds the limit for that year.

The primary benefit of nondeductible IRA contributions is tax-deferred growth of earnings. The problem is that withdrawn earnings are taxed at ordinary income rates, possibly as high as 35 percent. This holds true even for what would otherwise be long-term capital gains, which would be taxed at only 15 percent in a taxable account.

 Outside of using a nondeductible IRA to sidestep contribution limits on a Roth IRA, contributing to an IRA on a nondeductible basis is rarely a good strategy. Before contributing to a nondeductible IRA, be sure you've exhausted other more advantageous investment vehicles, such as your employer's retirement plan, a traditional or Roth IRA, and the 529 college savings plan. You'll also want to weigh the benefits of saving in a plain old taxable account.w

#34

Make the Most of Your Employer Retirement Accounts

By Barbara Camaglia, MBA, CFP, CFS, CPA

Your eyes may glaze over at retirement-plan numbers — 401(k), 403(b), 457 — but you want to be sure you understand yours. For most people, an employer-sponsored plan is crucial to accumulating enough for retirement.

The information here, which emphasizes the general rules rather than the exceptions, is intended to give you a basic understanding of employer retirement plans and some ways to make the most of them. Your employer can provide information on the specific provisions of your plan. Check with your financial planner and/or tax advisor on the state of current laws before making significant changes, withdrawals, and so on.

You have investment risk in your retirement plan. Manage this risk by working these accounts into your overall asset allocation and paying attention to the costs and performance of your investments in the plan.

Know Your Plans

401(k), 403(b), and 457 plans are governed by three sets of rules: Internal Revenue Service Code sections, other federal laws such as ERISA (Employee Retirement Income Security Act), and an employer's optional elections. Check with your tax advisor and human resources department to be sure you understand the features of your plan.

401 (k) and 403 (b)

401(k) plans are established by private-sector, for-profit employers. The employer decides whether its plan allows loans, hardship distributions, and Roth 401(k) contributions. 403(b) plans are similar to 401(k) plans but are found in public educational organizations, nonprofit organizations, and some religious organizations.

457

457 plans are most commonly government or private-sector deferred-compensation plans:

- ✔ **Government:** A state or local government offers the government 457 plan. These plans received a makeover from the Economic Growth and Tax Relief Reconciliation Act of 2001 and the Pension Protection Act, and now they work much like 401(k)s.

  The 457 plan lets government employees put away more pre-tax money to supplement their pensions and other retirement savings. It isn't subject to creditor claims of the employer, and funds must be set aside in a separate annuity or trust. The government plan may allow you to use money from your 457 account to purchase service credits to increase pension benefits. Contribution limits equal the employee deferral-contribution limits of 401(k)s ($15,500 as of this writing).

- ✔ **Private-sector:** The private-sector 457 plan serves as an additional way to defer compensation and taxes after you maximize contributions to a 401(k). To get the additional tax benefits, you have a substantial risk of forfeiture, which means you have a real risk of loss. These funds are subject to the creditor claims of the employer. If you have one of these plans, you can save more on a tax-deferred basis, even after you've deferred your maximum amount in a 401(k). You don't have a 10-percent penalty for withdrawals before age $59^{1}/_{2}$. The funds are taxed as ordinary income when you receive them.

Use the government 457 plan to supplement your pension; use the private-sector 457 plan when you want to defer more than your 401(k) allows. Understand that with a private-sector 457, your money isn't as secure because it's subject to creditors' claims against your employer.

Get Money into Your Accounts

So how do you invest money in your retirement plan? You have a few options:

- ✔ You contribute the funds through salary deferrals.

- ✔ Your employer contributes the funds.

- ✔ You have investment earnings in a retirement account.

- ✔ You roll another retirement account into the plan.

Employee contributions

You usually make your employee contributions before tax. Federal, state, and local income taxes apply when the contributions are distributed to you. Social Security taxes on your contributions aren't deferred. If you make post-tax contributions, you're usually taxed only on the earnings in the account upon distribution.

Your employer may allow Roth 401(k) or 403(b) contributions. (At the time of this writing, a bill allowing government 457 Roth contributions is pending.) You make Roth contributions after tax, and the earnings on Roth contributions should be tax-free. If Roth contributions are allowed, you can make your employee contributions Roth contributions, pre-tax contributions, or some of each.

In deciding whether to make Roth contributions, consider your tax rate now and in retirement. If your marginal rate in retirement will be significantly lower, pre-tax contributions may be preferable. If you think overall rates are likely to increase significantly, consider Roth contributions.

Employer contributions

Many 401(k) plans have an employer match based on a formula or per-centage. For example, perhaps an employer matches $0.50 for each $1 the employee contributes, up to a maximum of 6 percent of the employee's salary. This is free money, and you should take advantage of it. 403(b) plans may or may not have matching contributions. Employers can match contributions to a Roth account, but they must match the funds on a pre-tax basis. They can't make contributions into the designated Roth account. Here are a couple of tips:

- ✔ If your employer matches contributions, contribute at least as much as needed to get the entire employer match.
- ✔ Consider contributing enough to receive the match and then funding an IRA. Then continue contributions to the plan up to the maximum allowed, if you have enough income.

Investment earnings

The choices your employer made limit the investment options in your employer plan. Think of it as your menu. When choosing, consider the following:

✔ Don't put too large of a percentage of your assets into your employer's stock. Every individual stock you own is subject to company risk, which is compounded when the company is your employer.

✔ Look at your employer plan as part of your total portfolio. Choose plan investments that fit within your overall asset allocation and complement investments in your IRA and other accounts.

✔ Fees and other costs cut into your return. Look for investments with low fees and operating expenses.

Rollovers

Generally, employees can transfer employer plan account balances to another employer plan or to an IRA when they leave a job, without tax or penalty, regardless of age. However, if you don't transfer your balance as a trustee-to-trustee transfer, the plan customarily withholds 20 percent for taxes. Make sure your rollover is a trustee-to-trustee transfer if possible.

Prepare to Take Funds Out

When funds come out of employer plans, they're usually subject to ordinary income tax unless they're rolled over to an individual retirement account (IRA) or if an exception applies. (Also see Strategy #74 for more information.)

Usual distributions

Distributions are subject to ordinary income tax and can be subject to a 10-percent penalty tax unless they're qualifying distributions. You can take qualifying distributions only after age 59½ unless one of the following applies:

✔ Disability

✔ Death

✔ A qualified domestic relations order (divorce)

✔ A distribution covering medical expenses in excess of 7.5 percent of adjusted gross income (AGI)

✔ Separation from employment at age 55 or older

✔ Victim of a specific natural disaster (designated by the federal government)

✔ Other (check with the IRS)

NUA of employer stock in a 401(k)

If you have company stock in your plan and the stock is eligible, you may be able to take advantage of special tax rules. Basically, if the stock value has grown substantially, *net unrealized appreciation* (NUA) rules allow you to pay regular tax only on the original cost when the stock comes out of the plan and capital gains tax on the balance upon the sale of the stock. Any gain in value over your basis will be taxed at capital gains rates when you eventually sell the shares. Long-term capital gains rates are currently lower than the ordinary income tax rates for most people.

If you're eligible and if you and your tax advisor determine it's worth doing, you must take a lump-sum distribution of your retirement-plan within one calendar year. The account is split into a taxable account that receives the company stock, while the balance of the account (everything that's not employer stock) may be transferred into an IRA or other tax-deferred plan.

Withdrawals and loans in hard times

If you need money, you can explore these options to withdraw funds from your retirement plan:

- ✔ **Hardship withdrawals:** An employer may allow hardship distributions, but if it isn't a qualifying distribution, the 10-percent penalty applies.

- ✔ **Taking plan loans:** Although some plans allow loans, taking one is typically a bad idea. If you invest properly, you're likely to earn more in the account over the loan period than you'd pay in loan interest. Reducing your investment returns during the loan period can make a big difference later. You'll also be repaying the loan with post-tax money, which will ultimately be *taxed again* when you withdraw the money.

Bankruptcy protection is a critical reason not to take out a loan against plan assets. An employer retirement plan often protects your assets in the event of your bankruptcy, so if you take money out of the plan, you could be making an exempt asset nonexempt. Plans receive protection if they're covered under applicable federal statutes, such as being ERISA qualified, protected by the Bankruptcy Abuse Protection and Consumer Protection Act of 2005, or protected by the Federal Bankruptcy Code. Some states have applicable state statutes. Check with an attorney for applicability of statutes to your plan(s).

What if your company is in trouble and declares bankruptcy? Retirement funds in 401(k), 403(b), and government 457 plans are generally protected against your employer's creditors' claims. Consult with an advisor for the specifics on your plan and current laws. This doesn't protect against declines in the plan's investments.

Choose a Self-Employment Retirement Account

By Roland Mariano, CPA

*O*pening a retirement plan is a big decision for every business, especially for the self-employed. Even in uncertain times, the benefits outweigh the costs. This section explains retirement plans for yourself and any employees.

Self-Employment Retirement Plans

As a self-employed individual or small-business owner, you can choose from the SEP-IRA, SIMPLE IRA, individual 401(k), or Roth IRA.

SEP (simplified employee pension) IRA

A simplified employee pension (SEP) is a low-cost plan for the small business owner. These plans are easy to establish and have practically no IRS filing requirements. SEPs use IRAs as the trustee/custodian for the contributions.

The amount to contribute on behalf of an employee is 25 percent of the employee's wages or $46,000, whichever is less (2008 limit). The employer's contribution to the SEP-IRA must be uniform for all employees. For you, the self-employed individual/owner, the maximum percentage is 20 percent of your net self-employment income adjusted (see IRS Publication 560).

SEP-IRAs can be either fiscal year or calendar year, and you don't have to contribute to the SEP-IRA every year. New businesses considering setting up a SEP-IRA can wait as late as the due date of their tax return, including extensions. So a Schedule C (Form 1040) filer can wait until October 15 of the following year to open and fund a SEP-IRA.

If you have employees and you want to maximize your contribution versus your employees', you may be able to allocate contributions through a method called *Social Security integration* if your plan provides this option. You can do this if your earnings are greater than the Social Security wage base or $102,000 (2008). See your financial advisor for more on this computation and ask whether this provision is offered in the plan document.

For more information, IRS Publication 4333, "SEP Retirement Plans for Small Businesses," is a useful guide. Visit www.irs.gov or call the Internal Revenue Service at 800-829-3676.

SIMPLE (savings incentive match plan) IRA

Any business can set up a SIMPLE IRA if it has fewer than 100 employees and no other retirement plan in place. Under this plan, both the employer and employee contribute to an IRA. Employee contributions are pre-tax salary deferrals. Employees can contribute 100 percent of their salary or up to a maximum of $10,500 (for 2008). If the employee is age 50 or older, he or she is entitled to put away an additional $2,500 (called *catch-up*).

As the employer, you can fund the employee SIMPLE-IRAs in two ways:

- ✔ **Matching contribution:** The employer matches salary contributions dollar-for-dollar up to 3 percent of wages (with a maximum match of $10,500). The employer may choose to limit this to 1 percent for any two years in a five-year period.

- ✔ **Non-elective contribution:** The employer contributes a fixed 2 percent of wages (up to $4,600, or $230,000 × 2%) to all eligible participants, whether the employee makes contributions from his or her salary or not.

See IRS Publication 4334 for more information on the SIMPLE IRA. *Note:* Individuals deferring up to $2,000 of their salary may be entitled to a tax credit on their individual return; please see your tax advisor.

SIMPLE IRAs must be maintained on a calendar year basis. October 1 is the deadline to set up a SIMPLE IRA plan. If you're a new employer after October 1, you can still set up the plan, but do so as soon as possible. The IRS will allow this (see your tax advisor regarding IRS Notice 98-4, K-1).

Individual 401 (k)

If your business is a sole proprietorship, a corporation with no employees besides you and your spouse, or a partnership with no employees, then an individual 401(k) is an appropriate retirement vehicle. You can put away more for retirement with an individual 401(k) than you can with the SEP-IRA or SIMPLE IRA. The individual 401(k) allows you to contribute in two components:

- ✔ Salary deferral of $15,500 (for 2008) plus a catch-up contribution of $5,000 if you're age 50 or older

- ✔ A profit-sharing contribution limited to 25 percent of compensation; the contribution is limited to 20 percent of compensation for the self-employed individual

Here are some points to note about the individual 401(k):

- ✔ Plan loans are allowed (50 percent of the account balance or $50,000, whichever is less). But check with the financial institution to make sure the plan document includes this provision.

- ✔ You need to make your salary reduction choice by December 31.

- ✔ This plan has a 401(k) feature, so think about the annual limit. It's $15,500 (for 2008), so if you participate in another 401(k) plan and you put away $9,000, you can defer only $6,500 under the individual 401(k) plan.

- ✔ An individual 401(k) is designed for the owner and spouse only. If you expect to hire additional full-time employees, you shouldn't consider an individual 401(k) plan.

- ✔ An individual 401k plan is subject to filing IRS Form 5500EZ. But great news! You're not required to file this form until the account balance reaches $250,000.

Roth IRA

As long as you've earned income, you can set up a Roth IRA. Earnings are tax free, unlike in a regular IRA. No deduction is allowed on the individual tax return for Roth contributions. Also, the law allows you to contribute to this type of plan even after you reach age $70^{1}/_{2}$, the age at which you have to begin taking distributions from your retirement account.

You can contribute the annual limit of $5,000, plus $1,000 (for 2008) if you're age 50 and older. How much of this you can contribute is affected by the self-employed individual's adjusted gross income.

Decide Which Plan to Open

Your objective is usually to start with the cheapest plan that'll allow you to put away the most money into a retirement plan. The number of employees who qualify for your business's retirement plan affects overall cost. Table 35-1 compares eligibility requirements.

Table 35-1	Eligibility Requirements for Retirement Plans			
Plan	*Minimum Age*	*Time of Employment*	*Earnings*	*Exclusions*
SEP-IRA	21	Three of the last five years (not necessarily consecutive)	$500 or more during the current year	Union employees, certain nonresident aliens
SIMPLE IRA	None	Two years or more (not necessarily consecutive)	$5,000 during any two calendar years prior to the year the plan is set up, with expectations to earn at least $5,000 in the current year	Union employees, certain nonresident aliens
Individual 401(k)	None or age 21	Immediate, or 1,000 hours prior to entering the plan in a period of 12 consecutive months	Any	For owners and spouses only
Roth IRA	None	Any	Any	None

In the SEP-IRA plan, all eligible employees must participate. This includes your part-time employees and even those who quit during the year. Even employees who die are covered. There's no requirement that an employee has to be working on the last day of the year to receive a SEP contribution.

Part III

Demystifying Risk: Accumulating and Protecting Wealth

The 5th Wave   By Rich Tennant

Defining your investment risk with the:
TOAST RETRIEVING RISK TOLERANCE TEST

LOW RISK | Waits for toast to pop up even though it's burning.

MODERATE RISK | Goes after toast with wooden toast prongs.

HIGH RISK | Goes after toast with all metal butter knife.

ULTRA HIGH RISK | Goes after toast with metal butter knife wearing a wet swim suit and a stainless steel colander on head.

In this part . . .

Knowledge is comforting. The more you understand investment risks and how to minimize them, the better you're able to design a portfolio that'll allow you to accomplish your goals while sleeping well at night. In this part, you explore the types of financial risks, how to measure your risk-adjusted investment performance and your personal tolerance for risk, and how to design a portfolio that maximizes diversification so you can achieve attractive risk-adjusted returns in any market environment.

Understand Investment Risks

By Michael Knight, CFP

*S*ome risks can certainly be avoided; others cannot. The only certainty in investing — and probably in life — is *uncertainty,* and if you find that to be a little scary, you're in good company. Investing features risk, which means that preparing for long-term goals like retirement can really be an adventure. It's like a Lewis and Clark expedition: You may not be able to anticipate every step of the way, but you'll reach your destination if you understand the risks and you prepare for this long and exciting adventure.

With investing, it's easy to think that the only risk involves watching your investments lose their value when the market goes down. However, other risks — emotion, inflation, outliving your assets, and holding investments that you don't understand — are lurking in the shadows. These risks become less scary if you understand them better and develop a plan to deal with them.

Emotional Risks

The biggest threat to your financial freedom may be *you.* When the market went through its painful three-year downturn beginning in 2000, many investors decided to run for the exits and then missed out on the solid returns of the next five years. Fear and greed tend to drive markets, and it's easy to succumb to either of these powerful emotions. The worst thing that you can do is react to what happened in the market today or yesterday. You need a big windshield and a small rearview mirror.

Take a long-term, disciplined, and consistent approach to investing with an understanding that market volatility is to be expected.

If you know yourself and if you know how you've reacted in the past, you're in a better position to invest in a way that is right for you. Here's what to do:

- ✔ Understand your risk tolerance (see Strategy #38).
- ✔ The best plans are based on clear and specific goals, so use the help of a fee-only advisor to help develop an investment plan that fits your financial and emotional needs.

    ✔ During times of uncertainty, look at your monthly statements, but don't check your investments daily and don't panic. Stick to your plan.

Threats of Inflation

One reason you invest is to keep pace with inflation and shield you from lost purchasing power. When you invest for a long-term goal, such as retirement, you need to think about the impact inflation will have over 30 or 40 years.

The longer the time period, the more inflation will erode your buying power. With 4 percent inflation a year, $1.00 today will buy just 30 cents worth of goods or services in 30 years. In other words, at an annual 4 percent inflation rate, $100,000 set aside today for retirement will be worth just $30,800 30 years from now. If inflation jumps to 5 percent, your $100,000 will be worth $23,000 in 30 years. Now that's scary.

Another negative affect of inflation is that it reduces the value of long-term bonds as interest rates rise. This includes government bonds that may be backed by the federal government but are subject to a decrease in value when interest rates go up.

Here are some ways to protect yourself from inflation:

    ✔ The best strategy is to invest for long-term growth and inflation protection with a diversified mixture of stocks and high-quality short term bonds. For more information, check out Strategy #41.

    ✔ Invest in a diversified mix of investments that includes both U.S. and international stocks.

    ✔ When interest rates are rising, use high-quality short-term bond funds and high-quality money market accounts.

    ✔ To protect against unexpected inflation, invest a small portion of your investments in Treasury inflation-protected securities (TIPS). You can easily do this with a mutual fund that invests in TIPS.

Roller Coaster: Market Volatility

Volatility is a measure of how much a security rises or falls within a short period of time. Low volatility is best because the greater the volatility, the more difficult it is to achieve your goals.

Many investors felt the pain of extreme volatility when the technology bubble burst in 2000. For example, one technology mutual fund, the Janus Venture Fund, fell 60 percent between March 2000 and February 2001. This means that $10,000 invested on March 1, 2000, was worth just $4,000 a year later. Returning to the $10,000 original investment would require a 150-percent gain.

You can reduce the risk of big, volatile swings in the value of your investments through diversification. And because volatility seems to diminish over time, carefully consider how soon you'll need your money when making investment choices. Here are a couple of strategies:

✔ If you'll need a certain amount of cash within the next five years, don't invest it in stocks. Use money market funds, CDs, and high-quality short-term bond funds instead.

✔ Avoid concentrated investments in any one company or market sector. This includes your employer's stock, which should be limited to no more than 10 percent of your investments.

The Risk of Outliving Your Money

One of life's greatest uncertainties is how long you'll live. Retire at 65, and you could live 30 years or more without a paycheck, running the risk of depleting your nest egg. Consider a married couple, both age 59 and non-smokers: There's a 50 percent chance that one of them will live to age 92 and a 30 percent chance that one of them will live to age 95.

One of the best strategies is to prepare now for a long retirement by saving more and spending less. It also helps to plan ahead and think about ways to generate income during retirement. Understand your current and future cash flow needs.

If your cash flow plan includes a way to separate fixed and discretionary expenses, you'll be able to adapt to the unexpected. Here's how:

✔ Expense control is essential, so look for a system for tracking expenses. Personal finance software programs like Quicken or Microsoft Money are good options. You can also find free templates with a personal budget worksheet and a family monthly budget planner on the Microsoft Office Web site (office.microsoft.com/en-us/templates).

✔ Be careful about withdrawal rates. One rule of thumb is that you shouldn't be withdrawing more than 4 percent from your savings and investments during the initial years of your retirement.

✔ Consider a fixed annuity with a portion of your savings, say 25 percent, but wait until you're approaching age 70 to invest in it. (Read Strategy #19 to find out more about fixed annuities.)

✔ Delay collecting Social Security until at least your full retirement age and even as late as 70 if possible.

✔ Plan ahead so you can generate some income in retirement. A part-time job can be fun and take some pressure off your investments.

The Risk of Making Investments You Don't Understand

Investments are sometimes complicated because they're designed to be good for the company selling the product rather than for you. Make sure you do some research and know what you're buying. Find out what penalties you may face if you want to get your money back.

Understand the compensation policies for salespersons. If you're dealing with investment products sold by banks, brokerage firms, or insurance companies, watch out for a potential conflict of interest. The person representing the institution is receiving a salary and often commissions from guiding you to a short list of products that produce income for the institution. To avoid this risk, follow these tips:

✔ Don't invest in products you don't understand.

✔ Be sure you know how the salesperson or advisor across the table is being paid.

✔ Use a fee-only advisor willing to provide you with a written statement that says that loyalty to you is the top priority.

Sort Through an Investment's Return

By Jean Keener

*E*ver opened up your 401(k) statement and found yourself wondering, "Is this good?" Or seen the sales commissions being charged each time you invest in your mutual fund and thought, "How are these affecting my retirement savings?" But as you start thinking about all the percentages, ratios, and math involved in answering these questions, your eyes glaze over, and suddenly tomorrow sounds like a much better time to start answering these questions.

Well, in reality, you deal with return on investment daily in your life. It can be a question of how much effort you'd have to invest to lose 10 pounds. Or whether it's worth the time required to cut carrots and put them in small bags for school lunches to save the money on preassembled snack packs. You make these decisions constantly in a split second based on your priorities, knowledge, and resources of time, money, or energy.

Assessing financial return on investment really isn't much different. Figuring out your returns takes just a couple of minutes. This can mean a better retirement, a cooler vacation, or more money to spend on the things you really care about.

Calculate Your Return

The *return* is how much money you made or lost on an investment. You look at how much you invested and the total amount it's worth now. The difference in these amounts is your *absolute return* — either positive or negative.

Holding period return

Holding period return shows you the absolute return over the entire time you owned the investment, whether that's three months, a year, ten years, or some other time period. Here's how to calculate the holding period return:

Total worth of investment now – money invested = holding period return

With the holding-period-return formula, don't forget any dividends or other income received from your investment. If you reinvested the income, it's automatically included. If you didn't reinvest, you need to add the income to what your investment is worth now to calculate an accurate return.

After you figure out the dollar amount you made or lost (hopefully made!), you can convert it to a percentage. Percentages allow you to compare different investments to each other regardless of the dollar amount of money invested. Here's how to calculate your percentage return:

Holding period return ÷ money invested × 100 = percentage return

Annualized return

The rubber really meets the road with annualized returns. If a couple buys a house for $100,000 and sells it ten years later for $130,000, they may think they earned a really great return. They made $30,000, or 30 percent, according to the formula in the preceding section. But think about what that actually equates to each year.

Calculating annualized returns requires more math than holding period return because of compound interest. Each year, your investment's increase in value is based not only on the original investment amount but also on all the interest or increase in value gained in earlier years. Financial planners use software or a financial calculator to calculate annualized returns; no one does this manually. For the $100,000 house that sees a 30-percent holding period return over ten years, the annualized return comes out to 2.66 percent.

You can eyeball annualized return with this shortcut:

Percentage return (of holding period) ÷ number of years = ballpark annualized return

With the house example, the annualized return comes out to 3 percent when you use the shortcut method. (Just remember that this shortcut isn't exact.)

You can also use online calculators to get exact annualized return figures. If an online calculator asks for the *present value,* enter the value of the investment at the beginning. *Future value* is the value of the investment at the end. Some good online calculators are available at www.moneychimp.com, www.bankrate.com, and `finance.yahoo.com` (do a search for "compound interest calculator" for other options).

Don't forget the effect of expenses when calculating your returns. Here are the most common expenses:

✔ **Real estate:** Take into account commissions, property taxes, and interest on your mortgage, among other expenses. If you're calculating returns on your primary residence, also take into account that you need a place to live, so you would've been paying rent if you hadn't been paying your mortgage.

✔ **Mutual funds, stocks, or bonds:** Include any commissions or management fees as part the initial cost of your investment. If you're not sure whether you're paying commissions, you probably are. Ask for no-load funds if you want to avoid commissions, and be sure to understand how your advisor is being compensated.

Identify Good versus Bad Returns

After you calculate your annualized return, you're ready to determine whether your results are up to par. Three basic factors show you whether your returns are doing their job. The importance of each depends on your personal circumstances.

Achieving your goals

The first question you need to ask is whether this investment is returning enough to achieve your goals (see Strategy #13 for info on setting financial goals). When you set a goal to retire in 15 years, you make several assumptions about how much money you'll be saving and what kind of return you'll be earning on your savings. In financial jargon, this is your *required rate of return*. A required rate of return varies by individual, depending on the following:

✔ The length of time the money will be invested

✔ Your tolerance for risk

✔ Other options available to you as investment vehicles

If your investment is meeting your required rate of return, great! If not, you can adjust your goals, seek a better-performing investment, or take on more risk.

Beating the benchmark

How does your investment's return compare to its peers? In some years, a 2-percent return for a particular mutual fund is pretty good. In other years, a 2-percent return for the same mutual fund is terrible. It all depends on what other comparable funds did that year.

To accurately compare an investment to its peers, determine what the relevant benchmark is. You can usually find information on the benchmark and the average performance of similar funds on your brokerage's Web site. Here's how to define peers of various investments:

✔ **Stocks:** Compare with other companies of similar size in the same industry.

✔ **Bonds:** Compare with other bonds of similar maturity dates and credit ratings.

✔ **Real estate:** Compare real estate appreciation or depreciation in similar neighborhoods in the same or other markets. Sites such as www. zillow.com or www.realtytimes.com are good sources for market comparisons.

✔ **Mutual funds:** Three industry standard benchmarks are based on the size of company a mutual fund invests in:

  • **Large cap:** S&P 500

  • **Mid cap:** S&P 400

  • **Small cap:** Russell 2000

Look for choices that have consistently performed at or above their benchmark, but beware — you shouldn't jump to a fund just because it's had a really terrific year and wildly outperforms its comparison fund. You also shouldn't automatically dump a fund because of one bad quarter or year. A lot of investors chase returns, but when you do, you have a good chance of buying high and selling low rather than the other way around.

Assess Your Ability to Absorb Losses

By Ben Jennings, CPA/PFS, CFP

*E*very investment exposes you to some type of risk. Although you should consider each type of risk, the one that seems to dominate during uncertain times is shrinking portfolio values — what most people call "losing money." But if you have a well-diversified, long-term portfolio, you should look at portfolio declines as temporary. The long-term reality is that you won't lose all your money, contrary to what it feels like during volatile markets.

Over time, you'll have investment experiences that differ from your expectations; the real issue is *how much* and *for how long.* If the temporary losses exceed your willingness to maintain your strategy, you're likely to take actions such as abandoning stocks in favor of cash; or you may fail to take actions such as rebalancing the portfolio. Both paths result in worse long-term investment results than if you had a more stable, less anxiety-producing portfolio in the first place.

Evaluating your ability and willingness to maintain your portfolio strategy during downturns is critical. Here are two primary considerations:

✔ Making sure your expectations are realistic

✔ Knowing what your likely response will be in various scenarios

This strategy discusses realistic expectations and helps you gauge your risk capacity, risk tolerance, and risk requirements.

Line Up Your Expectations with Reality

Suppose you love coffee, grunge music, boating, and salmon. You consider moving to Seattle, but you've heard the rain is awful. You do some research and discover that Seattle gets fewer inches of rain than Houston. So this means Seattle's climate is pretty much like Houston's, right? Not so fast!

Average rainfall doesn't give the complete picture. To get a realistic view of Seattle's climate, you have to consider multiple perspectives (in this case, frequency of rain as well as amount). You may love living in the Northwest — millions do — but the odds go down if you don't have appropriate expectations before moving there.

In a similar way, looking at average returns in the stock market doesn't provide a reliable perspective on actual stock market behavior. For example, you may know that the long-term average return for the U.S. stock market is close to 10 percent. However, since 1926, investors have experienced negative annual returns about 30 percent of the time — temporary periods of loss for long-term investors.

Investing in stocks and simply expecting a 10-percent average return is like moving to Seattle and expecting it to be less rainy than Houston: Although it may be technically true, your actual experience will differ. A well-diversified long-term portfolio often shows declines in particular asset classes as well as overall declines.

Evaluate Your Risk Profile

When you have realistic expectations of market behavior, you're ready to implement an investment strategy. When determining your portfolio allocations, consider at least three perspectives:

- **Risk capacity:** How much risk *should* you take, assuming a worst-case scenario? Take the following into account:

  - Your age and how many income-earning years you expect to have left

  - Your ability to insure against risks to your financial security

  - Your net worth

  - Your expenses covered by future incomes not related to investments, such as pensions and Social Security

  - Your family situation

- **Risk tolerance:** How much risk *can* you take? Consider your ability to stick with your investment plan without lying awake at night. Your emotional reaction to volatility is much more of a trait (a long-term characteristic) than a state (a temporary response). Though your reaction to volatility may change as you gain investing experience, it's also related to how you're wired.

Free online questionnaires from mutual fund companies and brokerages can help you assess this aspect of your personality. Alternatively, an Australian company, FinaMetrica, offers two Web-based assessments for a fee (www.myrisktolerance.com).

✔ **Risk required:** How much risk *must* you take? The answer depends on your goals and objectives and on how much time you have to achieve them. Remember, your objective isn't necessarily to earn the highest return but rather to have the greatest likelihood of accomplishing your goals. It makes no sense to tolerate more risk and volatility than you need simply for the sake of potentially higher returns. Strive to plan for enough — not more — and your investments won't be cause for sleepless nights.

These three perspectives together make up your risk profile. Your portfolio design should be based on the lowest level of volatility indicated by these three elements.

Create a Portfolio You Can Grow and Consume

By Katherine Holden, ChFC, CFP

Creating a financial portfolio may feel daunting. A portfolio that's designed for simultaneous savings and withdrawals is challenging to put together, but growing a portfolio and consuming a portfolio at the same time is possible. The key is to divide your portfolio into sections that are dependent on when you'll need the funds.

Develop Goals with Varying Time Periods

Investment goals are generally either short-term or long-term. For a short-term goal, you save and invest money to be used within one to five years. In this situation, you want to grow your savings, but you're equally concerned about protecting what you're putting away because you'll need to spend it within a short time. You have much less tolerance for risk in your investment choices.

Longer-term goals may be 10 or 30 years in the future, so you'll be setting aside money regularly, growing it, and then using it either all at once or over a period of time. Your goal may be to save a sizeable down payment to buy a house; you'll use all your savings at one time in this scenario. You may choose to assume a higher level of risk because you have more time to reach your goal. But the closer you get to your goal, the less risk you want to take.

Or your goal may be to put money away for your children's college education. You'll be saving over 18 to 22 years if you start at the birth of each child, and you'll likely spend those savings over four to eight or ten years (depending on how many children you have).

Create the Portfolios

This strategy offers you four examples of short-term versus long-term goals to show you how investment choices may vary. Suppose you want to purchase a refrigerator, buy a car, save a down payment for a house, and fund a two-year trip around the world 20 years from now. You can reach these goals by investing the money differently for each.

Start with a list of the items you want to purchase or fund and prioritize them. These are your goals. Prioritizing your goals helps you decide which goals to fund and which ones to delay funding when you experience tough financial times.

Think about the cost of each goal and your time frame for each. You may

- ✔ Use one account to save for all four goals.
- ✔ Use several accounts based on the time to complete your goals.
- ✔ Use separate accounts for each goal.

Be sure to consider the account and transaction fees that your brokerage firm charges. Using one account for all four goals may end up being confusing when you try to track what amount and which investments are linked to each goal.

Goal #1: Save $1,200 for a fridge in a year

For money you need soon, carefully choose the savings vehicle. Avoid stocks! If the stock market is down, you won't have the funds you need for the purchase.

Consider an FDIC (Federal Deposit Insurance Corporation) insured account, such as a savings or money market account, at a bank or credit union. Accounts are insured up to $100,000 per depositor; individual and joint accounts are insured separately. Or you can use a money market mutual fund, which isn't insured (see Strategy #17 for more information). Research interest rates at bankrate.com.

If the refrigerator you want to buy in a year currently costs $1,200, how much should you save per month? Here's how it breaks down:

Ultra Short-Term Savings

You need $1,248 ($1,200 adjusted for one year of 4 percent inflation).

Save $100/month (assuming a return of 3 percent).

You're primarily saving for this purchase out of your current income while earning only a small return on your savings. But your focus is on preserving your savings because you'll be using it all on this purchase.

Goal #2: Save $5,000 for a deposit on a car in three years

Because you don't need the money in this example for three years, you may be willing to accept a slight risk, although there's no guarantee you'll be rewarded with a higher return. After evaluating the current bond market, you could invest in a short-term high-quality bond mutual fund for the first two years. Then transfer your savings and contributions to a money market fund for the last 12 months. How much should you save per month?

Short-Term Savings

You need $5,624 ($5,000 adjusted for three years of 4-percent inflation).

Save $138/month (assuming a 4.45-percent return compounded monthly).

Set up an automatic withdrawal from your checking account into your car–down payment account. It'll save you time and ensure you save every month.

You're still funding the majority of the car down payment from your current income, but you're also trying to achieve a small amount of growth by accepting a small amount of risk. If uncertainty in the economy creeps in, you may want to transfer your savings to a money market account sooner.

Goal #3: Save $60,000 for a down payment on a house in ten years

Because the time period in this house example is longer than in the previous examples, you can take on more risk with diversified investments in large- and small-cap value equities, international equities (developed countries), short- and intermediate-term high quality bonds, and real estate mutual funds. Be sure to diversify and not limit yourself to one or two holdings.

Long-Term Savings

You need $88,815 ($60,000 adjusted for ten years of 4-percent inflation).

Save $406/month (assuming a diversified portfolio with approximately 50 percent equity and 50 percent fixed income with an average annual rate of return of 8 percent).

As with the first two goals, you'll use all your savings at one time when making the down payment. So you may choose to get more conservative with your investment choices when you're two to three years away from your goal. Monitor economic forecasts on a regular basis so you can make adjustments to a more conservative allocation if things are becoming more uncertain.

Goal #4: Save $300,000 for a two-year world trip in 20 years

Because you won't need the funds in this world-trip example for 20 years, you can assume even more risk with a diversified portfolio of large- and small-cap value and growth equities, international equities (developed countries), short- and intermediate-term investment-grade and government bonds, and real estate mutual funds.

Extra Long-Term Savings

You need $657,337 ($300,000 adjusted for 20 years of 4-percent inflation).

Save $755/month (assuming a diversified portfolio with approximately 60 percent equity and 40 percent fixed income with an average annual rate of return of 9 percent).

This goal differs from the first three because you'll be using your savings over a period of two years to fund your travel and living expenses. As with Goal #3, you may choose to use a more conservative allocation when you're within a couple of years of meeting your goal. When you're consuming your savings, you'll want to continue to pursue a conservative amount of growth and keep a certain percentage of your portfolio available as cash. Because this goal covers 20 years, you can be almost certain of experiencing economic ups and downs. Track what's happening with the economy on a regular basis. Good, sound investing practices can help you ride out the down periods.

Altogether, the examples show setting aside $1,399 each month for the first year. As you achieve each goal, the savings you need per month drops, allowing for additional goals. For the long-term goals, remember to make your asset allocation more conservative in the last several years.

#40

Allocate Your Assets to Minimize Risk

* * *

By Deidra Fulton, CFP

* * *

*B*uilding a portfolio is like cooking: You start with several basic ingredients, and the way you combine them can lead to something delicious or a hard, inedible mess. You may use all your ingredients or only a few. Or you may use most of them but in varying amounts. This strategy describes how to best allocate your assets for the most appetizing result: maximum returns with minimum risk.

Combine Asset Classes

Multiple asset classes in your portfolio can improve returns and decrease volatility. Large-cap U.S. stocks, real estate, and bonds are a few examples of different asset classes.

Here are some ideas about asset classes to keep in mind:

- ✔ Different asset classes perform differently during the same time period. When large-cap stocks are performing poorly, performance results from bonds may be stellar.

- ✔ You can't predict the best- and worst-performing asset class. Investment results are unpredictable — as is life! Over the last 30 years, all asset classes have had their day and then some.

- ✔ Combining multiple asset classes can help reduce risk within a portfolio; however, risk can't be totally eliminated. Losses will occur occasionally. The goal for a well-diversified portfolio is that losses be small and infrequent.

If you diversify by investing across multiple asset classes, you needn't worry about which asset class is the best performer this week or this month. Here's how to get the best combination.

Look for low correlation

Good investors seek asset classes with low correlation to each other. *Correlation* is a measure of the relationship, if any, between the returns of different asset classes. If they move in the same direction, they're positively correlated; asset classes that move in opposite directions are negatively correlated.

In Table 40-1, the higher the number, the stronger the correlation. You can see from this table that large-cap stocks are most closely correlated with small-cap stocks, because they generally move in the same market direction.

Note that large-cap stocks are positively correlated with every other asset category in Table 40-1. However, this isn't the case with all other asset classes. For example, international stocks and small-cap stocks are negatively correlated with intermediate government bonds and Treasury bills, though in varying degrees.

Using combinations of asset classes that have low or negative correlation with most other holdings within a portfolio should improve performance and reduce volatility.

Table 40-1	Correlations of Historical Annual Returns (1970–2006)							
	Equity REITs	Internat'l Stocks	Large-Cap Stocks	Small-Cap Stocks	Long-Term Corp. Bonds	Long-Term Govt Bonds	Intermed-Term Govt Bonds	Treasury Bills
Equity REITs (real estate)	1.00	0.31	0.46	0.75	0.26	0.18	0.13	−0.08
Internat'l stocks	0.31	1.00	0.59	0.41	0.08	0.06	−0.07	−0.13
Large-cap stocks	0.46	0.59	1.00	0.66	0.33	0.27	0.20	0.04
Small-cap stocks	0.75	0.41	0.66	1.00	0.13	0.04	−0.01	−0.02
Long-term corp. bonds	0.26	0.08	0.33	0.13	1.00	0.95	0.91	0.01
Long-term govt bonds	0.18	0.06	0.27	0.04	0.95	1.00	0.91	0.04
Intermed.-term govt bonds	0.13	−0.07	0.20	−0.01	0.91	0.91	1.00	0.31
Treasury bills	−0.08	−0.13	0.04	−0.02	0.01	0.04	0.31	1.00

Source: Stocks, Bonds, Bills and Inflation 2007 Classic Edition Yearbook by Morningstar, Inc.

Watch out for asset class volatility

Keep in mind that some asset classes are more volatile than others. Their potential for higher returns can be appealing, yet those higher returns also bring greater potential for major losses. Think of this cooking metaphor: A little chile pepper can add a wonderful taste, but too much of it can ruin the dish. So it is with investing. Use the more volatile asset classes sparingly.

Consider your time horizon

Generally speaking, the shorter the time horizon, the more conservative the investments should be because you have less time to recover from a market downturn. For example, if your son will be entering college in two years and you've saved $50,000 for college expenses, you should keep the majority of that $50,000 in less volatile holdings, such as cash or bonds.

If you leave the majority of the $50,000 in aggressive stock holdings, your risk is much greater because your funds will be subject to much higher volatility and declining values during that two-year period. The value of the funds could decrease just at the time you need the money.

Rebalance Your Asset Allocation

By Deidra Fulton, CFP

*R*ebalancing is the process of modifying subsequent allocations back to target weightings. In its simplest form, rebalancing involves selling some of the holdings in asset classes that have become overweighted and using the proceeds for buying additional holdings in underweighted categories.

Reasons to Rebalance

Asset classes perform differently over given time periods, just as do individual investments. When the economy is performing well and credit is easily attainable, smaller and mid-sized capitalization companies may perform especially well. Large-cap companies — with their stronger balance sheets and greater diversification — may have the edge during periods with tighter credit and greater economic uncertainty. Bonds may hold a distinct advantage during recessionary periods. And international stocks may have an edge during periods when the domestic economy is pressured.

Here's why you should rebalance:

- ✔ **Distorted allocations:** Initially established asset allocations may become distorted over time and need occasional adjustments.
- ✔ **Risk:** Balanced diversification can help minimize risk. Although it's tempting to let a high flyer remain unbridled, doing so increases risk in the long run.
- ✔ **Improved returns over time:** Rebalancing helps minimize your portfolio's overall risk and improve returns over time.

You can choose one of several criteria as a standard for rebalancing:

- ✔ **Time period:** This method uses some predetermined interval of the calendar as the trigger for rebalancing, typically quarterly, semiannually, or annually. Asset class allocations are adjusted back to original target weightings at the selected calendar interval.

✔ **Absolute percentage weighting:** This method employs a simple standard for making future modifications: Rebalance at any point in the future when the actual asset class weightings have shifted from the original target allocations. Note that this method may result in almost constant rebalancing of your holdings — not to mention incurring higher trading costs — due to the continual movement of markets as a whole.

✔ **Tolerance window range:** This method allows for some judgment in deciding whether to rebalance. For example, you may have a threshold of 3 percent as your criteria for a tolerance window. If the weighting is more than 3 percent above or below your target weighting, you rebalance.

✔ **Combination:** For example, you can combine both a percentage tolerance window and an annual calendar interval. In that case, you may rebalance once a year if any holding is more than 3 percent off the original target.

Ways to Rebalance

There's no single correct approach for rebalancing. Regardless of the rebalancing method you use, you need to regularly review and adjust your portfolio's asset allocations to maintain proper diversification and reduce risk. Here are some common methods:

✔ **Sell and purchase:** Sell your overweighted investments and purchase underweighted ones.

✔ **Withdraw or invest:** Take regular withdrawals from overweighted categories or direct future investments to underweighted asset classes.

✔ **Redirect:** Redirect payouts, such as dividends or capital gain distributions, from holdings in overweighted asset classes to investments in underweighted asset categories.

During an uncertain economy, thinking about rebalancing may be even more difficult. Your gut instincts may be to cut and run. But to make money in the long term, it's essential to stick to the discipline. When the stock market is falling rapidly, selling bonds and buying stocks may just be the right thing to do because suddenly your portfolio is more heavily weighted in bonds and stocks are relatively cheap. Conversely, when the stock market is soaring, it's time to sell off some of your winners and buy bonds. Remember the old adage: Buy low and sell high. Sticking to the rebalancing discipline can help you accumulate wealth and hang on to it.

An Example of Rebalancing in Action

This section presents an example of rebalancing. Suppose your target asset class allocations are the following:

✔ **Large cap stocks:** 30 percent

✔ **Small cap stocks:** 15 percent

✔ **International stocks:** 25 percent

✔ **Long-term government bonds:** 5 percent

✔ **Intermediate-term government bonds:** 10 percent

✔ **U.S. Treasury bills:** 15 percent

Assume you invested $100,000 at the beginning of 2005 and you rebalance annually, using a 3-percent tolerance window. Table 41-1 shows your original asset category weightings and the amounts invested by asset class.

Table 41-1	Original Investments by Asset Class (Start of 2005)	
Asset Class	*Target Weighting*	*Amount Invested*
Large-cap stocks	30%	$30,000
Small-cap stocks	15%	$15,000
International stocks	25%	$25,000
Long-term government bonds	5%	$5,000
Intermediate-term government bonds	10%	$10,000
U.S. Treasury bills	15%	$15,000

Table 41-2 shows the original amounts invested, returns for the year, the amounts invested by asset class at the end of 2005, the end weightings, and the original target weightings. Although weightings have changed, no category exceeds the 3-percent tolerance window, and no rebalancing is needed.

Table 41-2	Returns at the End of 2005					
Asset Class	*Beginning Amount Invested*	*Returns by Asset Class*	*Ending Amount Invested*	*Ending Asset Class Weightings*	*Target Weighting*	*Adjustment Needed with 3% Window*
Large-cap stocks	$30,000	4.9%	$31,470	29%	30%	0
Small-cap stocks	$15,000	5.7%	$15,855	15%	15%	0
International stocks	$25,000	14.0%	$28,500	27%	25%	0
Long-term government bonds	$5,000	7.8%	$5,390	5%	5%	0
Intermediate-term government bonds	$10,000	1.4%	$10,140	9%	10%	0
U.S. Treasury bills	$15,000	3.0%	$15,450	14%	15%	0
Total	$100,000		$106,805	100%	100%	

Table 41-3 shows the year-end results following 2006.

Table 41-3	Returns at the End of 2006					
Asset Class	*Beginning Amount Invested*	*Returns by Asset Class*	*Ending Amount Invested*	*Ending Asset Class Weighting*	*Target Weighting*	*Adjustment Needed with 3% Window**
Large-cap stocks	$31,470	15.8%	$36,442	30%	30%	0
Small-cap stocks	$15,855	16.2%	$18,424	15%	15%	0
International stocks	$28,500	26.9%	$36,167	29%	25%	−4
Long-term government bonds	$5,390	1.2%	$5,455	4%	5%	1

Asset Class	Beginning Amount Invested	Returns by Asset Class	Ending Amount Invested	Ending Asset Class Weighting	Target Weighting	Adjustment Needed with 3% Window*
Intermediate-term government bonds	$10,140	3.1%	$10,454	8%	10%	2
U.S. Treasury bills	$15,450	4.8%	$16,192	13%	15%	2
Total	$106,805		$123,134	100%	100%	

Applied to target asset class weighting for revised total portfolio value. Note that international stocks are now beyond the 3-percent tolerance window and have triggered the need for rebalancing. Notice further that three other asset classes are below their respective targets.

To rebalance, you sell international stocks and purchase intermediate government bonds and U.S. Treasury bills. Table 41-4 shows the updated portfolio.

Table 41-4	Your Rebalanced Portfolio					
Asset Class	Ending Dollar Amount 2006	Adjustment Needed with 3% Window*	Adjustment (Dollars)	Revised Amount Invested	Revised Weighting after Rebalancing	Target Weighting
Large-cap stocks	$36,442	0.0%	$0	$36,442	30%	30%
Small-cap stocks	$18,424	0.0%	$0	$18,424	15%	15%
International stocks	$36,167	–4.0%	–$5,384	$30,783	25%	25%
Long-term government bonds	$5,455	0.0%	$0	$5,455	4%	5%
Intermediate-term government bonds	$10,454	2.0%	$2,692	$13,146	11%	10%
U.S. Treasury bills	$16,192	2.0%	$2,692	$18,884	15%	15%
Total	$123,134			$123,134	100%	100%

Applied to target asset class weighting for revised total portfolio value.

Diversify Your Stock Portfolio by Size

By David McPherson

You can break down stocks into an almost endless number of categories. You can find growth stocks and value stocks, blue chips and orphans, industrials and financials. The list goes on and on. But the basic starting point is market capitalization, or size; that is, how much is a company worth? How big is it?

Using the market-capitalization measure, stocks are categorized into three broad groups: large caps, mid caps, and small caps. These terms frequently appear in the names of mutual funds that focus on particular segments of the stock market.

In this strategy, you look at one of the best ways to ease the uncertainty of investing in good times and bad: being sure your portfolio includes portions of large caps, mid caps, and small caps. This type of diversification can help you capture the strong performance of one category and offset the declines in another. For most individual investors, the best way to diversify by cap size is through mutual funds or exchange-traded funds (ETFs) rather than individual stocks. (See Strategy #21 for info on mutual funds; Strategy #23 discusses ETFs.)

Know the Market Cap Categories

The *market-capitalization* measure that people use to categorize stocks as large caps, mid caps, or small caps is a simple calculation that involves multiplying the number of outstanding shares in a company by the price of a single share. For example, a company with 100 million shares worth $10 each has a market capitalization of $1 billion.

In defining market cap categories, different institutions use different standards that can change with market conditions. But in general, sizes are defined in the following manner:

- ✔ **Large cap:** These stocks represent the largest companies trading on Wall Street and usually feature companies with market capitalization of $5 billion or more. They include some of the best-known companies in the United States, such as General Electric, Microsoft, and Bank of America. They also include lesser known companies such as Schlumberger Ltd., an oil-field services company, and Avery Dennison Corp., a label maker.

  This category accounts for about three-quarters of the overall U.S. stock market in terms of value. A frequently used gauge of U.S. large cap stocks is the Standard & Poor's 500 Index, or S&P 500.

- ✔ **Mid cap:** This category encompasses stocks that fall within a market capitalization range of $2 billion to $5 billion. Though considered medium size by Wall Street, a number of nationally known companies such as 3Com Corp., American Eagle Outfitters, and Netflix, Inc., are mid caps. Mid cap benchmarks include the Standard & Poor's MidCap 400 Index and the Russell Midcap Index.

- ✔ **Small cap:** This group encompasses publicly traded companies with market capitalizations of less than $2 billion. Though they account for only about 10 percent of the U.S. stock market in dollar value, small caps make up the majority of the nation's publicly traded companies. Chances are you recognize few of the names on this list — they include U.S. Concrete, Inc., Kosan Biosciences, Inc., and Illumina, Inc.

  A subcategory of small caps known as *micro caps* makes up the smallest of the small in terms of market capitalization. The definition of a micro cap varies widely, with some people starting at a market capitalization of $500 million or less. Others use a $100 million starting point. Either way, these are the riskiest of stocks and are best avoided by most individual investors. Many micro caps qualify as *penny stocks* because their shares regularly trade for less than $1.

Get the Right Mix in Your Portfolio

Different types of investors may be drawn to one category over another based on the traits of large caps, mid caps, and small caps, particularly in times of market turmoil. See Table 42-1 to see how the stock categories compare.

Table 42-1		Comparing Large, Mid, and Small Cap Stocks		
Size	*Makeup*	*Returns*	*Dividends*	*Ideal for*
Large caps	Older and better-established companies; in difficult times, they stand a better chance of surviving than young upstart companies	Less risk for investors also means less potential for future growth. The chances of seeing a stock price double or triple in a short period aren't great.	They typically feature higher dividend payments than mid caps or small caps, which can make large caps particularly appealing during periods of uncertainty.	Those who want the inflation-beating returns of stocks without taking on too much risk
Mid caps	Both companies on the way up and those unlikely to grow any larger	Though less risky than small caps, mid caps over the last ten years have delivered higher average annual returns.	They tend to pay investors little, if anything, in the way of dividends.	Investors who seek higher growth potential but can't stomach the volatility inherent in small caps
Small caps	Less-established companies that contain tremendous growth potential but also run a higher risk of failure	Historically, this category has featured the highest returns in exchange for higher degrees of volatility.	They tend to pay little, if anything, in the way of dividends; there may not be enough cash to go around, or the companies are hoarding it to finance growth.	Investors with appetites for risk who plan to buy into this category after prices fall and are ready to hold for the long haul

Under most circumstances, you should own a little bit of each category to counter the uncertainty that surrounds money and markets. The right mix of large caps, mid caps, and small caps depends on your risk tolerance, goals, and circumstances. Traditional asset allocation models call for higher portions of large caps and smaller portions of mid and small caps. More-aggressive investors who seek higher returns and can withstand the volatility may want to allocate larger shares to mid caps and small caps.

If you're seeking diversification and simplicity at the same time, consider a total stock market fund or an extended market index fund. A *total stock market fund* invests in large, mid, and small caps in proportion to their overall representation in the market — that is, large caps make up about 75 percent of the fund. An *extended market fund* replicates the mid and small cap markets in a single fund but leaves out the large cap companies. Both options reduce the number of holdings needed to diversify your portfolio and simplify the investing process. The trade-off is that you have less flexibility in overweighting or underweighting a given category.

#43

Diversify Your Stock Portfolio by Valuation

By David Anderson, CFA

*I*n uncertain times, which is better — growth investing or value investing? Everyone agrees that the purchase price of an investment ought to represent good value; that is, the anticipated return should justify the associated risk. However, *good value* doesn't have a universal definition; it becomes obvious only after the fact.

Undaunted, the ever intrepid consultants divide the universe of investment managers into three style categories: value, growth, and a combination of the two labeled *blend* or *core*. This strategy explains how value and growth investing compares and advises you on how to protect yourself from manic changes in the market.

Value versus Growth: Taking Lessons from History

So what's the difference between value and growth investors?

- ✔ **Value investors generally look backward at history.** They examine financial statements to estimate an intrinsic value of a stock and compare it to the current price. If the current price is significantly lower than the estimated intrinsic value, the value investor purchases the stock, anticipating that other investors will recognize the disparity and *their* purchases will drive up the market price so that it equals or exceeds the estimated intrinsic value. The fly in the ointment is getting everyone to agree on the definition of *intrinsic value*.

- ✔ **Growth investors look forward.** They postulate that companies growing at above-average rates will provide above-average returns. Generally, the higher the anticipated growth rate, the more investors are willing to pay. The fly in their ointment is the realization of that growth. For the stock price to appreciate, the company has to achieve the growth expectations.

A growth investor's most disconcerting moment is discovering that a stock declined 10 percent in one day because the company's earnings missed analysts' forecasts by 5 cents. Wiping out 10 percent of the market value for such a minor shortfall seems awfully excessive. However, the strong reaction suggests that investors believe the company's growth rate has hit a turning point and will begin to slow.

A value stock's earnings typically fluctuate with the economy; these stocks tend to do well when the economy is accelerating out of a recession. Growth stocks are expected to be impervious to economic fluctuations. However, what makes economic sense can be trumped by Wall Street's propensity for manias. Read on.

Growth manias

Wall Street's mantra is "anything worth doing is worth overdoing," and growth versus value is no exception. In the uncertain times of the last 40 years, growth-stock investing has twice been taken to extremes. In the early 1970s, Wall Street became enamored with *one-decision stocks:* Companies such as IBM, Xerox, and Polaroid were projected to grow at above-average rates indefinitely, and analysts believed that stock valuation was irrelevant. Investors merely had to make the one decision to purchase and hold. Of course, they were blindsided by the 1970s inflation that drove up expenses faster than revenues. Rather than growing, profits declined and so did stock prices, as much as 80 to 90 percent in many cases.

In the second episode of growth stock mania, the advent of the Internet drove huge demands for technology products. On top of that, as the year 2000 approached, corporations had to deal with the dreaded Y2K issue and the fear of global software malfunctions. It was a perfect storm for the demand of technology products and services. However, January 1, 2000, came and went, leaving behind a tremendous supply of unneeded products and services. The result? Stock price declines of 80 to 90 percent for many.

Value manias

Value stocks aren't immune to manias. The value sector contains a large percentage of bank and financial services stocks. The inflation of the 1970s generated a lot of real estate lending by banks and savings and loans. However, when Congress shortened the real estate depreciation schedules in 1986, many real estate projects became untenable. Stock prices of major banks declined as much as 75 percent from 1989 to 1990.

Because value-oriented stocks sat out the growth stock mania of the late 1990s, they didn't have major gains to surrender in the bear market of 2000 to 2002. However, they made up for it by funding the mania in housing prices from 2004 to 2007. After the marginal buyers were sucked in with teaser adjustable-rate mortgages, no was one left to buy. Supply overwhelmed demand, which in turn started the decline in home prices. Financial panic ensued when bonds backed by shaky mortgages turned bad as housing prices declined. Again, stock prices declined dramatically.

However, one segment of the value-oriented universe did extremely well through the housing debacle of 2007 to 2008. Energy and commodity prices soared beyond anyone's wildest expectations. Ten years ago, the price of oil was scraping $10 per barrel. The low prices of the late 1990s caused oil companies to de-emphasize finding new energy sources because of the low return on investment. But as demand from emerging nations such as China and India increased, supply couldn't keep up with demand, and energy and commodity prices skyrocketed along with their associated stock. But high energy prices sow the seeds of their own decline. At some point, the economic dislocations caused by higher energy prices will overwhelm the growth in demand for energy, and prices will decline. The only question is when.

Find the Right Balance and Avoid Manias

Should you invest in growth funds or value funds in uncertain times? Fortunately, you don't have to choose one over the other. Managing your portfolio can be a matter of shifting the emphasis as you participate in growth and value funds as well as blended funds:

- ✔ Emphasize growth funds when economic growth is slowing.

- ✔ Emphasize value funds when the economy begins to accelerate. These periods are usually accompanied by a steep yield curve, when short-term interest rates are much lower than long-term rates. Banks are a large component of the value sector, so a steep yield curve usually precedes higher bank profits.

How do you approach the value-growth question and protect yourself from manias? Here are some guidelines:

✔ **When purchasing either kind of fund, examine how well the current portfolio manager navigated debacles of the past.** Keep in mind, however, that past performance doesn't guarantee future results.

✔ **Don't believe the hype.** Exercise common sense. Investment management is a closed world, and managers feed off of one another. When an investment theme looks extreme, head for the exits; if it looks too good to be true, it probably is.

✔ **Read a mutual fund's annual and semiannual reports to get a sense of the fund management's thinking.** Watch out for language that echoes some of the more hyperbolic language used by the talking heads on the business news channels.

✔ **Examine a fund's holdings for style drift.** In the late 1990s, value managers suffered because their funds were dramatically underperforming their growth counterparts. In desperation, value managers added growth stocks to improve performance. Unfortunately, many did this at the market peak, which caused their value funds to decline like a growth fund in the following bear market. Value funds that remained true to their style performed much better in the bear market of 2000 to 2002.

In all cases, develop your own investment policy with a target asset mix based on your tolerance for risk (see Strategy #38 for information on assessing your risk tolerance). Rebalance your portfolio when asset-class weightings experience significant gains and declines. The decision to emphasize growth or value stocks or funds should be only a nuance in a long-term strategy of diversification that matches your investing goals with your risk tolerance.

#44

Diversify Your Stock Portfolio by Country

By Corry Sheffler, MBA, CFP, CFE

*T*oday's investment world probably isn't the same as it was for your parents. You live in a global economy, as reflected in your investment options.

Domestic markets are the equity investments in your own country, and *foreign markets* are all the equity investments found outside your country. This strategy shows you ways to diversify your investment portfolio by investing in foreign markets.

Get Your Feet Wet in Foreign Waters

A global portfolio is a more diversified portfolio, so over time, it tempers your overall volatility. Being globally diversified in troubled economic times is especially important because when the U.S. market is struggling, other markets are often soaring. For example, while the domestic U.S. stocks soared during the late 1990s, many foreign markets were in the doldrums. Conversely, while U.S. stocks languished or returned less than double-digit gains from 2003 to 2007, foreign markets had outstanding performance. Portfolios that lacked foreign stocks lagged far behind those that did. Diversification and rebalancing are the perfect way to ensure that, on average, you're buying low and selling high.

Here are several ways to gain exposure to countries outside the United States:

- ✔ Invest in multinational companies.
- ✔ Invest directly in the stocks of foreign countries.
- ✔ Buy mutual funds that invest in foreign stocks.
- ✔ Buy exchange-traded funds (ETFs) that specialize in non-U.S. markets. (For info on ETFs, see Strategy #23.)
- ✔ Buy global funds that invest in domestic U.S. as well as non-U.S. equities.

For most people, investing in these markets through mutual funds and ETFs is best. If you don't have the time to research your mutual funds, consider hiring a fee-only financial planner to help you decide — or rely entirely on index funds. Also see Strategy #40 for more on tempering risk.

Decide How Much to Invest

How much of your investment portfolio should be in non-U.S. equities? To make this decision, do the following:

- ✔ Determine what portion of your total portfolio should be in equities in general.

- ✔ Determine your personal risk tolerance.

- ✔ Accept that by investing in foreign markets, you'll be taking on more short-term risk.

- ✔ Realize that you're taking on some currency risk because the total return on foreign investments includes not only the underlying investment but also the foreign currency exchange gains or losses during the investment holding period.

For the stock portion of your portfolio, experts vary in their opinions on how much of your investments should be domestic or foreign. Still, depending on your stage in life, a good rule of thumb is to invest between 10 and 15 percent of your portfolio in non-U.S. equities.

Diversify within Your Foreign Allocation

Just as in your domestic investments, you want to have the appropriate allocations between large-cap, mid-cap, and small-cap investments. Here are a variety of ways to go:

- ✔ Invest in funds that specialize in an individual country, such as Canada, China, or Japan.

- ✔ Invest in funds that specialize in regions like Latin America or Europe, Australasia, and the Far East (EAFE) (**Note:** *Australasi*a includes Australia and New Zealand.)

- ✔ Invest in an investment fund or ETF that captures a good part of foreign markets, such as a total market index or a World (Excluding U.S.) SPDR (Standard & Poor's Depository Receipt).

In foreign markets, investing in both developed and emerging markets is also important. Think of this as the difference between domestic large-cap and small-cap stocks:

- ✔ **Developed markets:** Like large-cap domestic stocks, developed markets are more established than emerging markets. Developed markets are considered less risky than emerging markets. Examples include Germany, Japan, and the United Kingdom.

- ✔ **Emerging markets:** Emerging markets are more like the rapid-growth domestic small-cap stocks. Emerging market stocks are newer to the global investing scene. Examples include Mexico, South Korea, and Taiwan.

The bulk of your foreign investments should be in developed markets, with a small percentage, perhaps 2 to 5 percent, in emerging markets. Like country-specific or regional markets, developed and emerging market stocks can be bought individually, through mutual funds, or through ETFs.

Diversify Your Portfolio by Industry

By Robert Friedland, PhD

*W*hen buying a share of stock in a company, you buy into a particular industry. For a well-diversified stock portfolio, consider not only the size, valuation, and geographical coverage of the companies (see Strategies #42, #43, and #44) but also the industries. A portfolio of large and small capitalized firms allocated nicely between growth and value stocks in the same industry does little to diversify a portfolio. Predicting which industries will best weather an economic storm is nearly impossible, so the best long-term strategy is a portfolio broadly diversified across industries.

Industry: A Concept of Shared Risks

An industry reflects the collection of businesses that comprise a particular sector of the economy. The sector includes competitors of the firm in which you own stock and many related companies, such as companies that sell to and buy from the company whose stock you own.

An industry reflects a group of different businesses whose financial fortune or demise is likely linked. These links may be in shared labor markets, related regulations, a common purpose, or a shared technology. Hence, changes in technology, government regulations, or the marketplace may fundamentally change the business of the company you own.

Industry boundaries aren't straightforward. More importantly, many companies do business in more than one industry. Many automobile manufacturers, for example, are also in the financial services industry. A few automobile manufacturers also make jet engines. At least one jet engine company also makes medical equipment.

Understand the Industry Life Cycle

Industries, as well as the firms in them, evolve and change. Major evolutionary leaps are often marked by a technological or scientific advancement. Rapid growth within the industry often follows. Eventually, industry-wide growth may decline. Finally, the industry reaches a period of maturity and sometimes overall decline. Of course, firms enter the industry at different stages in the life cycle, so there can be considerable diversification of size and valuation among different firms in the same industry.

Products of some industries are vulnerable to the normal movements of the overall economy. Industries that move in the same direction with the economy are considered *cyclical*. Industries that move in the opposite direction are considered *countercyclical*. The extent to which an industry is cyclical or countercyclical creates a relationship between the stock price and the business cycle.

Use Sector Funds to Add Exposure to an Industry

Adding exposure to a particular industry sector is easier than ever. By purchasing either a mutual fund or exchange-traded fund (ETF) that focuses on a specific sector (see Strategies #21 and #23), you gain concentrated exposure to an industry through one investment. Often called *sector funds, specialty funds,* or *single industry funds,* they provide a cost-efficient and effective avenue for buying a large number of companies within a specific industry. Purchasing or selling sector funds enables someone with an already diversified portfolio to quickly add or reduce exposure to a specific sector.

Sector funds alone aren't well-diversified investments. A single event affecting the industry may quickly decrease the value of the sector fund. However, the volatility of a sector fund is likely to be less than the volatility of just one or two companies in that industry sector.

Know How Sectors Fit into the Economic Cycle

The inevitable contractions in the economy result in loss of employment for many and fear of job loss for many more. Fortunately, every contraction has been followed by an expansion, which means new jobs, less fear of losing a job, and less anxiety about spending to replace durable goods or expand inventory or equipment. These contractions and expansions cause stock prices to rise and fall.

Many investors manage their portfolios by moving in and out of certain industry sectors based on their assessment of the economic cycle. Their goal is to buy at the low point of a contraction and sell at the high point of an expansion:

1. When they believe the market has bottomed out, they buy in the financial and transportation industries when those industries are at their expected lows and expansion is on the horizon.

2. As the economy improves and heads toward a peak, the capital goods industries appreciate.

3. Soon thereafter, the basic industries appreciate, followed by precious metals and the energy sector.

4. At the peak, the only way to go is down into a contraction! Now, noncyclical and consumer goods — such as food, cosmetics, and healthcare — look good.

5. As the economy moves deeper into contraction, utility and consumer cyclical sector goods look more attractive — until just about the time the economy hits the bottom and the cycle begins anew.

Unfortunately, knowing just where the economy is in the business cycle isn't easy. People can speculate, sound knowledgeable, and even be correct about it by accident. Knowing when the economy has hit the peak or the bottom is like driving on a road you've never seen before while looking in the rearview mirror. You can easily see where you came from, but knowing what lies ahead is impossible.

If you buy individual stocks, buy companies in industries you understand. If you buy mutual funds or exchange-traded funds, pay attention to your portfolio's overall allocation to a given industry.

#46

Diversify Your Bond Portfolio

· ·

By Jennifer Luzzatto, CFA, CFP

· ·

*M*ost investors can best buy the bond portion of their portfolios by purchasing bond mutual funds. Because the best prices on bonds are usually in very large increments (think $1,000,000 per purchase), individuals benefit from being able to participate in a pool of professionally managed funds invested in the bond market. (For information on individual bonds, see Strategy #27.) Your approach to diversifying your bond portfolio depends upon whether you're in the accumulation phase or the retirement phase of your life.

Bond fund returns are especially sensitive to the fees of mutual funds because they typically don't see the high returns of stock funds. Keep an eye out for expense ratios of less than 0.30 percent.

Advice for Early- and Mid-Life Accumulators

Early- and mid-life accumulators can benefit from exposure to all parts of the bond market. Because of their long time horizon, they don't have to be as defensive against hard times in the investment cycle. An early accumulator should invest bond money as follows:

- ✔ **Short-term bond fund:** 35 percent
- ✔ **Intermediate-term bond fund:** 35 percent
- ✔ **Inflation-protected securities:** 20 percent
- ✔ **High-yield bonds:** 10 percent

Different sources define short-, intermediate-, and long-term differently. But generally, *short-term* bonds have maturity dates of five years or less, *intermediate-term* bonds have maturities of five to ten years, and *long-term* bonds have stated maturities that are longer than ten years. *Inflation-protected securities* are a relatively new type of security and are generally called TIPS (Treasury Inflation

Protected Securities — see Strategy #18). *High-yield bonds* are usually less creditworthy, which means they have to pay a higher rate to attract investors. These
investments are riskier, but they can be appropriate for accumulators because
the long-term horizons can temper the risk.

In this section, you discover how to allocate your bond investment if you
have ten or more years until retirement.

Let returns and volatility direct allocation

Standard deviation is one way of measuring the volatility of bonds and other
securities. A standard deviation of 4 percent means that historically, the
actual returns of a given security class have ranged from 4 percent below the
category average to 4 percent higher. The lower the standard deviation, the
lower the volatility and therefore the lower the market risk.

Table 46-1 shows that shorter-term bonds have lower volatility and that long-
term, mortgage, and high-yield bonds have greater volatility. For a long time
horizon, an ideal allocation is a blend of short-term bonds, intermediate-term
bonds, and in some cases, mortgage bonds.

Table 46-1	Average Bond Returns and Volatility	
Bond Category	**Historical Average Return**	**Standard Deviation**
Short term	7.34%	4.14%
Intermediate term	8.24%	6.83%
Long term	8.63%	10.94%
Mortgage	9.49%	10.64%
High yield	8.86%	10.60%

Source: MoneyGuide Pro

As an individual investor, you don't get enough additional return from purchasing long-term bonds over intermediate-term bonds, given the dramatic
rise in volatility for long-term bonds. Long-term bonds are generally better
suited for businesses such as insurance companies that need to match the
maturities of their assets with their liabilities. High-yield bonds can at times
be appropriate in an individual portfolio, but their risk and return profile fits
more into a stock allocation than bond allocation.

Set up an ideal allocation among bonds

For most investors, an appropriate bond allocation puts equal amounts of money in short-term and intermediate-term bonds, as Table 46-2 shows.

Table 46-2	Bond Allocation for Early to Mid Life	
Allocation	*Historical Return*	*Historical Standard Deviation*
50% short term	7.34%	4.14%
50% intermediate term	8.24%	6.83%
Total bond allocation	7.79%	5.48%

Source: MoneyGuide Pro

Unless you need to invest in tax-exempt bonds, the short- and intermediate-term bond funds should be invested in Treasuries, agencies, corporate bonds, and mortgages. You want exposure to all parts of the bond market with these funds. (For info on government bonds and Treasuries, see Strategy #18.)

Table 46-3 shows a slightly more aggressive bond allocation that includes mortgage bonds. If mortgage bonds are appropriate for your portfolio given your risk profile, Government National Mortgage Association bonds, or GNMA bonds (sometimes referred to as *Ginnie Maes*), are preferable. *GNMA* is a U.S. federal government agency that issues bonds to fund housing loans. Other government agencies issue bonds, but only GNMA bonds are backed by the full faith and credit of the U.S. federal government. This makes them similar in credit quality to Treasury bonds, although their *coupon* (the amount of interest paid) and maturity structure is different.

Table 46-3 Short, Intermediate, and Mortgage Bond Allocation		
Allocation	*Historical Return*	*Historical Standard Deviation*
35% short term	7.34%	4.14%
35% intermediate term	8.24%	6.83%
30% mortgage	9.49%	10.64%
Total bond allocation	8.28%	7.03%

Source: MoneyGuide Pro

If you go aggressive and invest in high-yield bonds, remember that high-yield bonds tend to be the most volatile. When times get rough, hold off allocating more money to these bonds until the storm begins to blow over. It's impossible to know when things may turn around, so don't abandon your high-yield funds completely — just don't add new funds until the crisis of the day is no longer on the front page.

Bond quality

The quality of the bond also affects bond volatility. The higher the bond is rated, the less sensitive it'll be to uncertain economic times. Table 46-4 explains the ratings of two of the largest rating agencies, Standard & Poor's and Moody's.

If you're an accumulator with a higher risk tolerance and a number of years before retirement, some lower-quality bonds may be appropriate. The higher yield and growth opportunities of lower-rated bonds come at the expense of more risk. If you're an investor with a shorter time frame, this risk may be unacceptable, so your mixture of bonds should tend toward the higher-quality side.

Table 46-4		Bond Ratings
Standard & Poor's Rating	**Moody's Rating**	**Meaning**
AAA	Aaa	Lowest risk
AA	Aa	Slight long-term risk
A	A	Possibly vulnerable to changing economic conditions
BBB	Baa	Currently safe but possibly unreliable over the long term
BB	Ba	Somewhat speculative issue that offers moderate security
B	B	At risk of default in the future
CCC	Caa	Clear danger of default
CC	Ca	Highly speculative or may be in default
C	C	Poor prospects for repayment even if currently paying
N/A	D	In default

Source: Forefield Advisor

Advice for Almost-Retirees and Retirees

If you plan to retire in about one to three years, your time horizon is a bit shorter, but by no means short! Inflation may be your biggest enemy because the cost of living will most likely exceed your income after a few years of retirement. Stocks and stock funds can help take care of the dreaded effects of inflation, but you should use your bond portfolio to hold down the volatility of the overall portfolio. Thus, you need to be a bit more conservative. Your bond portfolio should look like this:

- ✔ **Short-term bond fund:** 45 percent
- ✔ **Intermediate-term bond fund:** 35 percent
- ✔ **Inflation-protected securities:** 20 percent

This bond allocation should be sustainable throughout most of your retirement years. After it's clear you're in your final years and that your current assets will sustain you for the rest of your life, a 100-percent short-term bond allocation is advisable.

Short-term bond funds suffer the least in turbulent times. So if in doubt, go short! But remember that you may be giving up growth or yield if you put too much in or stay in the short-term arena too long.

Diversify Your Portfolio with Alternative Vehicles

By Kevin O'Reilly

*I*n unpredictable times, knowing that your portfolio is well-diversified is comforting. So besides diversifying among different flavors of traditional investments such as stocks, bonds, and mutual funds, why not consider different investments altogether? So-called *alternative investments* can perform very differently from stocks and bonds. This strategy discusses some of these alternative investments, which span a broad set of choices: Common vehicles include real estate, private equity, and hedge funds.

Private Equity: Some Privacy, Please

Most people understand that public companies raise money by issuing stock that's bought and sold on exchanges. Less well-known are the various ways that owners of private companies secure capital to grow their businesses. They do this through *private equity*. You have to have significant assets and/ or income to participate in this arena.

Private equity vehicles are generally required by law to accept money only from individuals who are accredited investors. The Securities and Exchange Commission (SEC) defines an *accredited investor* as one of the following:

- A person who has individual net worth, or joint net worth with his or her spouse, that exceeds $1 million at the time of the purchase

- A person with income exceeding $200,000 in each of the two most recent years, or joint income with a spouse exceeding $300,000 for those years, and a reasonable expectation of the same income level

Investing in private equity can be very lucrative. For example, Table 47-1 shows historical returns for Thomson Financial's U.S. Private Equity Performance Index (PEPI). However, the range of private equity investments is broad, and the return can vary significantly. Investing in this manner can be complex and frustrating. A financial advisor can help with the how-to as well as suitability issues.

Table 47-1	Private Equity Performance				
	1 Year	*3 Year*	*5 Year*	*10 Year*	*20 Year*
Private equity	22.5%	13.4%	3.6%	11.4%	14.2%
NASDAQ	5.6%	10.2%	0.0%	6.2%	11.7%
S&P 500	6.6%	9.2%	0.7%	6.6%	9.79%

Source: Thomson Financial/National Venture Capital Association

Hedge Your Bets with Hedge Funds

Hedge funds — which are designed to maximize gains while minimizing risks — employ many different strategies in pursuit of superior returns. For instance, they may be made up of assets that don't move in the same direction as traditional investments, or they may be short-selling those assets.

You can't look at hedge funds as a homogenous asset class, because they're lightly regulated and invest in a broad spectrum of vehicles to meet a wide range of objectives. Nonetheless, looking at the overall performance of hedge funds over time, they clearly stack up well against more traditional investments. As Table 47-2 indicates, hedge funds can provide a solid alternative during periods of poor stock market performance.

Table 47-2	Hedge Fund Performance in a Down Market	
Year	*S&P 500*	*All Hedge Funds*
2000	–9%	9%
2001	–12%	7%
2002	–22%	6%

Like private equity (see the preceding section), hedge funds come with steep requirements, and you have to be an accredited investor to participate.

Fortunately, one approach brings hedge funds within reach of a broader group of investors: the *fund of funds* (FoF). The managers of these funds of funds wade through the sea of hedge fund information to identify a handful of hedge funds that, together, may best meet your stated objective. They then bundle these various hedge funds into a single investment vehicle, which they offer to the public.

Investing in a fund of funds can be very expensive. The underlying hedge funds themselves may charge something along the lines of 1 percent plus 20 percent of the profits of the fund. If you're investing through a fund of funds, the manager of *that* fund will charge up to 1.5 percent of assets plus 10 percent of their profits. Note, however, that despite the high fees, investors who can afford to invest in a hedge fund may benefit from the diversification a fund of funds provides.

Seek Diversification with Real Estate

Don't let recent housing market slides scare you away from real estate investing. Depending on where you invest, long term returns can be attractive. For investors who have much of their retirement savings in the stock market through an employer's 401(k) plan or IRAs, real estate investing can offer good diversification.

Get in it for the long haul

Single-family rental housing can be a solid hedge against an uncertain future — just make sure you view the investment as a long-term proposition. If you purchase a rental house tomorrow and the economy experiences a period of significant inflation, your investment will likely appreciate at a rate at least close to inflation. The rent you collect will also grow with inflation while your mortgage payments remain static.

The idea that all real estate is local is a cliché in the industry — and it's true! Even in the recent real estate debacle, some U.S. housing markets rose in value. In less extreme examples, it's common for some markets to rise while others fall, regardless of what happens in the overall economy and stock market.

Proceed with caution with residential real estate

You may have several reasons to think twice about investing in residential real estate:

- Housing isn't liquid.
- This is a hands-on investment. Houses require maintenance, and rent needs collecting. You need to perform upkeep to prepare the house for new renters. You can hire a management company to perform these services for you, but this expense comes out of your profits.

✔ Renters are short-term visitors in your house. You can protect yourself through security deposits and lease provisions, but it's unlikely that your investment will be treated as gently as if your renters owned it.

✔ Rent checks don't always arrive as stipulated by the rental contract. Sometimes, rent checks bounce. People choose to rent for many different reasons, but the fact is that renters are sometimes renters simply because they're unable to buy a home for cash flow and/or credit score reasons. You can mitigate these problems by carefully screening renters, but that'll reduce your market for potential renters.

If you still think residential real estate investing is for you, check out *Real Estate Investing For Dummies* (Wiley).

Commercialize with corporate buildings

Commercial real estate is an option for real estate investors. Although far from certain, rent checks tend to be a bit more reliable coming from established corporate entities rather than individuals. Typically, a third party handles management of the property, making the investment easier to deal with on a day to day basis. On the other hand, you have to pay for that property management, which eats into your returns.

The commercial real estate market is more efficient than the residential market. Investments are typically valued based on the *capitalization rate* (cap rate), which is simply the net cash flow divided by the investment cost. Prevailing cap rates change over time, but finding bargain prices in commercial real estate is less common than it is in residential properties. In short, people buy and sell houses for many different reasons, only some of which are profit-oriented; however, profit motive is generally the biggest driver for commercial real estate transactions.

Look to REITs

Perhaps the easiest way to diversify your portfolio with real estate is through real estate investment trusts (REITs). Think of REITs as mutual funds that invest in real estate. Numerous specialty REITs invest in apartment buildings, strip malls, and office buildings.

Historically, REITs haven't correlated to the stock market. They've moved in the same direction as equity markets less than 50 percent of the time. See Strategy #24 for a more thorough review of investing in REITs and how they may fit into your portfolio.

Employ a Conservative Portfolio

· ·

By Peggy Creveling, CFA

· ·

*W*hat is a conservative portfolio? Is it what you need? This strategy delves into the building blocks used in designing a conservative portfolio, highlights the historical returns and risk profile of each component, and provides you with guidance on developing a conservative portfolio that'll serve you through all economic climates.

Determine Whether a Conservative Portfolio Is Right for You

You should consider a conservative portfolio if the following applies:

✔ **You need the money in the next five to ten years.** For goals less than five years away, you want to avoid exposure to the markets. The risk of a loss is too high. Instead, use a money market account, CD, or ultra short-term bond fund to finance short-term goals.

✔ **You're unable to bear much risk.** If you can't accept the consequences of your investments' not producing results in the time period needed, you can't bear much risk. For example, a retiree dependent on investments for essential living expenses can't accept much risk, but one who has covered those living expenses with pensions, Social Security, and/or annuities can afford to take more risk.

✔ **You're an inexperienced investor.** Almost all people overestimate their ability to handle market volatility. If you don't have much investment experience, start conservatively. You'll be less likely to sell your portfolio when the market drops.

✔ **You're averse to risk (market volatility).** If dips in your portfolio keep you up at night, stick with a more conservative portfolio. You'll sleep better and be better off than if you were outside your comfort zone.

Although less volatile than a more-aggressive portfolio, a conservative portfolio can still produce negative returns in any given year, or in rarer instances, for more than one year in a row. And of course, the trade-off for lower volatility is lesser returns.

Decide Which Asset Classes to Use

An enormous number of asset classes are available. Many, however, don't belong in a conservative portfolio. Table 48-1 gives examples of the more traditional asset classes for a variety of increasingly complex portfolios. If you're just starting out, stay with the simple portfolio; as your nest egg grows, add additional asset classes as illustrated in the more-complex and complex portfolios.

Table 48-1	Asset Classes for Model Portfolios	
Simple Portfolio	*More-Complex Portfolio*	*Complex Portfolio*
Cash	Cash	Cash
Bonds	Short-term bonds	Short-term bonds
U.S. total stock market	Intermediate-term bonds	Intermediate-term bonds
International equity	U.S. large cap	High-yield bonds
	U.S. small cap	Global bonds
	International developed	U.S. large cap value
	Emerging markets	U.S. large cap growth
		Small cap
		International developed
		Emerging markets
		Real estate
		Commodities

Increasing the number of asset classes potentially increases your long-term return while decreasing volatility. After 8 to 12 asset classes, the value of adding additional asset classes actually diminishes. You need to weigh the additional benefit against the increased management complexity.

Know How Much to Allocate to Each Asset Class

The split between fixed income (bonds) and equity (stocks) has the biggest impact on the likely long-term returns and volatility. There's no one right answer, but because the goal is a less volatile portfolio, the range for cash and fixed income should be about 55 to 80 percent. Equity and alternative investments should fill in the remaining 20 to 45 percent.

To further lower volatility, consider swapping riskier asset classes (which have a higher standard deviation) for less-risky asset classes under the broad bond/equity split. For example, use intermediate-term bonds instead of long-term bonds, large-cap stocks instead of small-cap, and so on.

The following table provides data on various asset classes. Use this information to decide how conservative you need or want to be.

Consider breaking your investments into a number of mini-portfolios, each with an allocation suited for that particular time frame and objective. You'll remove much of the stress of trying to fund a number of diverse goals from the same portfolio.

Asset Class	Holding Ranges (%)	Long-Term Historic Returns*		Standard Deviation** (%)
		Nominal (%)	Real (%)	
Fixed Income	**55–80%**			
Cash*	0–10%	6.0	1.4	±2.9
Short-term bonds	20–40%	7.3	2.7	±4.1
Intermediate-term bonds	20–40%	8.0	3.3	±6.5
High-yield bonds	0–5%	9.2	4.8	±9.1
Global bonds (unhedged)	0–5%	8.4	3.7	±6.7
Equity	**20–45%**			
Large cap	10–25%			
Value		10.7	6.1	±15.4
Growth		10.2	5.6	±18.1
Small cap	0–10%	14.3	9.7	±22.2
International developed	5–15%	11.7	7.1	±21.4
Emerging markets	0–3%	11.6	7.0	±28.0
Alternative	**0–6%**			
Real estate investment trusts	0–3%	13.0	8.4	±17.1
Commodities	0–3%	11.7	5.6	±24.2

Source: Long-term historic returns and standard deviation figures from MoneyguidePro/PIE Technologies for time period 1972–2007.
*Nominal returns are returns before inflation. Real returns exclude inflation (average 4.63 percent per year for the period 1972–2007.)

**One standard deviation describes the range that returns will likely fall within two-thirds of the time.

Finally, here are sample portfolios along with historical performance.

Conservation Portfolios

70% Cash and Fixed Income : 30% Equity and Alternative

55% Cash and Fixed Income : 45% Equity and Alternative

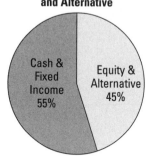

Six Asset Class		Twelve Asset Class		Six Asset Class		Twelve Asset Class	
Cash	8%	Cash	8%	Cash	6%	Cash	6%
Short-term bonds	28%	Short-term bonds	23%	Short-term bonds	21%	Short-term bonds	16%
Intermediate-term bonds	34%	Intermediate-term bonds	29%	Intermediate-term bonds	28%	Intermediate-term bonds	23%
Large cap	16%	High-yield bonds	5%	Large cap	25%	High-yield bonds	5%
Small cap	5%	Global bonds	5%	Small cap	5%	Global bonds	5%
International	9%	Large cap value	7%	International	15%	Large cap value	11%
Total	**100%**	Large cap growth	7%	**Total**	**100%**	Large cap growth	10%
		Small cap	5%			Small cap	5%
		International developed	5%			International developed	10%
		Emerging markets	2%			Emerging markets	3%
		Real estate	2%			Real estate	3%
		Commodities	2%			Commodities	3%
		Total	**100%**			**Total**	**100%**
Expected return	8.7%	Expected return	8.8%	Expected return	9.2%	Expected return	9.4%
Real return	4.0%	Real return	4.2%	Real return	4.6%	Real return	4.8%
Standard deviation	6.1%	Standard deviation	5.7%	Standard deviation	7.9%	Standard deviation	7.2%

Source: Portfolio expected returns and standard deviation figures from Moneyguide Pro/PIE Technologies based on historic performance during the period 1972–2007

#49

Employ a Moderate Portfolio

By Peggy Creveling, CFA

The moderate portfolio shifts up the risk, volatility, and return scale when compared with the conservative portfolio, including perhaps more years of loss and an increased chance of multi-year losses. The reward for bearing more risk is the increased chance of a higher long-term return when compared with the conservative portfolio (refer to Strategy #48). The difference between an expected return of 9.94 percent for a moderate portfolio and 8.96 percent for a more conservative one may not look like much, but it can really add up. Figure 49-1 shows the range of possible values that $100,000 invested in a moderate and conservative portfolio may earn over time. In the long term, the moderate portfolio's expected or *mid value* is higher than that of the more conservative portfolio, and the potential range of values is wider.

Choose to Create a Moderate Portfolio

A moderate portfolio is appropriate if you meet the following criteria:

- ✔ **You won't need the money for about ten years.** In general, the longer time horizon allows you to add more equity and other risky assets, which should increase your long-term return. With a longer time frame, extreme up and down years tend to cancel each other out, and your return will trend much closer to the expected long-run return.

- ✔ **You have increased ability to bear risk.** Someone in his 20s or 30s with decades of earnings ahead of him — and not dependent on income from the portfolio — can afford more risk in search of a higher return than a retiree with her working years behind her. Similarly, a retiree with adequate health and long-term care insurance and a hefty retirement pension can bear more risk than a retiree dependant on his portfolio to fund essential expenses.

- ✔ **You can tolerate a moderate amount of market volatility.** You already have some experience in the market and are comfortable with some volatility, but you're unwilling to accept the more extreme movements that come with a more aggressive portfolio. For example, a moderate portfolio with an expected annual long-term return of 9.6 percent may be expected to return between 1.8 and 17.4 percent two-thirds of the time.

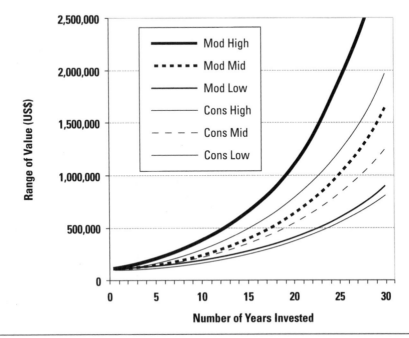

Figure 49-1:
Range of possible ending-portfolio values, moderate versus conservative.

Expected range of values for a Moderate Portfolio with an expected return of 9.94% per year and standard deviation of 10.10% and a Conservative Portfolio with expected return of 8.96% per year and standard deviation of 7.02%, assuming returns are log normally distributed. Portfolios are expected to earn above the lower boundary 90% of the time and below the upper boundary 90% of the time.

Construct a Moderate Portfolio

Building a moderate portfolio follows the same process as constructing the conservative portfolio. You use the same asset classes for the level of portfolio complexity you prefer (see Strategy #48); only the weightings change.

Keeping equity and alternative investments in the 45-to-65-percent range, and cash and fixed income investments in the 35-to-55-percent range, is a good idea.

The same steps apply as with the conservative portfolio:

1. **Keep the overall split between equity and fixed income within the ranges for a moderate portfolio as specified in the following table.**

2. **Balance the number of asset classes with the size of your portfolio and your ability to manage it.**

   Having more than 8 to 12 isn't necessary.

3. **Allocate funds to the various asset classes within the ranges indicated in the table, depending on how much risk you're willing to take in the attempt to earn a higher return.**

   Focus on overall portfolio performance. By design, you'll always have some asset classes in your portfolio doing better than others. The impact of having some investments zigging while others are zagging lowers overall portfolio volatility and potentially increases portfolio return. (See Strategy #40 for more on diversification.)

4. **Choose one or two mutual funds for each asset class, depending on the size of your portfolio.**

   If most active fund managers have trouble beating the market or their respective benchmarks in a one-year period, what chance do they have of beating their benchmark over longer periods? And what chance do you have of choosing that manager ahead of time? By choosing passively managed funds (index funds and exchange-traded funds) over actively managed ones, you may improve your chances of earning the market return over the long run. See Strategies #21 and #23 for details.

5. **Rebalance periodically back to your target allocation.**

   In volatile markets in particular, ensure you don't stray too far from your target weightings. This may mean you have to sell assets that are doing well and buy those that are doing poorly, but you'll be well positioned when the market recovers because you've bought low and sold high along the way.

The following table gives suggested asset class percentages.

Asset Class	Holding Ranges (%)	L/Term Historic Returns		Standard Dev (%)
		Nominal (%)	Real (%)	
Fixed Income	**35-55%**			
Cash^	0-10%	6.0	1.4	±2.9
Short Term Bonds	15-25%	7.3	2.7	±4.1
Intermediate Term Bonds	15-25%	8.0	3.3	±6.5
High Yield Bonds	0-5%	9.2	4.8	±9.1
Global Bonds (unhedged)	0-5%	8.4	3.7	±6.7
Equity and Alternative	**45-65%**			
Large cap	20-40%			
Value		10.7	6.1	±15.4
Growth		10.2	5.6	±18.1
Small cap	5-10%	14.3	9.7	±22.2
International developed	5-20%	11.7	7.1	±21.4
Emerging markets	0-5%	11.6	7.0	±28.0
Real estate	0-5%	13.0	8.4	±17.1
Commodities	0-3%	11.7	5.6	±24.2

^ *Cash allocation is needed for portfolios where you'll be making withdrawals. L/T historic returns and standard deviation figures from Moneyguide Pro/PIE Technologies, 1972-2007. Real returns based on long term US inflation of 4.63%*

Note the Historical Performance of Moderate Portfolios

We provide two examples of moderate portfolios. The first portfolio illustrates a moderately conservative allocation using both 6 and 12 asset classes, and the second example shows the same historical results for a portfolio that has more opportunity for growth. The key statistics are shown on the bottom line — you want the highest return with the lowest amount of volatility (as measured by standard deviation) for your personal comfort level.

Note that the additional asset classes in the more complex portfolio result in a higher expected return and lower standard deviation in both cases, although the simple portfolio captures most of the benefits of diversification.

Moderate Portfolios

50% Equity and Alternative : 50% Cash and Fixed Income

Equity & Alternative 50%

Cash & Fixed Income 50%

Six Asset Class		Twelve Asset Class	
Cash	6%	Cash	6%
S/T Bonds	19%	S/T Bonds	15%
Int Bonds	25%	I/T Bonds	21%
Large Cap	31%	High Yield	4%
Small Cap	7%	Glbl Bonds	4%
Int'l	12%	Lg Value	14%
Total	**100%**	Lg Growth	11%
		Small Cap	7%
		Int'l Dev	9%
		Emg Mkts	3%
		REITs	3%
		Cmmdities	3%
		Total	**100%**
Exp Rtn	9.4%	Exp Rtn	9.6%
Real Rtn	4.8%	Real Rtn	5.0%
Std Dev	8.3%	Std Dev	7.8%

65% Equity and Alternative : 35% Cash and Fixed Income

Equity & Alternative 65%

Cash & Fixed Income 35%

Six Asset Class		Twelve Asset Class	
Cash	5%	Cash	5%
S/T Bonds	12%	S/T Bonds	9%
Int Bonds	18%	I/T Bonds	15%
Large Cap	40%	High Yield	3%
Small Cap	10%	Glbl Bonds	3%
Int'l	15%	Lg Value	17%
Total	**100%**	Lg Growth	16%
		Small Cap	10%
		Int'l Dev	10%
		Emg Mkts	3%
		REITs	4%
		Cmmdities	3%
		Total	**100%**
Exp Rtn	10.0%	Exp Rtn	10.2%
Real Rtn	5.4%	Real Rtn	5.6%
Std Dev	10.7%	Std Dev	9.9%

^ Portfolio expected returns and standard deviation figures from MoneyguidePro/PIE -Technologies, based on historic returns from 1972-2007

Employe an Aggressive Portfolio

By Peggy Creveling, CFA

An aggressive portfolio bears nearly the full brunt of market volatility in an attempt to achieve higher long-term returns. There'll be more years of losses and more periods of multi-year losses, countered by some extremely good years of positive returns. You'll need to stomach large swings in the value of your portfolio, sometimes on a daily basis, without losing your nerve and bailing out on your portfolio. Your returns in any one year can vary widely, but the longer you hold the portfolio, the closer your return will approach the long-run expected return.

Is a portfolio that's earning only 1 to 2 percent more than a less volatile one worth the stress and anxiety? Over the long haul, yes. That additional 1 to 2 percent doesn't seem like much on its own, but compounded over a 20- to 30-year time period, the impact can be huge, as shown in Figure 50-1. For longer time periods, an aggressive portfolio is likely to do better than more conservative ones. The trick is having the ability to stay invested for long periods despite the turmoil you'll most likely experience. In this strategy, you explore aggressive portfolios.

 Don't forget about mutual fund fees. You can sometimes add nearly 1 percent to your return by simply swapping your high-cost actively managed fund for a low-cost index fund or exchange-traded fund — and you don't need to take on any additional risk to get it.

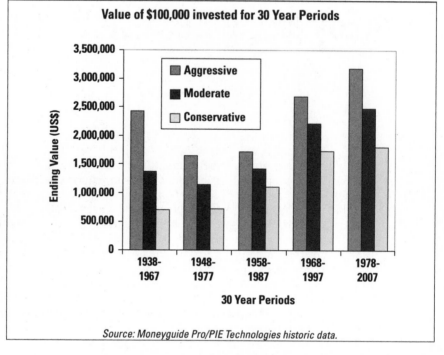

Figure 50-1:
Comparing ending values of aggressive, moderate, and conservative portfolios.

Know Whether an Aggressive Portfolio Is Right for You

Consider an aggressive portfolio only if you meet the following conditions:

✔ **You have a long time horizon.** You need the extremely bad and good years to cancel each other out and settle around the longer-run expected return.

With an aggressive portfolio, the long run should be 15 to 20 years or more. Anything shorter and your returns may be significantly lower than your expected return.

✔ **You have a high capacity to bear risk.** In other words, you can weather the storm financially if your investments don't work out within the time period expected. This may be because your goal is flexible or because you have a way to make up the shortfall by adding savings, extending the time period, or funding the goal from another source.

✔ **You're an experienced investor and know that you can stomach a lot of volatility.** The returns of an aggressive portfolio in any one year may vary widely. If you've invested during a prolonged period of market uncertainty before, you have a good idea of how you'll react when the financial media starts churning out stories of impending financial Armageddon. If you stuck through past periods without panicking and selling out, an aggressive portfolio allocation may be for you.

An aggressive portfolio isn't appropriate for all goals — the risk of shortfall is too high. Using an aggressive portfolio to fund college for your 13-year-old wouldn't be a good idea, but it may be appropriate for a younger person saving for retirement or even a retiree whose living expenses are covered by a pension or other income and is growing the portfolio to pass on to heirs.

If you're dependent on income from your portfolio, the risks of an aggressive portfolio may be unbearable. Making regular withdrawals, especially in years of bad returns, can devastate your portfolio and your life (see Strategy #68 for details). On the other hand, if you have an emergency fund in place, you have adequate health and long-term care insurance, and your essential living expenses are covered by Social Security, pensions, or other sources of income (not part-time work), then you may be able to take some additional risk with your portfolio. If you're primarily dependent on your portfolio to cover your basic living expenses, you don't.

In a household where more than one person is affected by the investment decisions, both need to be comfortable with the portfolio's level of volatility. Go with the risk tolerance level of the more conservative person.

Constructing an Aggressive Portfolio

Building an aggressive portfolio follows the same process as building moderate and conservative portfolios. You use the same asset classes for the level of portfolio complexity you prefer (see Strategy #48); only the weightings change.

An aggressive portfolio has a greater percentage invested in equity and alternative holdings and a lower percentage in fixed income. Experts suggest keeping equity and alternative investments in the 70-to-90-percent range and fixed income investments in the 10-to-30-percent range.

The same steps apply as with the conservative and moderate portfolios:

1. **Keep the overall split between the broad fixed income, equity, and alternative asset classes within the ranges shown in the following table.**

2. **Balance the number of asset classes with the size of your portfolio and your ability to manage it.**

   Use no more than 8 to 12.

3. **Allocate funds to each selected asset within the suggested ranges, ensuring that the total doesn't exceed the recommended range for the broader asset classes (fixed income, equity, or alternative).**

   Consider index funds and exchange-traded funds (ETFs) for each asset class to keep fees low. (See Strategies #21 and #23 for more on these funds.)

This table gives you some idea of how to split out the asset classes.

Asset Class	Holding Ranges (%)	Long-Term Historic Returns* Nominal (%)	Real (%)	Standard Deviation** (%)
Fixed Income	**10-30%**			
Cash*	0-5%	6.0	1.4	±2.9
Short-term bonds	0-15%	7.3	2.7	±4.1
Intermediate-term bonds	0-15%	8.0	3.3	±6.5
High-yield bonds	0-5%	9.2	4.8	±9.1
Global bonds (unhedged)	0-5%	8.4	3.7	±6.7
Equity	**60-90%**			
Large cap	25-50%			
Value		10.7	6.1	±15.4
Growth		10.2	5.6	±18.1
Small cap	10-20%	14.3	9.7	±22.2
International developed	10-20%	11.7	7.1	±21.4
Emerging markets	0-10%	11.6	7.0	±28.0
Alternative	**0-20%**			
Real estate investment trusts	0-20%	13.0	8.4	±17.1
Commodities	0-5%	11.7	5.6	±24.2

*Cash allocation is needed for portfolios where you'll be making withdrawals. L/T historic returns and standard deviation figures from Moneyguide Pro/PIE Technologies, 1972-2007. Real returns based on the historical US inflation rate of 4.63% per year during the same period.

Examples of Aggressive Portfolios

Following are some sample portfolios of differing complexity along with their historical performance. Find the portfolio that's most comfortable and appropriate for your needs by focusing on the bottom line — most return with lowest volatility or standard deviation.

Aggressive Portfolios							
75% Equity and Alternative : **25% Cash and Fixed Income**				**90% Equity and Alternative :** **10% Cash and Fixed Income**			
Six Asset Class		**Twelve Asset Class**		**Six Asset Class**		**Twelve Asset Class**	
Cash	2%	Cash	2%	Cash	2%	Cash	2%
I/T Bonds	23%	S/T Bonds	7%	I/T Bonds	8%	I/T Bonds	5%
Large Cap	35%	I/T Bonds	10%	Large Cap	45%	Glbl Bonds	3%
Small Cap	15%	High Yield	3%	Small Cap	15%	Lg Value	19%
Int'l	15%	Glbl Bonds	3%	Int'l	20%	Lg Growth	15%
REIT	10%	Lg Value	18%	REIT	10%	Small Cap	15%
Total	**100%**	Lg Growth	14%	**Total**	**100%**	Europe	10%
		Small Cap	15%			Asia Pacific	10%
		Int'l Dev	10%			Emg Mkts	8%
		Emg Mkts	5%			REITs	10%
		REITs	10%			Cmmdities	3%
		Cmmdities	3%			**Total**	**100%**
		Total	**100%**				
Exp Rtn	10.8%	Exp Rtn	10.9%	Exp Rtn	11.3%	Exp Rtn	11.4%
Real Rtn	6.2%	Real Rtn	6.2%	Real Rtn	6.6%	Real Rtn	6.8%
Std Dev	11.8%	Std Dev	11.2%	Std Dev	13.9%	Std Dev	13.4%

Source: Portfolio expected returns and standard deviation figures from Moneyguide Pro/PIE -Technologies, based on historic returns from 1972-2007

Structure different portfolios to fund different goals. Your goals vary in terms of time horizon and importance and therefore impact your ability to handle a shortfall and market volatility.

Part IV
Investing for Accumulators

The 5th Wave · By Rich Tennant

"It's surprising considering his portfolio is so conservative."

In this part . . .

In this part, you look at everything from what you need to save to be prepared for a major life event, such as raising children and paying for their education, to making sure you're saving enough so you can retire someday if you choose. You also discover investment vehicles and strategies that are appropriate whether you're just beginning to invest or you have a good-sized nest egg and want to make sure you don't lose all you've accumulated.

Save for Emergencies

By Dylan Ross, CFP

*E*ven if you've never had to quickly come up with money for something you weren't expecting, you always face the possibility of needing money in an emergency. Emergencies are unplanned expenses that require more money than you can cover with your paycheck, even if you cut some expenses until next payday. When you don't have enough in savings, emergencies can put you in debt or deeper in debt. An emergency fund helps protect your finances.

Unexpected expenses may be one-time or recurring. Potential uses for emergency funds include car repairs, paying bills if you're out of work, large medical costs, insurance deductibles, critical home repairs, legal defense fees, travel to attend a funeral, natural disasters, and so on.

Figure How Much to Set Aside

At an absolute minimum, set aside enough money in your emergency fund to pay for at least three to six months of *basic living expenses* (the regular and essential expenses you must pay to live). These expenses don't include discretionary items like entertainment, dining out, or spa treatments. Keep at least six months of basic living expenses in your emergency fund if you're single or living on one income, or if one income in your two-income household varies a lot from month to month or isn't secure.

Your emergency fund does more than just cover expenses in case you lose your job, so resist the temptation to keep a smaller emergency fund if your job is stable or if you think you could find work quickly if you're laid off. Basing the size of your emergency fund on monthly expenses establishes a guideline, but the fund covers other emergencies, even while you're employed.

If you anticipate more frequent or more severe emergencies than three to six months of basic living expenses can cover, increase the size of your emergency fund. For example, you may need a larger emergency fund if

     ✔ Your job security is questionable.

     ✔ You're about to have a baby or purchase a new home.

     ✔ You have numerous, aging household appliances.

     ✔ You drive an older car.

     ✔ You live in an area prone to severe weather, earthquakes, or other disasters.

     ✔ You engage in activities that may result in frequent trips to the emergency room, doctor's office, or the first aid aisle of your local pharmacy.

Your emergency fund is handy when you need to make insurance co-payments or pay for charges not covered by a health, dental, or vision plan. Sometimes you may need cash until you're reimbursed by an insurance company or flexible spending account. Consider any unreimbursed medical expenses from the past few years when deciding whether to increase your emergency fund.

If you're feeling especially uncertain, add to the size of your emergency fund. You can always reduce it after you're through the rough patch.

When purchasing household appliances, decline the offers for extended warrantees and add that money to your emergency fund instead. If you self-warranty several appliances, you spread out the risk of needing to repair any one of them. If you don't need to make repairs, you get to keep the money!

Handle Your Emergency Fund with Care

The tricky thing about financial emergencies is that you don't know what they'll be, when they'll happen, or how much you'll need in order to cope until you can recover. All these unknowns make your emergency fund an important part of your financial profile and one that you should treat with special attention and care.

Make your fund a high priority

The harder you think it is to come up with money for an emergency fund, the more you need one. If coming up with money to start an emergency fund now will be a sacrifice, imagine how tough it will be when you have to pay for the costs of an emergency situation.

If you're trying to pay off credit cards or high-interest loans, start with an emergency fund that could cover one month of basic living expenses. After you save one month of expenses, put extra money toward your debt payments. When your debt is paid off, build your emergency fund as quickly as possible. Otherwise, a sudden emergency could send you right back into the red.

Keep your fund liquid

Keep your emergency fund in cash types of investments (see Strategy #17 for more on cash investments). This money should be quickly available with no risk of decreasing in value at any time. An emergency fund is self-insurance, not an investment. You want your money to be accessible, but you also want to earn some interest on it so that you offset inflation at least partially, if not completely. The next section tells you where to invest your money.

Invest your fund

Some places to keep your emergency fund savings include the following:

- **High-yielding direct savings accounts:** Online savings accounts often pay a higher than average interest rate. You can, and should, establish an electronic transfer link (called an ACH or Automated Clearing House link) to your checking account.

- **Savings and money market accounts:** These are interest-bearing accounts at banks or credit unions. Being able to electronically transfer money to your checking account is best.

- **Money market funds:** Not to be confused with money market accounts, these are funds offered by mutual fund companies and brokerage firms. You redeem fund shares to get cash out. Some accounts allow you to write checks to access the cash.

- **Interest-bearing checking accounts:** These accounts may pay less interest than savings accounts.

- **Certificates of deposit (CDs):** These banking deposits guarantee a specific interest rate if you hold them for a specified period of time. They aren't an ideal place to keep emergency fund money because you usually have to pay a penalty to get your money out early.

When deciding where to keep your emergency funds, make sure you know how and when you can access your cash. Can you get to your money after business hours? What about on weekends and holidays? Can you use checks, an ATM, or a debit or check card? Also, make sure you're comfortable with whether or not the account is insured.

Don't use available credit as an emergency fund! Credit cards and home equity lines of credit could serve as a backup to your emergency funds in the event of a catastrophe, but the whole idea of an emergency fund is to keep you from adding debt. Some emergencies could affect your ability to make minimum debt payments, and missed payments, late penalties, and finance charges can easily snowball out of control.

Keep a small amount of cash (enough for some groceries or to get out of town in an evacuation) stashed away at home for emergencies. During local emergencies like storms and blackouts, nearby merchants may not accept checks or be able to process credit and debit cards.

Use your fund wisely when the time comes

Create a plan for dealing with emergencies. Prioritize what expenses you could cut or reduce in an emergency. Know what you have to do, whom you have to call, and how long it will take to cancel unnecessary services. Write it all down and keep it somewhere you can find it when you need it.

Sooner or later you'll have a large, unexpected expense you can't cover with your paycheck. First, decide whether it's a real emergency. Do you need to spend the money right now? Can you make do until you can save up to meet the expense? Your answer may be influenced by other events. For example, if your dishwasher bites the dust, you may decide to save up for a new one while you handwash dishes because of layoff rumors at work.

When you face a real emergency, access only the minimum amount of money necessary to get you through the emergency. Cut any unnecessary expenses and direct any available income toward your emergency before accessing the emergency fund. When the emergency is over, rebuild your emergency fund as quickly as possible, before reinstating nonessential expenses.

Provide for Large Expenses

* * *

By Eileen Freiburger, CFP

* * *

*I*n a perfect world, you'd have funds saved long before you needed them for a large outlay. However, the world isn't perfect, and national or local economic uncertainty can challenge your purchase decisions. Having a plan or a set of guidelines for funding large purchases can help you make better decisions when the time comes. An obvious decision with large expenses is to delay the purchase until the economy turns around. However, with careful planning ahead of time, that may not be your only choice. Read on for some options.

Buying a Car

Whether you buy a car every three years or drive the one you have until it falls apart, you generally know well ahead of time that you'll make this purchase. Because ego and emotions often influence the decision of which car to purchase, developing guidelines for yourself can keep you from buying a car that's more than you can afford — one that may create a debt crisis when the economy gets tough.

Do your prep work

Start with a review of your current assets. Do you have enough saved in a car fund to pay cash for the car? If not, review your current spending. If you take out a loan to buy the car, how much monthly payment can you add to your current expenses? Choose an amount that you can afford not only now but also if your finances get tough.

If you know today that you'll be replacing a car in the future, start saving toward the down payment. (See Strategy #17 for information on where to invest your savings.) Because you'll use this money within a short time and won't have time to recover from a dip in the stock market, you need to invest these funds in a way that protects what you're putting aside and provides modest growth.

Next, comparison shop. Here are some useful Web sites:

- ✔ **Edmunds:** www.edmunds.com
- ✔ **Kelly Blue Book:** www.kbb.com
- ✔ **CarBuyingTips.com:** www.carbuyingtips.com

For the vehicle you're considering, research the retail price as well as each dealer's invoice price and whether the dealer may be receiving incentives or rebates on that vehicle. Knowing this information beforehand can help you choose a dealer and give you a stronger negotiating position. That'll also help you reduce your total cost, as well as your loan payment. Do this step for both new and used cars.

Because car values depreciate quickly, buying a two- to three-year-old used car with a service warranty may make the most financial sense for getting the best bang for your buck.

Pay for your car

You have three options for buying a car:

- ✔ Save and pay outright.
- ✔ Prearrange a loan.
- ✔ Use dealer financing.

Having a sizable down payment saved may help you obtain better terms on a loan. Also, check your credit score at www.myfico.com because it'll affect the loan terms you're offered and therefore the monthly payment you'll make. You also want to check your credit report; see Strategy #12.

You can use www.bankrate.com to see what the loan rates are nationally and in your area. Shop local lending institutions for their rates, check the interest rate each dealer offers, and compare all rates to find the lowest. Table 52-1 shows how different loan rates impact your monthly payment based on a $25,000 loan.

Table 52-1	**Monthly Payments on a $25,000 Loan**		
Rate of Loan	*3-Year Loan*	*4-Year Loan*	*5-Year Loan*
0%	$694	$520	$416
3%	$723	$553	$449
5%	$749	$575	$471
5.5%	$754	$581	$477
6%	$760	$587	$483

Getting a House

Whether to buy or rent is a major financial decision. For a worksheet to compare the pros and cons of owning a home — as well as worksheets on mortgages and the like — see *Personal Finance Workbook For Dummies,* by Sheryl Garrett (Wiley).

Determine your tax savings

If you own a house and you itemize deductions on your tax return, you can deduct your property taxes and the interest from your mortgage payment. Look at this savings as money that can be put into your emergency fund or into savings for another large purchase.

For example, suppose you have a $250,000 30-year mortgage at a 6-percent interest rate and your property taxes are 1 percent of your home value. The total interest paid over the first year (assuming you bought on January 1) is $14,916, and your property taxes are $2,500. If you're in the 28-percent tax bracket, this would give you a $17,416 tax deduction and result in a tax savings of $4,876.

Decide what can you afford

You need to have both feet on the ground when you figure out what kind of monthly house payments you can afford.

Don't buy a house that's more than you can afford just because the initial monthly payments look affordable, and don't rely on a lender to tell you what an affordable monthly payment is.

Be sure you understand all the terms and conditions of the type of mortgage you're committing to, especially if the interest rate will be level for the length of the loan or if it'll vary and under what conditions. Loans that are interest-only for a limited period of time or that have a variable interest rate can create great financial problems during financially difficult times.

Note how long you'll stay in the house and whether you can afford this loan into retirement. If you plan to live in this house for a long time, look seriously at a fixed-rate mortgage payable over 15, 20, or 30 years. Table 52-2 gives you an idea of what your monthly payment could be on a 30-year fixed-rate mortgage.

Table 52-2	Payments on a 30-Year Fixed-Rate Mortgage	
Loan After the Down Payment	Interest Rate	Monthly Payment
$300,000	6.5%	$1,896
$300,000	6.0%	$1,799
$250,000	6.5%	$1,580
$250,000	6.0%	$1,499
$150,000	6.5%	$948
$150,000	6.0%	$899

Taking on higher monthly expenses than you should can quickly put you in debt and expose you to the risk of losing everything during bad times, so ask yourself these tough questions:

✔ How much down payment do you need to make? And do you have the cash to do so? If your credit is average or below average expect to need a down payment of 10 percent in most situations, unless you qualify for an FHA or VA loan. They require less of a down payment and are more lenient on credit scores. Before you go shopping for a home, obtain a pre-approval letter from your lender.

✔ What mortgage payment, property taxes, and insurance premiums fit into your current budget?

✔ Would you be able to make these payments if you were laid off, lost your job, or had an extended illness and couldn't work?

✔ Does the house need any repair or remodeling and if so, how soon? Will those costs be included in your mortgage?

✔ With these new expenses, can you still afford to contribute to your retirement accounts? Do you still have sufficient emergency cash reserves? Will you be able to put a reasonable monthly savings amount toward your children's college education?

For help with mortgage decisions, rates, and tutorials for home purchases and loan considerations, www.mgtprofessor.com is a wonderful source.

Doing Home Repairs and Remodeling

Your options for financing home repairs, updates, and additions can present a challenge. You may choose to borrow the money you need by using a fixed- or variable-rate home equity line of credit or a second mortgage. Or you may consider refinancing your current loan for a larger amount and take cash out. Or you may decide to use money you've set aside for taking advantage of opportunities that may come up. First consider the following:

- ✔ **A home equity line of credit** gives you ongoing access to money. But after you tap into a line of credit, the payments add up. Also, keep in mind these are interest-only loans. Ask your lender to confirm what payment you'd make and how long it would take you to pay it off. Don't kid yourself; $40,000 at 5-percent interest and a $166.66 payment per month sounds reasonable, right? But this payment means the loan is *never* going away during your lifetime. By adding another $100 for a $266.66 payment, you still have more than 19 years before you pay the loan in full. Know the payoff schedule before you commit!

- ✔ **Home equity loans** are also home loans, but with a fixed loan amount and a monthly payment plan. The amount of the loan is generally based on a percentage of the amount of equity you have in your home. If your home has appreciated in value, this loan can be a way to access that appreciation and use it to improve the value of your home even more. However, you should be fully aware of what's happening with the values of homes in your area, and whether they're currently moving up or down, as well as what's been happening over the last several years.

- ✔ **Refinancing your mortgage** for a larger amount and using the extra cash for home updates works for many consumers. Are you planning to stay in your house? Can you absorb the higher fixed costs? Look at this financing option with an eye toward the future. But note that when home prices are depreciating, many home owners won't qualify for refinancing due to tightened credit and income requirements. This option may not be viable during tough times.

Before refinancing, determine the new loan amount you owe and the repayment schedule. Could you buy a new house for less that has all the features you want to add? Fees to refinance are usually around 1 percent of the new loan amount. Is it worth it? Can your budget, livelihood, and future retirement handle the new payments? Don't make this decision lightly; it's very possible that you'll have a loan well past retirement on a significantly higher balance than you may have anticipated. Don't rush into this option without reviewing the financial merits ahead of time.

#53

Develop a Plan to Provide for Children

By Eileen Freiburger, CFP

Most of the considerable costs of raising children are blended in with your everyday living expenses, such as housing, food, clothing, transportation, healthcare, and childcare. However, you can plan for several large expenses. This strategy tells you how to make sure you're ready.

Having a Baby

Having a baby isn't always a planned event — surprises do happen! The cost of delivering a baby ranges from $7,500 to $10,000. Even with medical insurance, you'll pay deductibles, co-insurance percentages, and co-pays. (See Strategy #5 for information on medical insurance.) Plan ahead by doing the following:

- ✔ Contact your insurance company to find out the process for filing your claims and what you need to do when preparing to check into the hospital.

- ✔ Find out how long it takes for the hospital to file insurance claims.

- ✔ Ask your insurance company how long it takes to pay claims after they're filed. You need to know whether you'll be responsible for any payments before your insurance company has paid its portion of all expenses. Determine when you have to pay your portion of the expenses.

You can then figure out how much money you want to set aside ahead of time so that even if there are economic troubles at the time your baby is born, you'll be able to pay your bills.

If you aren't covered by medical insurance and don't have sufficient savings, you can work with the doctor's office and the hospital on a payment plan. You may also want to check out local or county health care clinics to see whether prenatal care is available. If you qualify, Medicaid may be available.

Having a baby may raise other financial questions, including the following

- ✔ When will Mom stop working?
- ✔ Will Mom and/or Dad stay home with the baby?
- ✔ Will Mom and/or Dad return to work? If so, when?
- ✔ Will anyone's career plans change?

Having an emergency fund large enough to cover three to six months' worth of living expenses can help to cover changes in jobs, time off, and loss of wages.

Setting Aside Pretax Dollars for Medical Expenses

According to a survey by the U.S. Department of Agriculture, the estimated cost of raising one child from birth through age 17 ranges from $125,000 to $250,000 (in 2001 dollars). Based on an inflation rate of 3.5 percent, this amount becomes $160,000 to $318,000 in 2008 dollars. Finding ways to reduce your expenses can help whether times are good or bad.

Take advantage of available *flex saving accounts* (FSA); these enable you to set aside pretax money from your paycheck for medical, dental, vision, and dependent care expenses, all of which add up very quickly. For example, an average family may have to pay for the following:

Category	*Cost*
15–20 doctor visits/year at a co-pay of $30	$450 to $600
Two sets of glasses	$300 to $800
Four dentist visits, out of pocket	$200 to $500
10–20 chiropractor visits at $75 each	$750 to $1,500
Annual medical prescription co-pays	$1,000 to $2,000
Total	$2,700 to $5,400

This family may potentially spend $2,700 to $5,400 annually.

You don't pay income taxes on money distributed from your FSA. For this example, if the contribution limit is $3,000 and your income tax rate is 33 percent, you'd save $990 per year by using an FSA. That savings can be money that you add to your contributions to your employer's retirement plan or an IRA. In tough economic times, you can use those savings to help cover other expenses.

If your employer offers an FSA, save your medical, dental, vision, and dependent care receipts to file for reimbursement. Compare your potential expenses to the limit you can put into an FSA, and make sure you use the entire amount you've withheld; you lose any amount you don't claim.

Saving for College

As you save for your kids' college, start as soon as possible with regular contributions. How much to save may be your first question. A calculator on www.savingforcollege.com came up with the estimates in Table 53-1. The example is based on an annual cost of $20,000 ($80,000 total for four years in today's dollars) with school costs increasing by 6 percent and a portfolio with an after-tax return of 7 percent. In these estimates, parents will pay 100 percent of expenses.

Table 53-1 Sample Estimates of How Much to Save for College

	Age 1	Age 5	Age 10
Future cost of school	$235,597	$186,615	$139,449
Years until the child starts	17	13	8
Monthly amount of savings	$498	$584	$776

Many parents are comfortable funding part of their children's college education and letting the kids pay for part of it. Two common ways to save for college today are the 529 college savings plan and the education savings account.

Students are expected to contribute a larger percent of their assets than their parents are, so some people recommend that you save in your name instead of your child's. You can save in normal, taxable accounts.

529 college savings plans

Every state offers a 529 college savings plan. These plans vary widely. For example, the total contribution varies from just over $200,000 to more than $300,000. States use different investment companies to administer their plans, and investment choices vary widely. You can use any state's plan, but most offer a state income tax deduction on contributions only for residents. Obtain a description of each state's plan that you're considering (www.savingforcollege.com enables easy comparison of several plans at a time). Be very careful to evaluate the expenses of each plan you consider — both plan and mutual fund expenses. When you withdraw money to pay for qualified college expenses, it's tax-free.

Education savings accounts

In a *Coverdell education savings account* (ESA), families may currently deposit $2,000 per year for each child under age 18. Contributions are not tax-deductible, but earnings accumulate tax-free, and no taxes are due on withdrawal for qualified expenses for tuition, fees, books, equipment, and room and board. The ESA is phased out for individuals and families with adjusted gross incomes between preset limits. Investing an ESA should be the same as you'd do within a 529 college savings plan in which you choose the mix of mutual funds. However, with an ESA, you have total control over the mutual funds you select because you choose the investment firm where you set up the account. You can set up an ESA with any discount broker, mutual fund company, and the like.

Loans

If you have to limit what you can save for college, one way to pay for college is with student loans. To qualify for loans, you submit a Free Application for Federal Student Aid (FAFSA) application. You should do this as soon as possible in January during your child's senior year. You can find more information at the following Web sites: `www.fafsa.ed.gov`, `www.myrichuncle.com`, and `www.finaid.org`.

Education tax credits

If you're already paying for education costs, you'll likely be able to claim a credit on your income tax return. The two education tax credit programs are the HOPE Scholarship and the Lifetime Learning credit.

The $1,800 HOPE Scholarship credit equals 100 percent of the first $1,200 of tuition and fees and 50 percent of the second $1,200 (the amounts will be indexed for inflation).

The Lifetime Learning credit is another option. Whether your student attends an eligible institution full time or part time, the credit is 20 percent of the first $10,000 (up to $2,000 per return) for eligible students in your family. The credit is reduced if your modified adjusted gross income is between certain income limits.

The Hope and Lifetime Learning Credits can't be used for the same student.

#54

Save for Retirement Regardless of the Shape of the Economy

By Christine Falvello, MS, CFP

*W*hat could be more gratifying than faithfully making your retirement contributions month after month and year after year while the value of your plan increases? Each good day in the market brings you closer to your retirement dreams. Making those contributions is easy when you're watching your account grow.

But what about when the economy's not so strong? In an uncertain economy, the financial markets can appear to be going nowhere, and your retirement plan seems to be sleeping. You keep pumping in your money and your plan repays you with a value that stays the same. Or even more nerve-wracking, you watch the value sink. You ask yourself, "Why should I keep giving my hard-earned money to this ungrateful retirement plan that doesn't reward me by growing?" This strategy explains why.

Buy Low: A Sale's the Best Time to Shop

Imagine that instead of an uncertain economy, the reverse is true. The economy is humming along as you continue to save; with few bad days in the market, your account grows nicely. How gratifying! The markets may even be doing so well that your family, friends, and colleagues talk about how they're investing and freely share that advice with you.

Now look at how investors behave in an uncertain economy. You know uncertain markets can be volatile and decrease in value, sometimes a lot. Those same people talk about ending retirement savings. Some may even change their investments to cash, figuring they'll wait for the market to bottom out and then jump back in. They assume they'll know the right time to start investing again. You may have even thought about doing this yourself.

This isn't a smart move. Here's why:

> ✔ Even the experts don't know when the market will hit a real bottom and start to move back up. If the experts don't know, how will you?
>
> ✔ On certain days throughout the history of the stock market, the market rallied quickly and dramatically. Those who were in cash and missed a key day had portfolio returns lowered, sometimes significantly. Out of the market, they got back in, often at higher prices.

Those who simply stopped making retirement plan contributions missed a great sale. And it's the right of all Americans, after all, to buy things on sale.

By continuing to save when the market is down, you purchase more shares for your money. When things improve, the additional shares you bought on sale increase the value of your account even more.

Take Five Steps to Retirement Accumulation

Here are five simple steps you can follow in any market to make your retirement dream a reality:

1. Save and invest regularly.

If you can, set up automatic payroll deductions for retirement contributions. If you don't have a retirement plan where you work, open an IRA (or a Roth IRA, if you qualify). Use a discount brokerage firm to save fees, and set up a monthly fund transfer from checking into your new account.

If you're self-employed, you have several retirement plan options, and some are fairly simple to open. They're often available through discount brokerage firms. Just be wary of bank and insurance plans that have high fees.

2. Start saving early.

The earlier you save, the more you'll enjoy the power of compounding. For example, a 30-year-old who invests $200 a month for four years at an 8-percent return will have $62,000 at age 55. A 40-year-old who saves $800 a month at the same return for four years will have $57,000 at age 55. The 40-year-old saved twice as much and had less money at 55. Remember, starting sooner means saving smarter.

3. Maximize contributions to qualified retirement accounts.

Always max out your retirement plan contributions. It'll give you more flexibility about when you can retire, and your retirement income will be higher. If you can save more than the maximum allowed, open an IRA, preferably a Roth IRA. If you can still save more after maxing out your IRA contributions, save in a taxable individual brokerage account.

Don't forget about the tax advantage to retirement plan contributions. Your federally taxable income for the year is reduced by the amount you contribute to your plan, so you'll pay less income tax. Think of it as having Uncle Sam subsidize part of your retirement savings plan!

4. Make sure your portfolio is diversified.

The old saying about not putting all your eggs in one basket is true in investing. Own a mix of different assets. Make sure you own a mix of stocks, bonds, and to a lesser extent, cash. Your stocks should include growth and value, as well as shares of large, medium, and small companies. For bonds, think about using a laddered bond strategy — short-, intermediate-, and long-term. Also, if your plan offers a stable value fund with a guaranteed interest rate, consider including it as an investment choice. A stable value fund will perform like a bond in your portfolio, stabilizing part of its value.

5. Choose good investments.

Make sure your investments are financially sound and perform well compared to other investments of the same type. If returns are compared to an index, look for funds that perform at least as well as that index.

If your retirement plan offers company stock or a company stock fund, limit it to 5 percent of your overall retirement plan. If your company does poorly, you risk not only your job but also the value of your retirement plan.

Seek More Information

To determine how much you'll need to save and get lots of other great information on retirement planning, visit the Retirement Savings Education Campaign Web site, www.dol.gov/EBSA/savingmatters.html, which is sponsored by the U.S. Department of Labor. The information ranges from tips for new workforce entrants to advice for workers within ten years of retirement. Links on the site direct you to advice on investing and diversification, employer retirement plans, and small business retirement plans.

If you don't have online access, use a library computer — ask a reference librarian to get you started. Or contact the Retirement Savings Education Campaign: U.S. Department of Labor, Employee Benefits Security Administration, 200 Constitution Ave., NW, Suite N-5623, Washington, D.C. 20210; phone 202-693-8664.

Determine How Much Money Is Enough for the Rest of Your Life

By Garry Good, MBA

*T*hink of your retirement as the most expensive purchase decision you'll ever make. Even more daunting: You have only one chance to get it right. A wrong decision has implications for the rest of your life. Before pulling the plug on a career and current income stream, develop a clear image of what you're buying and how much it's going to cost.

So what's a good retirement worth these days? How much do you need for the rest of your life? To solve this dilemma, the following formula should be useful:

> "Rest of life" cost = (annual expenses – retirement income) ×
> (life expectancy – retirement age)

In this formula, retirement income includes Social Security and/or pensions, and annual expenses should be adjusted for inflation.

The following sections look at these variables and discuss strategies you can use to take advantage of the variables you do control and manage the risk created by factors beyond it. ***Note:*** This simplified equation merely identifies the key factors involved and illustrates the basic concept of retirement planning; you need more actual number crunching to figure out that magic retirement number.

Create a Fact-Based Retirement Budget

How can you really predict your expenses over the remainder of your lifetime? Believe it or not, this is one area where you have considerable control. The following process can enable you to allocate enough funds to withstand the ups and downs of your retirement years:

1. **Establish a current budget based on actual expense data.**

   Five or six months' worth of data should be sufficient, but be sure the period you choose is representative of your average spending patterns.

2. **Develop a reliable post-retirement budget.**

   Don't factor in inflation. While focusing on the future, simply conduct a line-by-line review of your expenses:

   - Look for expenses that'll be reduced or eliminated at retirement (work clothes, commuting expenses, professional dues, and so on).

   - Identify spending categories that are likely to increase, such as healthcare.

   - Add a budget line for unforeseen expenses. You don't know exactly what or when, but count on the fact that unforeseen expenses will occur — auto repairs, appliance repairs or replacement, general home maintenance, and so on.

   - Envision your retirement on a day-to-day basis. What have you been looking forward to? How do you see yourself spending all that free time? Chances are this time won't really be free.

When you make budget cuts during the planning process, you leave no room to compensate later for events that are beyond your control. People tend to adopt optimistic assumptions to trick their plans into telling them what they want to believe. For example, to make an earlier retirement look viable, you may rationalize that you can easily get by with less. Making a deliberate choice to reduce your lifestyle can be a legitimate component of retirement planning — but only if you'll remain committed. Ideally, your budget should include expenses that you can trim to stay on track even in the face of change.

Imagine that you're retired and the economy isn't cooperating with your well-crafted plan. Inflation is heating up. The stock market (and your portfolio) is taking a dive. These events are all beyond your control. The good news? With appropriate planning, you can mitigate the damages. This is the time to beat your budget. You can tighten your belt by choosing to eliminate or delay selected activities — as long as these expenses were in your original plan.

Limit Your Reliance on the Unknown

After you estimate your retirement expenses, you can deduct any retirement income that you'll receive from Social Security and employer-paid pensions to determine your actual (net) cash flow needs. The balance will have to come from your personal retirement savings.

Social Security and pensions provide a valuable hedge against longevity because they promise an income stream that'll last as long as you do. Unfortunately, you have little control over these fixed income sources. But although the future solvency of Social Security is out of your hands, you do have a say in how much you rely on this "guaranteed" source of income.

Every year, you're provided a current estimate of your future monthly Social Security benefit. Most experts agree that this estimate is fairly reliable for those who are nearing retirement. But what if your retirement is years away? You can reasonably assume that the younger you are (and further from retirement), the greater the risk that your eventual payment will be reduced.

A proactive decision to adjust your Social Security expectations downward, based on age, can limit the downside risk to your planning assumptions. The following chart provides an example you may want to adopt:

Age	Expected Benefit
65	100%
60	88%
55	75%
50	62%
45	50%
40	38%
35	25%
30	12%
25	0%

Although time (years to retirement) may reduce your confidence in future benefits, time (and the principle of compounding) is also your biggest ally in accumulating money to supplement Social Security and any pension income you may have in retirement.

Estimate Your Life Expectancy — Then Plan to Live Longer

Fortunately, most people aren't born with an expiration date tattooed on their bottoms. Count your blessings. This is one uncertainty you should embrace! At the same time, the risk of longevity is one of the greatest challenges you face in retirement planning.

Plan to live longer than you expect to live. Consider this: The average person has a 50 percent chance of exceeding life expectancy. In other words, planning for your expected life results in a fifty-fifty chance of running out of money too soon.

What type of longevity should you plan for? This depends largely on how much risk you're willing to assume. The current life expectancy for a 65-year-old American is about 83 years. You can see this individual's likelihood of surpassing additional milestones in the following chart from the National Center for Health Statistics:

Age Reached	Likelihood (Percent)
Age 83	50%
Age 85	44%
Age 90	25%
Age 95	10%
Age 100	3%

Making financial provisions for your life expectancy plus 17 years doesn't even guarantee success! On the other hand, you may be reluctant to fund this contingency, fearing your financial sacrifice could be wasted if you live a normal life or happen to die prematurely. Think of longevity planning as buying insurance with an interesting twist: Insurance compensates you for a loss, but longevity planning pays off when you win!

Make the Final Call: When to Retire

Whereas life expectancy is the great unknown, the timing of your retirement (health permitting) is a decision that belongs to you. This call has the potential to stabilize your plan or jeopardize your financial life. Make an active decision considering all options and implications. Don't retire simply by default.

When contemplating retirement, ask yourself the following questions:

✔ Are you really prepared financially for a secure retirement?

✔ Would you still want to retire if you were very happy with your job? Your boss? Your employer? Your career?

Sometimes a retirement goal is merely an escape from a bad situation. If you still enjoy working (though not necessarily at your current job), you should consider a job or career change instead — or simply focus on doing your current job better. To expand your options and retire on your terms, invest in yourself through continuous education, network to tune in to new opportunities, and embrace change throughout your working life.

Strategies for Beginning Investors

By Robert Oliver, CFA, CFP

*I*f you're just getting started investing, you may wonder whether you should put any of your hard-earned money at risk during a period of economic uncertainty. You're not alone. Even the most experienced investors become uneasy when the economy stumbles and their portfolios hiccup.

However, some fundamental truths of investing will serve you well no matter the state of the economy. So don't be daunted by the thought of getting started in a period of economic uncertainty. Some of the best buying opportunities come during economic turmoil.

Pay No Attention to Timing Predictions

Before investing, the first and perhaps most important concept to understand is that no one can consistently or regularly predict peaks and troughs of economic or market trends. Yet many investment managers and information services claim they can, and they ramp up their marketing during periods of bearish economies. Keep in mind that if someone could regularly time markets or economic cycles, there'd be no need to sell the knowledge.

Focus on low-cost, buy-and-hold investment strategies and disregard market timing services that claim to predict market trends.

Instead of trying to decide the best time to move your money in and out of the market, spend your time and energy researching and understanding the cost of investments.

Consider Costs and Index Funds

For any investment you own or consider owning, you should understand two key elements of cost:

- ✔ **Transaction costs:** How much it costs to buy and sell an investment; brokerage and sales commissions fall into this category
- ✔ **Holding costs:** How much you're charged annually for holding the investment; mutual fund expense ratios are the most common example

For most people, mutual funds and exchange-traded funds (ETFs) are the best way to invest in securities. You can find fund expense data and other fund details on the Internet at morningstar.com or finance.yahoo.com.

One way to easily reduce the cost of your investments is by using passively managed funds, also known as *index funds*. Instead of trying to beat the return of a specific benchmark, such as the S&P 500, an index fund's goal is to mirror the return of its benchmark. An index fund can charge a low expense ratio because its managers don't spend time and money trying to determine the best companies within its benchmark. Actively managed funds, which do try to beat their respective benchmarks, pass along the cost of research to you — the investor — in the form of higher expense ratios.

You may wonder whether you'd be better off paying more for an actively managed fund that more than makes up for the higher fee with a higher return. If your name is Nostradamus, this may be a good plan. You could look into the future and see which funds are going to have superior returns and invest in them. In the real world, the only information you have is the past performance of funds, and research has shown that past performance is a poor predictor of future return. In other words, you have no way to know which actively managed funds will be worth the additional price of admission. The only thing you do know with a great deal of certainty is that you'll pay more to invest in an actively managed fund than you would an index fund.

Keep most of your mutual fund expense ratios below 1 percent, and use no-load index funds whenever possible to keep costs low. Low expenses are especially important or when markets are struggling.

Determine Your Asset Allocation

The cost of your investments is important, but research shows that over 90 percent of your portfolio's return will be determined by *asset allocation* — the process of determining how much you invest in each type of investment or asset class, such as stocks, bonds, and cash. To determine which asset classes are appropriate for you, consider the following:

✔ **Your risk tolerance:** Quantify the loss you can sustain in your portfolio's value before you change investments. Because most investors don't have a good sense of their tolerance for loss until they actually experience it, uncertain and volatile markets generally provide a clearer picture of risk tolerance than consistently increasing markets. Ask yourself what you would do if your portfolio lost 10 percent, 20 percent, or 30 percent, and choose your asset allocation accordingly.

✔ **Your goals and time horizon:** Why are you investing? When do you need your money? You may be building a nest egg for retirement or saving for your next vacation. The time between today and when you need your investment is your *time horizon.* If you're just starting your career and retirement nest egg, decades will pass before you'll need the money. Therefore, you can stand to wade through periods of volatility and take on more risk. However, if you're saving for a vacation six months from now, you may not want to put your vacation in jeopardy by investing your vacation savings in risky stocks. Generally, you should invest less of your portfolio in stocks as your time horizon shortens.

Allocate assets for short-term goals

If you want to invest some money that you plan to use in ten years or less, be careful how much you invest in volatile asset classes like stocks. If you plan to use the money in one year or less, such as for next summer's vacation, avoid investing in stocks altogether.

Use cash-like investment vehicles — such as savings accounts, money market accounts and funds, and certificates of deposit (CDs) — for money you'll need to use within a year. For more on cash vehicles, see Strategy #17.

As your time horizon lengthens, you can begin to invest a portion of your portfolio in stocks. In *The Intelligent Asset Allocator* (McGraw-Hill), financial theorist William Bernstein recommends investing no more than ten times the number of years you'll be invested in stocks. For example, if you'll need the money in three years, you should invest no more than 30 percent of your portfolio in stocks with the remainder invested in bonds and cash. This is a good rule of thumb, but you probably shouldn't invest more than 80 percent of your portfolio in stocks even if you won't need the money for ten years.

Avoid using tax-deferred accounts such as an IRA or 401(k) for short-term goals if you plan to use the money before you can take penalty-free withdrawals.

Allocate assets for long-term goals

Although many people want to be saving for short-term goals such as a trip to the Bahamas, the reality is that whatever savings you can afford should go toward retirement savings, especially in periods of economic uncertainty. For most beginning investors, retirement is at least ten years away.

With those factors in mind, Table 56-1 provides sample portfolios for retirement savings for investors with moderate risk tolerance.

Table 56-1	Sample Portfolios for Moderate-Risk Investors		
Years to Long-Term Goal	*10 Years*	*25 Years*	*40 Years*
U.S. stocks	**35%**	**35%**	**40%**
Large cap	30%	27%	30%
Small cap	5%	8%	10%
International stocks	**10%**	**15%**	**20%**
Developed markets	7%	10%	15%
Emerging markets	3%	5%	5%
Real estate (via a REIT)	**5%**	**10%**	**10%**
Bonds	**50%**	**40%**	**30%**
Investment-grade	30%	20%	15%
Inflation-protected	15%	10%	5%
High-yield	5%	10%	10%

Investors with a higher tolerance for risk may increase their overall exposure to stocks and riskier asset classes, such as high-yield bonds and real estate, but more-conservative investors would reduce their exposure to them.

Generally, you should invest in tax-deferred accounts for long-term savings. If you have limited dollars to invest, find out whether your employer-sponsored plan, such as a 401(k) or 403(b), provides a match on the dollars that you invest. If so, contribute at least enough to maximize the match.

After you determine your target portfolio and invest accordingly, rebalance your portfolio back to its target percentages annually. This discipline forces you to stay invested during the year and then to sell the asset classes that have done well (sell high) and buy those that have underperformed (buy low) at year-end. It also helps you remove emotions from your investment decisions. For ideas on asset allocation and rebalancing, see Strategies #40 and #41.

Investments for Beginning Investors

By William Keffer, ChFC, CFP

*I*nvesting when you're just getting started can be intimidating, especially in an uncertain economy. You face a tough balancing act. You can't ignore important long-term goals such as retirement or college. Maybe you're trying to bulk up reserves while paying off a credit card, too. But relax — you can build an investment plan that gets you up and running with confidence.

Getting Started

To begin building an investment plan, you need the following:

- ✔ A budget with dollars earmarked to invest
- ✔ Specific goals, with costs, due dates, and savings requirements for each (see Strategy #13 for help with this)

Your projected timeline helps determine how much risk you can take so you can choose the right investments. A goal chart, such as the one in Table 57-1, helps you focus on the key element of the time horizon for each objective.

Table 57-1	Sample Goal Chart		
Goal	*How Much*	*Monthly Allocation*	*Goal Date*
House down payment	$40,000	$450	4 years
Retirement savings	$2,750,000	$1,000	35 years
College for child	$120,000	$340	16 years

Matching Investment Types to Your Time Table

With the investment industry so anxious to sell stuff, people have come up with a dazzling number of products — so many that it's sometimes hard for even the experts to sort through all the options. So what'll it be? Hedge funds? Commodity futures? The mattress?

For most purposes, investments can be broken down into three categories:

- ✔ **Stocks:** Stocks are shares of ownership in a company that entitle you to part of the profits, and they produce the biggest returns. But they also carry the most risk. They go up and down in value more frequently. The swings, called *volatility,* are greater than in bonds and cash, too.

- ✔ **Bonds:** Bonds represent a debt that a company or government owes you, the investor. They give you more modest returns but a smoother ride than stocks. The company or government that issues the bonds agrees to pay interest and to return the principal.

- ✔ **Cash:** In investment terms, cash is a short-term store of value that's accessible, safe, and can pay interest. Cash doesn't change in value very much. The amount of risk to your principal is little or none, but the downside is that cash gives low returns. (Refer to Strategy #17 for details on the types of cash accounts available.)

Risk is the amount of volatility in returns over a given period — in other words, how drastically the value of your investment goes up and down. High risk generally leads to a higher return, but lower risk ensures the funds you need in the short term don't disappear just when you need them. So for your emergency fund (see Strategy #9), a low-risk fund such as cash is the best bet. For a retirement that may be 30 or more years off but will require a substantial pile of money, more stocks are a good choice. Bonds are a great fit for a goal coming due in an intermediate period of time.

Risk is a normal and even healthy part of the market cycle, and avoiding all risk isn't an option. Investments that are too conservative may mean you're just trading the risk of gut-wrenching market gyrations for the equally scary prospect of having to move in with your adult children. For long-term goals, get comfortable with investment risk and stay the course (but review your portfolio annually to make sure you're still on track).

In any economy, you should tie your investment decisions to when the money must be available. Check out Table 57-2, which matches time tables with acceptable levels of risk.

Table 57-2 Investments for Short-Term and Long-Term Goals

	Short-Term Goals	Intermediate-Term Goals	Long-Term Goals
Years until	0–3 years	4–10 years	11+ years
Acceptable risk	Low	Low to moderate	Higher
Type of assets	Mostly or all cash	Cash and bonds	Stocks and bonds
Investments you may pick	Savings account Money market fund CDs Short-term bond fund	CDs Short-term bond fund Intermediate-term bond fund Conservative allocation fund	Mostly stock and bond funds Growth and income funds Target date funds Target allocation funds
Accounts you may use	Bank or credit union Investment account	Bank or credit union Investment account 529 college savings plan	Retirement (401(k), Roth IRA) 529 college savings plan Investment account

Here's a guideline for the maximum percentage of a portfolio that should be invested in stocks, based on when the funds will be needed:

Time Horizon	Maximum Invested in Stocks (Percent)
0–3 years	0%
4–5 years	20%
6 years	30%
7 years	40%
8 years	50%
9 years	60%
10 years	70%
11–15 years	80%
15+ years	90%

Building a Foundational Portfolio

No one can reliably predict the markets. But because investment requires being *in* the markets, it's important to control what you can so you limit potential losses. The things within your control include the following:

- ✔ **Allocation:** Allocation is the portion of your treasure in each of the big three: stocks, bonds, and cash.

- ✔ **Diversification:** Diversification means owning enough different investment positions in each asset category.

- ✔ **Costs:** High investment expenses can eat away at your hard-earned dough.

As a beginning investor, you need just a few — or maybe even just one — investment vehicles to hit all your asset classes and to be diversified. And you don't want to pay big expenses and commissions. *Mutual funds* — investment companies that sell shares to the public, pool their money, and buy a large number of various stocks or bonds — are the best choice for beginning investors because they offer automatic diversification.

Mutual funds can be either actively or passively managed. *Actively managed funds* have managers who try to beat the market by stock picking and market timing. *Index funds* own shares of an entire sector, hoping to passively match the market. Fans of indexing believe that markets move randomly, so active managers can't accurately and consistently predict the direction or timing of markets. And because active management has higher costs, index funds may have a leg up. (For more on mutual funds, see Strategy #21.)

Following are a couple of ideas for foundational portfolios:

- ✔ **One-stop shopping:** A number of fund companies now offer life cycle, target date, or asset allocation funds that include large and small U.S. stocks, international stocks, bonds, and cash in one bucket. Some are geared for a particular objective, such as retirement or college, ratcheting back the riskier assets as the goal approaches. Others cater to specific asset mixes, from conservative to aggressive. These plug-and-play funds are good options if your funds are limited or if you just like the convenience. Look for one using index funds.

- ✔ **Simple index fund portfolio:** For beginning investors who want more leeway on allocations, try the following:
  - Total U.S. stock market index
  - Total U.S. bond market index
  - Total international (non-U.S.) stock market index

  Plunking 40 percent each into the U.S. stock and bond funds and 20 percent into the international fund can provide a moderate investor with broad diversification and a great start toward building long-term wealth. See Part III for strategies on getting the asset mix that's right for you.

Strategies for Intermediate Investors

By James Taylor, CFP and Buz Livingston, CFP

*M*aybe you just got the invitation to your 30-year high school reunion. Or perhaps the gray is showing around your temples. Whether you like it or not, you're getting older, and just as you (hopefully) mature, your investment strategy should, too.

Parts I and II of this book address building a secure foundation and employing different investment tactics, and Strategy #57 demonstrates the use of three basic portfolio building blocks: mutual funds covering international stocks, U.S. large companies, and bonds. Now, this strategy addresses additional investments to help further diversify and maximize your returns.

You don't have to be eligible for AARP membership to be an intermediate investor, but here are some asset classes you need to include as your portfolio grows:

- ✔ U.S. small company stock mutual funds
- ✔ Emerging market stock mutual funds
- ✔ International small company stock mutual funds
- ✔ Real estate investment trusts (REITs)
- ✔ High-yield bond funds
- ✔ Treasury inflation-protected securities (TIPS)
- ✔ International bond mutual funds

This strategy also discusses a couple of other options — micro-cap stocks and commodities — and gives you some general investment tips.

Own It: Equity Asset Classes

Equity asset classes are groups of stocks that have similar characteristics and perform the same in the marketplace. Here are the next four asset classes to add to your portfolio:

- ✔ **U.S. small company stocks:** U.S. small caps make up the first asset class you should add to your mix. Over the last 80 years, the U.S. Small Cap Index has outperformed the S&P 500, earning 12.2 percent annually versus the S&P's 10.4 percent. The tradeoff is volatility because the prices of small companies can swing dramatically in comparison to their larger counterparts.

- ✔ **Emerging markets:** These assets may make sense for a small portion of your portfolio, but their volatility is even more dramatic than small company U.S. stocks. For instance, the MSCI Emerging Market Index was up over 66 percent in 1999 and down over 30 percent the very next year.

- ✔ **International small company stocks:** Like their stateside cousins, international small cap stocks are more unpredictable than stocks of larger companies.

- ✔ **Real estate investment trusts (REITs):** From 2004 to 2006, REITs garnered returns of 31, 12, and 35 percent, as measured by the NAREIT (National Association of Real Estate Investment Trusts) Index. With the downturn in real estate in 2007, the index lost over 15 percent.

Emerging market stocks, international small company stocks, and REITs all can add a little punch to your portfolio, but they're also extremely volatile. Never let them reach a double-digit allocation in your portfolio. Experts recommend a higher allocation to large company stocks versus small company stocks.

Why include these additional investments? The answer is simple: diversification. In 2001, the S&P 500 was down almost 12 percent while the NAREIT Index was up almost 14 percent. The next year, the S&P was up 28.66 percent and the Russell 2000 (which measures small cap U.S. stocks) was up 47.25 percent.

Successful investors don't chase the highest performing asset class from one year to the next. Instead, they use investments that perform differently under the same economic conditions. In doing so, they diversify their portfolio and lower their risk.

Lend It: Bond Asset Classes

As with stocks, investors benefit by including different types of bonds or fixed income in their portfolio. Dissimilar asset classes of bonds perform in distinct ways:

- ✔ **High-yield bonds (junk bonds):** These pay higher yields and sometimes pay capital gains.

- ✔ **Treasury inflation-protected securities (TIPS):** TIPS provide stability during periods of high inflation.

- ✔ **International bond funds:** These funds allow an investor to profit from changes in the value of the dollar and fluctuations in overseas interest rates.

The best way to add these asset classes is through low-cost index funds or exchange-traded funds (ETFs — see Strategy #23). Unfortunately, none exist for high-yield bonds. Instead, consider Vanguard's High-Yield Bond Fund. For international bond exposure, consider State Street's recently released SPYR International Treasury Bond ETF (BSX).

Risk It: Other Asset Classes for the Intermediate Investor

Intermediate investors with high risk tolerance may want to consider two additional asset classes: micro-cap stocks and commodities. *Micro-cap stocks* are the smallest stocks trading in the U.S. stock market. They provide diversification but are also extremely volatile. Only the most aggressive and sophisticated investor should own this asset class. Bridgeway Funds has an index fund that tracks micro-cap stocks (BRSIX), and iShares has an ETF that tracks the Russell Micro-cap Index.

You may face uncertain times, but one thing is certain: Commodities frequently perform very well in periods of uncertainty. PIMCO and Oppenheimer have long-established mutual funds that track specific indexes. Investors also can use an ETF from iShares that tracks the GSCI Commodity Trust. This index and the two mutual funds invest in a basket of diverse commodities such as oil, agricultural products, and precious metals. Avoid investing in only one type of commodity.

Micro-cap stocks and commodities are among the most volatile of asset classes. Make sure your risk tolerance is suitable for either of them.

Follow It: Advice for Intermediate Investors

Investment decisions aren't easy for intermediate investors. You have plenty of opportunities but also a fair amount of risk. These tips may help:

- **Don't limit your investments to your company's retirement plan.** Most people begin investing via their employer's 401(k) plan. If that's all you have, it's not sufficient. Intermediate stage investors should have investments in taxable accounts (see Strategy #32) to take advantage of long-term capital gains rates and in Roth IRAs (Strategy #33) because qualified distributions aren't taxed.

- **Use 529 college savings plans for children or grandchildren.** Distributions for "qualified higher education expenses" are completely tax-free. Plus, 529 plans aren't controlled by the student, so you don't have to worry about the money going for pizza and beer. Students submit receipts for reimbursement to verify expenses, so you can use a 529 plan to teach young adults money management skills. In uncertain economic times, that talent can't be overemphasized. (See Strategy #53 for more on college saving.)

  Some states allow college tuition to be purchased at today's dollars using pre-paid tuition programs. This can help you hedge against rising college costs.

- **Make sure your insurance is appropriate.** You've worked hard to build a nest-egg — don't lose it! Not everyone needs or can afford long-term care insurance. However, everyone needs to plan for the possibility of long-term care (Strategy #7 can give you details). Your life, disability, and liability coverage should be suitable.

- **Avoid mutual funds and ETFs that are country-specific (such as Brazil or China) or sector-specific (such as healthcare or technology).** Diversifying reduces risk, so don't concentrate your investments. Make sure you have adequate cash reserves for emergencies.

Investments for Intermediate-Stage Investors

By Thomas Arconti, CFP

*Y*ou've now been investing for a while. You have your asset allocation in place and have already rebalanced your portfolio a few times. You know the ups and downs of the stock market and even feel comfortable with the swings in the value of your portfolio. Now, like that basic food recipe you've cooked countless times, you're ready to kick it up a notch.

Supplement Your Core Portfolio: The Satellite Approach

As you look to add additional investments to your portfolio, the first thing to remember is not to dismantle your well-balanced, diversified portfolio. Instead, consider this your core portfolio — the one to hold for the long term and that will continue to stand the test of time. Supplement your core portfolio with one or more satellite portfolios, made up of more narrowly focused holdings that you believe will enhance your overall risk/return profile.

The satellite portfolios can be constructed with mutual funds or exchange-traded funds (ETFs). Some examples of satellite funds include the following:

- Commodity funds
- Emerging market bond funds
- Foreign currency funds
- High-yield bond funds
- Long/short funds
- Mega or micro cap funds
- Preferred stocks
- Real estate investment trusts (REITs) of varying kinds
- Sector funds

Uncertain economic times create anxiety about overall market performance, but they also provide opportunities. The challenge is to assess what's happening now, predict what's likely to happen, and select an investment that may profit from the upcoming changes — no easy task and not something to make large bets on. Use only a small percentage of your investable funds in your satellites; this percentage should be an amount that you can comfortably risk.

Invest in the next hot sector

Sector funds are mutual funds or ETFs that invest only in companies belonging to the same industry. You can choose from hundreds of sectors; some can be narrowly focused on a subsector of a particular industry (for example, Fidelity Select Medical Equipment [FSMEX] is a subsector of healthcare, investing mainly in companies involved in the development, manufacture, and sale of medical equipment and devices).

Here's a small sampling of some of the sectors you can invest in:

- Biotechnology
- Consumer discretionary
- Consumer staples
- Defense and aerospace
- Financials
- Gaming
- Healthcare
- Information technology
- Nanotechnology
- Oil and gas exploration
- Real estate
- Solar energy
- Transportation
- Utilities
- Water resources

When investing in sector funds, keep the following in mind:

- If the sector is already hot, it's probably too late.
- Know the sector weighting in your core portfolio; choose something that may be missing or underrepresented in your core. (Refer to Strategies #48 through #50 for more on sector weighting.)
- Be aware of the typically higher management fees and any short-term redemption fees.
- Be prepared to pay closer attention to the sector funds on an ongoing basis; you need to know when to get out.

Not sure you can predict which sectors may come into favor? Consider a *sector rotation fund* and leave it to professional money managers. They may not choose any better than you would, but at least you're transferring the research to others. Of course, you'll pay higher fund management fees. Some examples of sector rotation funds are Claymore/Zacks Sector Rotation ETF (XRO) and Rydex Sector Rotation (RYISX).

Invest in long/short funds

In an uncertain economy, stocks go up and down. Sophisticated investors have long employed strategies to take advantage of both movements, through short selling, options, and hedge funds (see Strategies #27 through #30 for more info). As an intermediate investor, you can tiptoe into this arena with long/short mutual funds or ETFs (sometimes also referred to as *market neutral* or *130/30* funds). Basically, the fund manager buys some stocks she anticipates will go up (long positions) and sells (actually borrows and sells) other stocks she anticipates will go down (short positions). Long/short funds may be a good diversifier in a down economy.

When investing in long/short funds, keep the following in mind:

- ✔ Minimum purchase requirements may be high.

- ✔ Returns may be mediocre at best when the overall market is good.

- ✔ Be aware of the typically higher management fees and any short-term redemption fees.

- ✔ These funds will have higher turnovers and subsequently higher tax consequences.

- ✔ These funds are relatively new and don't have long track records.

Some examples of long/short funds include Hussman Strategic Growth (HSGFX), Fidelity 130/30 Large Cap (FOTTX), and Powershare S&P 500 Buy/ Write (PBP).

Bet on the value of currencies

As the overall U.S. economy rises and declines, the value of the U.S. dollar rises and declines in relation to other currencies. You can purchase mutual funds or ETFs that track a single currency, such as the Swiss franc, or that track several currencies. If you think the U.S. dollar is weakening relative to the euro, you could profit by purchasing an ETF like the CurrencyShares Euro Trust (FXE) or a mutual fund like the Merck Hard Currency Fund (MERKX), which invests in multiple currencies. If you think the strength of the U.S. dollar is on the rise, you could consider the Powershares DB U.S. Dollar Bullish (UUP).

When investing in currency funds, keep these points in mind:

✔ You need to be concerned with economies and market factors in two or more countries (the U.S. and all the foreign currency countries involved).

✔ You may be introducing new types of risk into your portfolio. Examples include political issues, trade deficits, interest rates, and national debts — both at home and abroad.

✔ Current events may drastically affect currency rates in a matter of days.

Currency funds are usually a zero sum game, meaning one side wins at the expense of the other. Accurately predicting whether the value of the U.S. dollar will rise or fall, and investing accordingly, is important.

Add an income-producing satellite

Perhaps you're content with your core portfolio and merely want additional income. Accomplish this goal with investments beyond the traditional fixed-income holdings in your core. Intermediate-level, income-producing investments may include the following:

✔ **Municipal bonds (held in taxable accounts only):** These bonds usually pay a lower interest rate than corporate or agency bonds, but they're generally safe (check credit ratings). The income is free of federal income tax and possibly state tax. Check the tax equivalent yield (TEY) to make a sound comparison.

✔ **High-yield bonds (a nice way of saying *junk bonds*):** These bonds typically pay more interest than investment-grade bonds, but they also carry a higher degree of default risk.

✔ **Preferred stocks:** These securities are somewhat of a cross between a stock and a bond. They generally pay a relatively high yield in the form of quarterly dividends.

✔ **High-grade corporate or government agency bonds:** The quality and interest rates paid by these bonds vary by their credit ratings, length of their term, and the general interest-rate market.

When investing in bonds or preferred stock, you should

✔ Become familiar with the credit ratings issued by Moody's and Standard & Poor's (Aaa/AAA = the best, C/D = the worst).

✔ Understand the effect that buying a bond at a discount, at par, or at a premium has on your expected yield to maturity (YTM).

✔ Be aware of call features associated with your bond.

✔ Diversify your investment among several income-producing holdings to reduce risk.

Increase Your Tolerance for Risk

New investments in your portfolio bring new risks as well. Continue to analyze the risk/reward profile of any new investment and fully understand its place in your portfolio. Follow this advice:

✔ **Knowledge is power, so go beyond the basics and commit to learning as much as you can about the interactions between your investments.** Develop a good understanding of risk and performance measurements, such as standard deviation, beta, correlation, alpha, and the Sharpe index. Know where your aggregate portfolio falls on the Efficient Frontier.

✔ **Don't go it alone.** Get a buddy or mentor with the same interests in investing. Bounce ideas, concerns, and new knowledge off one another. Things are often more easily understood when you have a sounding board and two heads thinking about an issue instead of one. Better yet, join or start an investment club.

✔ **History often repeats itself, so take some time to gain historical perspective of the U.S. economy and the stock market.** Look specifically at difficult periods in U.S. history (see Strategy #2) and find out how the market performed leading into it, during it, and afterward.

✔ **Seek a professional opinion.** Find an hourly, fee-only financial advisor in your area to provide a second opinion. The fee may well be worth the validation of your assumptions or the discovery of hidden issues.

#60

Take Advantage of Retirement Plan Catch-Up Provisions

• •

By Brooke Salvini, CPA/PFS, CCPS

• •

*W*ho says nothing good comes with age? If you turn 50 by the end of the calendar year (or are already 50+), you have an opportunity to make a significant difference in your retirement savings by taking advantage of the catch-up provisions the IRS has given you for your 50th birthday.

Catch Up with Age-50 Allowances

Taking advantage of the age-50 catch-up provisions can really add up over time. For example, if you contribute an additional $5,000 to your retirement plan at the beginning of each year from ages 50 to 65 and you make a modest return of 5 percent, you'll have an additional $113,287 in your retirement savings account at age 65. That's nothing to sneeze at.

Go beyond the annual limit

The catch-up provisions detailed in Table 60-1 effectively increases the maximum contribution to most retirement plans and IRAs for people 50 and older. You make the catch-up allowance in addition to the annual employee-plus-employer limit.

Table 60-1	Age 50 Catch-Up Allowances (2008)		
Retirement Plan	**Employee Contribution Limits**	**Age-50 Catch-up**	**Total Maximum Employee Contributions**
401(k)/Roth 401(k) 403(b)/Roth 403(b) 457(b), SAR-SEP	$15,500	$5,000	$20,500
SIMPLE 401(k) and IRA	$10,500	$2,500	$13,000
IRA (traditional and Roth)	$5,000	$1,000	$6,000

In other words, if your employer contributes to your retirement plan through profit sharing, matching, or bonuses, the total contributions can reach the combined employee-plus-employer limit ($46,000 for 2008). But if you're 50 and you use your age-50 catch-up allowance, you and your employer together can actually contribute a total of $51,000 — or $48,500 if your plan is a SIMPLE 401(k) — to your retirement plan. Wow!

Note: The age-50 catch-up is available for 457(b) plans only if they're governmental. If you work for a nongovernmental organization that offers a 457(b) plan, you can still take advantage of the special catch-up provision described later in the section titled "457(b): Last three years before retirement."

Deal with multiple retirement plans

If you participate in more than one retirement plan, either at the same or different employers, you can make only one age-50 catch-up contribution for all your plans combined (except for 457(b) plans). Here are a few examples:

✔ **Two 401(k)s:** You're 50 years old, have two part-time jobs, and participate in the 401(k) plans of two employers. You must apply the age-50 catch-up allowance to both plans together. That is, you can't contribute more than $5,000 catch-up contributions in total between the two plans.

✔ **A 457(b) and plus a different plan:** Your employer offers a 401(k) and 457(b) plan. You participate in both plans. The catch-up limits are applied to these plans separately. In 2008, you can defer an additional $5,000 catch-up to both your 401(k) and 457(b) plans for a total of $10,000 extra retirement savings.

✔ **Two 457(b)s:** You're 50 years old, work for two separate employers, and participate in the 457(b) plan of each employer. You apply the age-50 catch-up allowance to both plans together. This means that in 2008, you can't contribute more than $5,000 in total catch-up contributions between the two 457(b) plans.

Play Catch-Up with Special Provisions for 457(b) and 403(b) Plans

If you participate in either a 457(b) or a 403(b) retirement plan through your employer, you should be familiar with a couple of special catch-up provisions that aren't related to turning age 50. Taking advantage of these 457(b) and 403(b) catch-up provisions can play an important part in securing your retirement savings against the inevitable uncertainties of these (and most other) economic times.

457 (b): Last three years before retirement

The 457(b) has a special rule saying that for the three years prior to normal retirement age (as defined by your employer), you can increase your salary deferrals by up to twice the regular limit — up to $31,000 in 2008 — to make up for previous years in which you didn't contribute the full deferral.

If you're also eligible for the age-50 catch-up, you can choose either the special rule or the age-50, whichever gives you the higher catch-up in any year. Compare these examples:

- **High "unused contributions":** You're 62 and you intend to retire at 65, the normal retirement age at your company. Throughout the years, you haven't maximized your 457(b) retirement plan contributions, so you have $75,000 of "unused contributions" available for this calculation. In 2008, you can contribute $31,000 to your 457(b) retirement plan.

- **Low "unused contributions":** You're 66 and you plan to retire next year at 67. For the last two years, you've taken advantage of the special 457(b) catch-up allowance, so you have only $4,000 of "unused contributions" remaining for the calculation. In this case, you'd choose the age-50 catch-up allowance because it's greater than the special catch-up provision.

403 (b): Fifteen years of service

You're eligible for a special $3,000 annual catch-up in your 403(b) (with a lifetime max per employer of $15,000) if you meet both of the following conditions:

- You have 15 years of service (not necessarily consecutive years) for the same hospital, health agency, public school system, or church.

- Your average annual contributions to all the retirement plans offered by this employer are less than $5,000 annually.

You can be eligible for both the 15-years-of-service and the age-50 catch-ups for a total allowable catch-up in 2008 of $8,000. The 15-years-of-service special catch-up is included in the calculation of the employee-plus-employer limit ($46,000 in 2008). Compare these scenarios:

✔ **Employee contributions only:** You're 64 and have worked in the church office of your parish on and off over the past 25 years, for a total of 15 years of service. During this time, you've never contributed more than $5,000 to the church 403(b) retirement plan in any one year. The church doesn't contribute to your 403(b) plan. In 2008, you're eligible to contribute $8,000 in catch-up contributions — $3,000 special catch-up and $5,000 age-50 catch-up — in addition to a regular contribution of $15,500.

✔ **Employee-plus-employer contributions:** Same facts as in the first example, except the church has contributed $28,500 to your plan. Your special catch-up contribution is limited to $2,000 because it's included in the calculation of the employee-plus-employer maximum addition limit ($46,000 for 2008). You can still contribute your age-50 catch-up for a combined addition of $51,000.

Part V
Heading into Retirement

The 5th Wave   By Rich Tennant

"I've been working over 80 hours a week for the past two years preparing for retirement, and it hasn't bothered me OR my wife, what's-her-name."

In this part . . .

*J*ust as retirement draws nearer, you may be faced with unforeseen expenses, such as assisting aging parents or adult children. And long-term healthcare is a risk that can derail your best intentions. In this part, you find out how to prepare for these possibilities and how to position your investment portfolio to provide the flexibility you need. You also discover how to maximize your employer-provided retirement plans, understand your Social Security benefits, and explore other assets you may not have considered.

Be Prepared to Fund Large Expenses

By Corry Sheffler, MBA, CFP, CFE

*Y*our retirement looms on the horizon. Are you dreaming of that little cabin on the lake? Maybe you're planning to buy a boat and cruise the coast. Are your golf clubs going to get a workout on the nation's premier courses?

If you're thinking about how to fund such large expenses, you're taking an excellent first step! Now — during your peak earning years — is the time to look ahead and prepare for those big pre- and post-retirement expenditures.

This strategy tells you how to determine how much you'll need, how much to put away to reach your goal, and where you can put it to grow along the way. Because of the appearance of the first large *sandwich generation* — those who face caring for both aging parents and their own children — you also see some specific planning information on those topics.

Figure Out How Much You May Need and How to Get It

Many large expenses come with a known price tag: what they cost today. However, inflation will likely increase that cost when it's time to buy. Use an inflation calculator such as the one from Bankrate.com (www.bankrate.com/brm/calculators/savings/inflation_calculator.asp) to determine the future cost of a large expense.

The cost of some large expenses, such as long-term care or medical expenses, are more difficult to estimate. But again, your first step should be to find out what something costs today. This may involve a number of assumptions, but you have to start somewhere. For example, to plan for in-home care for elderly parents, you can check with local service providers for current costs. Account for inflation based on when you estimate care may begin, and you have your target amount.

This section explains how to figure out what you need to reach your goal and helps you decide whether to save that money or invest it.

Calculate periodic savings

To figure out how much you need to save, you need to know at least three of the following four items:

- ✔ How much money you'll need (remember to account for inflation)
- ✔ When you'll need it
- ✔ How much you'll earn on the money you save
- ✔ How much you can save, either today and/or each month until you reach your goal

With this information in hand, you can use one of the following online calculators to determine what you need to reach your goal: `dinkytown.net/java/Savings.html` or `apps.finra.org/investor_Information/Calculators/1/SavingsCalc.aspx`.

Money you don't spend now is money saved, but money you do spend now is lost savings.

Decide whether to invest or save

When you know how much you need to sock away, the next step is deciding where to put that money to make it grow. If your time horizon is short, say six years or less, consider an FDIC-insured high-yield savings account, money market account, or certificate of deposit (CD) (see Strategy #17). A good site to shop for rates is `www.bankrate.com`. Online banks typically offer the best rates, and most are FDIC-insured.

If you have a longer time horizon before you need the money, the higher expected returns of balanced or growth-and-income no-load mutual funds may make more sense. (See Strategy #21 for more on mutual funds.)

As you approach the time when you'll need this money, shift your invested money into savings. Otherwise, if the market drops shortly before you need the money, you may not have enough for your goal.

Prepare to Assist Family

You may face large expenses if your parents or children need financial help. If you plan and save well, and if your finances are secure, you may be in a position to offer that help. Extra money gives you the option of helping your parents, kids, or both if they need it. Consider the following:

- ✔ **Adult children:** As you approach retirement, you may see a need to help your adult children. Their issues may include job loss, house foreclosure, divorce, or health problems. Some people give money to their children with no strings attached. Others loan their children money. If you opt for a loan, companies that manage loans between relatives, such as Virgin Money (www.virginmoneyus.com), may help.

- ✔ **Elderly parents:** Besides offering financial support, you may eventually need to run all of your parents' financial affairs. If that happens, consider the services of a financial planner. A financial planner can help you understand the complete financial picture as well as estate matters.

Keep lines of communication open to be aware of any pending financial issues with your adult children or your parents. If you anticipate your help being needed, you can estimate an amount as a savings goal. Communicating with your kids and parents about money can give you a picture of their situations and may allow you to help them avoid bad financial decisions as well as determine whether they may need help in the future.

#62

Consider Working in Retirement

By Cynthia Freedman

Some people discover retirement isn't what they anticipated, leaving them bored and constantly underfoot around the house. And studies show that older people who stay physically and mentally active have longer, happier, and healthier lives. Your emotional well-being can also improve as you engage with other people, make new friends, and become a part of your workplace community.

Personal fulfillment is just one reason to consider returning to work. For others, reentering the workforce provides a number of concrete benefits, especially in uncertain economic times:

- **Income:** Maybe you were downsized unexpectedly or your portfolio has lost value. Working in retirement can help make up the shortfall. Working part-time during retirement means you can reduce or delay withdrawals from your retirement nest egg. Earning $20,000 a year in retirement is the equivalent of withdrawing a safe 4 percent per year from a $500,000 nest egg. And if income isn't a pressing issue, working can boost your standard of living and provide a little more money to live that life of leisure you've always wanted.

- **Health insurance:** If you're looking for help on the insurance front, seek out employers that include part-timers in their group health plan. Healthcare expenses often rise during retirement years, and Medicare requires co-payments and deductibles and may not cover all your medical costs. You need a Medicare supplemental policy (at an additional fee) to help pay some of the healthcare costs not covered under the original Medicare plan.

You're not eligible for Medicare coverage until you're age 65. Although you may be able to continue your existing group health insurance under COBRA for up to 18 months, you'll lose any employer subsidy. Your only option may be an expensive individual policy. Getting a job with an employer who offers a group health plan benefit can cover that gap in your healthcare. Check with the benefits administrator of your employer to see how your group health insurance coordinates with Medicare.

Note the Drawbacks

Even if you want to go back to work, getting pack on payroll may not be your best option. Here's why:

- ✔ **Current pension benefits:** If you're receiving an ongoing pension benefit, receiving employment income from another source may affect your benefit. Check with the pension benefit administrator to see what the impact will be. (This isn't an issue if you received a single lump-sum pension benefit.)

- ✔ **Leisure time:** If you're still working, you can't take off on a trip whenever you feel like it; you have to comply with the schedule constraints of your workplace. And when the holidays arrive, you may be the one who has to tend the store while your boss is home with his family.

- ✔ **Taxes:** If your job provides you with a high enough salary, you may be pushed into a higher income tax bracket. Contact a CPA, Enrolled Agent, or other qualified tax professional to see what impact working in retirement will have on your taxes.

As soon as you hit age 70½, you have to start taking your IRA Required Minimum Distributions (RMD), whether you're working or not. These distributions are taxed as ordinary income and are added to your other income when computing your total taxable income. And if you're receiving Social Security benefits, up to 85 percent of those benefits may become taxable, depending on your other income. Also, if you haven't yet reached your full Social Security retirement age, your Social Security benefit is reduced if your earnings are above a certain threshold.

If returning to the workforce isn't essential for your budget, consider volunteering. Many seniors gain the satisfaction of knowing they've made a significant impact on someone's life when they work in areas such as sports, tutoring programs for youth, or a women's shelter.

Make the Transition

So you've decided you want to work, but you don't want to go back to the same old grind you retired from, and you don't want to become a greeter at the local big box store. What should you do?

- ✔ **Consider your likes and dislikes.** Do you like to be with people, or do you like to work alone? Are you more productive when you focus on a single task, or do you need variety throughout your day? What social or philanthropic causes excite you? What hobbies are you passionate about?

✔ **Assess your skills and strengths.** Think about your job skills in general terms to help you see how the skills can transfer to other industries. For example, an effective teacher may become a corporate trainer. Also consider personal skills. Are you organized? Do you speak well in front of groups?

✔ **Realistically consider your physical limitations.** Certain jobs may not be physically appropriate. Some older people start to lose their mental acuity and find it more difficult to learn new procedures, use a computer, or remember where specific items are located. (And your boss may not appreciate it if you need to take a nap every afternoon!)

For info about possible careers, see the Department of Labor Occupational Outlook Handbook (www.bls.gov/OCO), which lists training and education needed, earnings, expected job prospects, what workers do, and working conditions.

After you decide what you want to do, you can gear up to reenter the workforce:

✔ **Network.** Join a professional organization. E-mail friends and family, telling them about your plans and asking them whether they know of any openings or if they can introduce you to someone who works in your target field.

✔ **Gain any needed training or experience before you start the job.** Check course offerings at local colleges or an online university. Volunteering, interning, and working through a temp agency are all great ways to get experience.

✔ **Polish your resume.** Many books and articles discuss how to write a resume, what to expect in job interviews, and other job search issues. (Check out *Resumes For Dummies,* 5th Edition, by Joyce Lain Kennedy [Wiley] or visit www.dummies.com.)

After you find that dream job, enjoy. And remember that at some point, you'll be able to walk away from this job, too, and resume that date with leisure time.

Provide for Potential Long-Term Care Expenses

By Louise Schroeder, CFP

*R*emember being in high school when becoming a senior was something you happily anticipated? You looked forward to the rest of your life and all the wonderful possibilities you could imagine. Sure, you may have felt some uncertainty and a bit of trepidation, but mostly excitement. Thinking this same way can make a real difference when you prepare for the senior years of your life — regardless of the current economic environment. Planning to make these years the best years of your life helps you focus on all the possibilities that can be open to you.

Improve Your Home

The next part of your prevention plan involves looking at your home as if you were currently disabled. Most people would prefer to be cared for in their own homes. But most homes, sadly, aren't equipped to assist with functional limitations, such as being in a wheelchair or using a walker to get around. Home modifications can help you live independently for a longer time, as well as make caring for you easier if and when you need assistance. For example, you may consider more complex structural renovations like widening hallways to 4 feet, widening exterior and interior doorways to 3 feet, renovating your bathroom by putting in a walk-in shower or bathtub, or installing a stairway chair-lift system.

Learning at this stage in your life about potential home modifications to make your home more comfortable in the future provides you with a few advantages:

> ✔ **You may want to complete some modifications before you retire, and pay for them with current income.** Changes can be as simple as adding grab bars where needed and changing round doorknobs to the lever style.

> ✔ **You may want to cover larger projects by using specific assets to finance the costs.** Learning about these potential costs can help you in setting aside certain assets to preserve, and invest more conservatively, for use whenever you may have a need.

This part of your prevention plan should also involve learning about assistive technology devices. Hundreds of devices and systems are available to help individuals with disabling limitations to continue to function on their own. Information from the National Council on Disability says that 80 percent of elderly people who used assistive technology were able to reduce their dependence on others. You can learn more about assistive technology programs in your state at www.resna.org/content/index.php?pid=133.

Review Your Options for Paying for Long-Term Care

How are people paying for their long-term care costs these days? A 2006 study by the American Association of Homes and Services for the Aging showed these results for the financing of long-term care (in nursing homes, assisted living facilities, and at home):

> ✔ 52 percent received unpaid care from family and friends (the "I'll go live with my kids" approach)

> ✔ 20 percent paid with Medicaid

> ✔ 15 percent paid out-of-pocket

> ✔ 8 percent paid with Medicare and other public programs

> ✔ 5 percent paid with private long-term care insurance (discussed later in this strategy) and other private resources

The following sections look at each of these financing possibilities so you can understand better the consequences of relying on each resource, especially in light of the demands baby boomers will place on all resources, public and private.

Moving in with the kids

"I'll just go live with my kids." How many people you know have made this statement when talking about long-term care? What they don't realize is that caregivers end up bearing costs, whether care takes place in the individual's home or in the adult child's home.

The financial impact is currently an average loss of $660,000 over the caregiver's lifetime due to lost promotions and raises, loss of benefits (especially retirement plan contributions), and increased sick days due to caregiver stress–related health problems. Donated care by your family and friends is an important resource, but planning well ahead of time to include additional resources as part of your plan can reduce the impact — physically, emotionally, and financially — on them.

Medicaid and Medicare

Medicare and Medicaid should be considered limited resources, especially 10 to 15 years from now. Medicare pays only for long-term care related to an illness or injury that you're expected to recover from. When you're no longer improving, Medicare stops paying. Medicaid is intended to provide care for people with very low incomes and very limited assets. You can visit with your local Medicaid office to find out whether that may be an option for you. Keep in mind that when baby boomers reach their mid- to late-80s, demands on government programs and services will likely be unsustainable.

Some government services and programs that are currently available to individuals who need long-term care services aren't restricted by income and asset limitations. An excellent resource is the nearest Aging and Disability Resource Center, if your state has one. If not, contact your nearest Area Agency on Aging office. These agencies can tell you what services are available in your living area. These offices are a part of the federal Administration on Aging network. You can find contact information and locations at www. eldercare.gov.

Saving on your own

Some long-term care expenses either will occur before you'll qualify for long-term care insurance benefits or won't be covered by long-term care insurance. Setting aside a portion of your own assets to pay for these expenses will provide you with more control over your quality of life in your later years. It will also provide you with a level of comfort when facing the uncertainty surrounding this potential financial need.

Although you should use a more conservative asset allocation when investing these assets, inflation will be a large factor in developing your investment strategy. When you're determining what average annual rate of return you want to try to achieve for these investments, look at the inflation rate associated with long-term care costs. Inflation for these costs is higher than the general inflation rate (currently at 6 percent versus 4 percent for general inflation). For asset allocation suggestions, see Strategy #79.

Purchasing long-term care insurance

Having long-term care insurance provides you with a level of financial flexibility (see Strategy #7 for more information on the ins and outs of this type of insurance). But what you may consider "long-term care expenses" may not meet the insurance company's definition. So you need to do your homework.

When long-term care insurance pays

Long-term care policies pay benefits only when you need substantial assistance with at least two activities of daily living or substantial supervision due to mental impairment for 90 days or longer. These activities include:

- ✔ Eating
- ✔ Dressing
- ✔ Bathing
- ✔ Transferring (from a bed to a chair or wheelchair)
- ✔ Toileting (using the toilet)
- ✔ Managing incontinence

When long-term care insurance doesn't pay

Later in life, many people need assistance — on a regular basis — that doesn't reach the level of incapacitation covered by insurance. These kinds of limitations often require assistance with daily activities that are unrelated to personal care, such as:

- ✔ Preparing meals
- ✔ Home maintenance, inside and outside
- ✔ Laundry
- ✔ Help with managing money, investments, and legal decisions
- ✔ Transportation
- ✔ Shopping
- ✔ Making and traveling to and from appointments
- ✔ Taking medications correctly

You'll pay for a lot of your long-term care out of your own pocket. Your success in doing so depends on careful planning for retirement to make sure you have enough assets to cover your potential costs.

Use Your Home as a Source of Income

By JamesTaylor, CFP, and Robert Friedland, PhD

*Y*our home is more than just the place where you hang your hat and raise your family. It's one of your biggest investments and an important part of the foundation of your financial security. For most people, paying for a home takes decades. But when you've accumulated a lot of equity or have paid off the mortgage, your home could start paying you back. This strategy shows you how.

Have the Lender Pay You with a Reverse Mortgage

If you have a home, you probably had a mo
rtgage. In a forward mortgage, you pay the lender every month. With a *reverse mortgage,* the lender pays you! You have a choice of a lump sum, a monthly payment, or a line of credit with which you can take out funds when needed. Any combination of these choices is also an option.

You don't have to meet any medical, income, or credit requirements, and there's no income tax liability; however, the amount of the loan increases each month because interest accrues on the loan balance. In addition, you have to keep the home maintained and insured, and all real estate taxes must be paid. The home remains in your name, and no repayment is required until maturity of the loan. Maturity occurs

✔ When the last borrower no longer resides in the home due to death or sale of the home

✔ When the last surviving borrower fails to live in the home for 12 consecutive months

---

Getting a federally-insured reverse mortgage

Federal Housing Administration (FHA) insured reverse mortgages, also called *home equity conversion mortgages* (HECM), are limited to HUD's 203(b) borrowing limits for your county. In 2008, these limits ranged between $200,160 and $362,790.

To obtain an FHA-insured reverse mortgage, you have to be at least 62 and occupy and own the house (or owe so little that it'll be paid off with the proceeds of the reverse mortgage). Single family homes, cooperatives, and mobile homes may be eligible for reverse mortgages if they meet HUD standards. The borrower, however, must meet with an approved reverse mortgage counselor.

Most reverse mortgages allow a six-month period after maturity for repayment and/or sale of the property. Naturally, if the loan isn't paid off, the lender owns the home.

Reverse mortgages are insured either in the private market or by federal, state, or local governments. The vast majority of reverse mortgages are federally insured by the Federal Housing Administration (FHA). A few states, such as Connecticut and Montana, have state-insured reverse mortgages, and a few local governments throughout the country also have programs. Private or proprietary reverse mortgages are available nearly everywhere.

State and local government reverse mortgages are often the least expensive, and private reverse mortgages — which often offer the highest borrowing amount — cost the most. The interest rate is likely to be higher along with the insurance premiums.

What does a reverse mortgage cost? They ain't cheap! Here's an example cost estimate:

- **Origination fee:** 2 percent of the value of the home or $2,000, whichever is less

- **Appraisal fee:** $350 to $500

- **Credit report fee (to verify whether there are any liens against the property):** $20

- **Flood certification fee (is the home in a flood zone?):** $20

- **Recording fees:** $75 to $225

- **Title insurance:** $500 or more

- **Pest inspection:** $75 to $150

- **Survey:** $250 to $750 (although you can sometimes use a recent survey)

- **Escrow and settlement fees:** $150 to $450

Keeping it in the family: A couple more reverse mortgage options

You may consider arranging your own reverse mortgage with a family member who has the resources to provide you the stream of income you need. That family member would place a lien against your home — just as any other lender would — to protect his or her "investment"

when you eventually pass away or the home is sold.

Here's a similar alternative: If a family member is willing and able to purchase your home, he or she can make mortgage payments to you and let you live in your home as long as you want.

> ✔ **Document preparation fees:** $75 to $150
>
> ✔ **Closing costs:** Whatever is common in your area with regular mortgages

The total cost begins around $4,250 and goes up depending on the value of the home. You may pay these costs with proceeds of the loan. These high costs should make a reverse mortgage an option of last resort.

Some advisors encourage eligible seniors to get a reverse mortgage and put all the proceeds into an annuity. This offers the advantage of a guaranteed income for life, whereas monthly income from the reverse mortgage can run out before the borrower dies. In addition, the reverse mortgage lender can charge up to $35 per payment to the home owner. However, the annuity can have income tax consequences. Furthermore, the costs of the fees and commissions of the combined reverse mortgage and annuity can exceed 20 percent of the funds available.

Good sources of information on reverse mortgages include the following:

> ✔ **Department of Housing and Urban Development (HUD):** www.hud.gov/offices/hsg/sfh/hecm/rmtopten.cfm
>
> ✔ **AARP:** www.aarp.org/money/revmort

Keep Property Rights with a Grantor-Retained Annuity Trust (GRAT)

If you have an estate consisting of real or personal property that has appreciated rapidly, you can establish a grantor-retained annuity trust

(GRAT) or a grantor-retained unitrust (GRUT). With both, you retain rights to your property, get income from the property, and minimize or even eliminate taxes when you die. These trusts, however, aren't for the faint-hearted or most middle-income families. They're irrevocable (meaning you can't change your mind) and require that you have other sources of income besides the income generated from the trust.

These trusts are considered *grantor retained* because you retain access to the earnings for a defined period of time. You transfer your property (real and/or personal) into the trust when you set it up and receive income during the retained trust period. These payments can be a fixed amount (GRAT) or can vary annually based on the trust's assets (GRUT). During the trust period, you receive taxable payments. At the end of this fixed period, the payments stop and any property remaining in the trust passes to your trust's beneficiaries.

The payouts you receive from a GRAT or GRUT reduce the size of the trust, enabling you (the grantor) to bypass gifting limits and lessen tax consequences from highly appreciated assets such as your home, commercial property, or equities. Therefore, you need income and income-producing assets outside the GRAT or GRUT to pay trust taxes during the trust period and to provide income after the property has moved from the trust to your beneficiaries.

Although you may have good reasons to establish an irrevocable trust, you also face some risks:

- ✔ **Dying before the term of the trust expires:** If you set up the GRAT for five years but die after one, all property remaining in the trust is included in your federal estate-tax calculation. Not only do you lose the tax advantage for setting up the GRAT, but the cost of creating and administering the GRAT is also wasted.

- ✔ **Needing trust assets to appreciate:** If assets don't appreciate at rates similar to government bond rates — or if they depreciate — you get no tax savings. Be sure to have a diversified portfolio in the trust.

GRATs and GRUTs are sophisticated estate planning techniques, so get the help of specialized estate planning attorneys.

Make the Best Use of Your Retirement Plan

By Robert Friedland, PhD

*1*f you've been working for many years, you've probably changed employers a few times. Each employer may have had a retirement plan; some may have had more than one. One or more may even have had a post-retirement health plan. Now is the time to be sure you'll get all the benefits you're entitled to when you retire.

Defined Benefit and Defined Contribution: What's the Difference?

The array of plan types is staggering, but most qualified retirement plans fit into one of two basic types. People often refer to both types of plans as *pensions,* but one is really a pension and the other is a tax-deferred savings plan. The pension plan is a *defined benefit* plan, and the tax-deferred savings plan is a *defined contribution* plan. See Strategy #34 for more info on qualified plans.

- ✔ **Defined benefit:** In a defined benefit pension plan, the pension benefit is defined by a specific formula. The formula determines your pension benefit. Formulas vary, but most are based on the number of years you worked and your salary.

- ✔ **Defined contribution:** In a defined contribution plan, your retirement benefit is defined by the contributions made to the plan and the growth of those contributions over time. If you didn't contribute very much, didn't contribute regularly, and didn't maintain a diversified portfolio, or if you contributed sporadically, your retirement benefit may not be as large as it could've been. This strategy covers catch-up provisions later on; they were created just for this situation and recently enacted into law.

Stake Your Pension Claim

If you worked many years for a company that provided a defined benefit plan, you're likely eligible for a pension benefit. If you left after a few years, you may have gotten a check from the pension plan. That check effectively ended your future pension benefit. (We hope you put it into an IRA.) If you didn't receive a check or lump-sum distribution, your former employer may be on the hook to start sending you monthly checks when you reach the age defined in that plan. You just need to let the employer know when and where to send the check.

If you've been getting updates from this employer or the pension plan administrators, they know you're out there. If you no longer receive those updates, or if you never received them and are fairly sure you were participating in the defined benefit pension plan (and didn't receive a lump-sum distribution), let your former employer know you're getting ready to receive your monthly checks.

Because your former employer may not remember you hanging out by the water cooler, you may need to refresh their memories. Before you contact them, do a bit of homework. Look through those piles of paperwork for info on the company defined benefit plan and for evidence that you worked there. That old pay stub may work, as will the W-2 you filed with your taxes. If they still don't believe you, you may need to hire a lawyer to help you make your claim.

Tabulate Your Defined Contribution Accounts

Defined contribution plans come with a lot of clever names like 401(k), Money Purchase Plan, 403(b), 457(b), TSA (tax-sheltered annuity), SEP (simplified employee pension), SARSEP (salary reduction simplified employee pension), SIMPLE (savings incentive match plan for employees), and stock bonus plans, to name just a few. Although these plans have important distinctions — particularly to your employer — from your perspective they tend to operate in the same way.

You — the employee — now have a key role. You choose whether and when to start participating in the plan, how much to contribute (typically through payroll deferral and subject to annual limits), and how to invest your contributions among the choices provided in the plan. Some employers also contribute something, usually matching a fraction of your contributions.

If you had a defined contribution account with a former employer, the account is still yours. Depending on the plan design, the employer contributions (matches) to your account may also be yours. With some plans, you get to keep the employer matching regardless of how long you worked for them (immediate vesting); with others, you get to keep employer contributions after working there three years (cliff vesting) or six years (incremental vesting).

When you left the company, you may have been able to leave the money invested where it was (if the balance was large enough), or you could've moved that money (or "rolled over") to another employer plan or to an individual retirement account (IRA). Either way, you should be receiving regular statements (at least quarterly) informing you of the value of your account holdings. If you've moved and stopped receiving statements at some point, check your old account documents to submit your current address. You don't want to lose money because the plan administrator can't locate you. If you haven't included the money from old employers and accounts in your ongoing monitoring and asset allocation, now is the time to include those funds in your investment planning.

Maximize Your Benefits for Defined Benefit Plans

If you're in a defined benefit plan, be sure you understand how the benefit formula works. Generally, defined benefit plans are designed to retain company-specific skills under the assumption that it takes time to acquire the necessary skills that the employer values but that older workers are eventually too expensive. Consequently, benefit formulas tend to reward workers more during the years employers see your skills as being the most valuable. This may be, for example, after five years but before 18 years. Continuing with this example, after the fifth year, each year of service will result in a significant increase in the promised monthly pension amount until the 17th year of service. Subsequently, each additional year of service doesn't contribute as much of an increase in monthly benefits as in the previous years. Knowing how this formula works may help you decide when to retire.

In doing your homework on former employer plans, you may discover that you have a former employer for whom a few more years of service will make a substantial difference in your monthly checks. You may want to consider employment with this former employer so you can increase your years of service and, therefore, your monthly pension.

If you're already collecting benefits from a former employer and you have sufficient savings, you may want to consider paying the benefits back. Some employers, and public employers in particular, let you in effect buy service credits. When you're older, your life expectancy is shorter, and therefore the monthly benefits will be higher. This will be particularly beneficial if you're in excellent health and were fortunate to have long-lived parents and long-lived grandparents.

Maximize Your Benefits for Defined Contribution Plans

You can't add years of service to a former employer's defined contribution plan, but you should make sure you're getting the full matching contribution from your current employer. Check with human resources to ensure you're deferring enough of your pay to at least get the full employer match. If your plan is relatively low cost with decent investment options, contribute as much as you can. In most cases, funding a Roth IRA is a better choice after you've deferred enough to get the employer match.

In 2008, federal law limited your 401(k), 403(b), 457(b), Roth 401(k), Roth 403(b), and other SARSEP-type plan contributions to the lower of 100 percent of compensation or $15,500. However, starting in the year in which you turn 50, you can catch up by contributing another $5,000 per year. For SIMPLE 401(k) plans and SIMPLE IRA plans, the 2008 limits are the lower of $10,500 or 100 percent of your compensation, but if you're age 50 or older, you can make additional catch-up contributions of $2,500 per year.

Contributing the maximum allowed to your 401(k) starting the year you reach age 50 and continuing until age 67 is likely to add more than $650,000 to your retirement savings.

Contributing to your defined contribution plan doesn't mean you can't also contribute to an individual retirement account (IRA). You may not be able to deduct those contributions, but at least the earnings will be compounding tax-deferred or even tax-free (if you have a Roth IRA). For more details on defined contribution plans and IRAs, check out Strategies #33, #34, and #35.

Before you retire, be sure you know what your retirement benefits will be, not only from your current employer but also from all your former employers. In the meantime, keep making those monthly contributions, especially while the market is moving down or sideways.

Understand Retirement Resources

By Janice Swenor, MBA, CFP

*W*hen people retired in the 1970s, their sources of retirement income were few. They may have had a nice pension and Social Security. Their medical care was covered by Medicare and perhaps a company-sponsored supplemental plan. Boy, have things changed! Employer pension plans are being replaced by retirement plans to which both employers and employees contribute. Social Security and Medicare both face financial problems in the future. So what are your retirement resources, and how do you plan for them so you don't sink in retirement? This strategy has you covered.

Collect Social Security

Even in the best of times, uncertainty pervades the Social Security system. Planning for your retirement gets more difficult the younger you are, because projections show the system running short of funds in the decades ahead. Today, Social Security replaces between 20 and 40 percent of what a retiree earned before retirement. Changes in 1983 resulted in a range of full-retirement ages (65 to 67) for those born in 1938 and later.

Review your statement

Grab your most recent Social Security statement. You should receive one annually a few months before your birthday. If you don't have one, or if you notice earnings discrepancies, contact your local Social Security office immediately. On your annual statement, you'll find your projected benefit for age 62, for your full retirement age (65 to 67), and for age 70.

If your spouse hasn't worked or earns considerably less than you do, he or she will receive half of your benefit or his or her estimated benefit, whichever is higher. The same applies if you divorce after ten or more years of marriage and your spouse hasn't remarried.

Make some plans

By 2041, Social Security benefits will fall if current funding problems aren't addressed. How much should you count on when planning your retirement? Here are some guidelines:

- ✔ If you're under 40, assume you won't receive any of your retirement benefit.
- ✔ If you're between 40 and 60, assume you'll receive 50 percent of your benefit.
- ✔ If you're 60 or over, assume you'll receive all of your benefit.

These guidelines will change if Congress passes legislation to improve the financial strength of Social Security. When that happens, adjust your plan accordingly.

Know what your benefits are

The following circumstances can affect your Social Security benefits:

- ✔ If you retire at age 62 or before your *full retirement age* (FRA) and choose to take your Social Security benefit then, it'll be permanently reduced based on the number of months until your FRA.
- ✔ If you continue to earn an income while drawing Social Security before your FRA and the amount is over the permitted limit, you'll be required to pay back some or all of your benefit.
- ✔ Your Social Security benefits may be taxable, up to 85 percent. If your total income is above the limit for a single individual or for a couple, you'll pay income tax.
- ✔ If you work or have worked for an employer who doesn't withhold Social Security tax and who has a pension plan, your benefits may be reduced or eliminated due to the Windfall Elimination Program (WEP) or the Government Pension Offset (GPO).

Visit your nearest Social Security office or go to the Social Security Web site at www.ssa.gov to find answers to individual questions.

Wade through Medicare and Medicaid

Medicare is a federal government health insurance program targeting U.S. citizens and permanent residents 65 and older, those under age 65 with certain disabilities, and those of any age with end-stage renal disease; *Medicaid,* on the other hand, is a federal medical insurance program administered by each state. It targets financially needy people. Limits are placed on the income and amount of assets an individual or couple may have in order to qualify for Medicaid benefits. Medicare and Medicaid aren't specifically sources of income, but you can use these resources to pay for expenses you incur.

Find more information on Medicare at www.medicare.gov. Resources there include the latest "Medicare and You" booklet. You can find more information on your state's Medicaid program at your local Medicaid office.

Table 66-1 shows the three parts of Medicare.

Table 66-1	Medicare Benefits Summary		
	Part A	*Part B*	*Part D*
Coverage provided	Basic coverage for hospital stays; may also cover some skilled nursing, hospice, and home healthcare if certain conditions are met	Medically necessary costs for doctors and outpatient services; also helps cover some preventive services	A portion of prescription medication costs
Program cost	$0 if you or your spouse paid into the system for at least ten years	Minimum premium is $96.40/month (2008)	Varies depending on the plan you choose
Benefit cost	None	Co-pay is 20% or more of doctor's bills, plus an annual deductible	25% of your prescription costs after meeting the deductible; coverage gap during which you must pay 100% of total costs until max reached

Medicare doesn't cover a number of items and services, such as deductibles, co-insurance, co-payments, yearly physicals, hearing aids, foot care, insulin, long-term care, and so on. To help pay out-of-pocket costs, consider a Medigap policy and a long-term care policy. Remember, though, that these policies typically cover only one person, so if you and your spouse both want coverage, you each need a policy. An alternative is a Medicare Advantage Plan, which combines Part A and Part B and sometimes Part D. These plans are managed by private insurance companies approved by Medicare. They can charge different deductibles, co-payments, or co-insurance.

You have to enroll in Medicare three months prior to turning 65. If you wait, your premium may go up 10 percent for each 12-month period that you could've had it but didn't. If you're still covered by your employer's health plan, you can delay coverage, but you still need to sign up.

Medicare is in worse financial condition than Social Security. Major changes in benefits and/or costs are likely to occur in the near future.

Know Your Employer Pension Plans

Employer pension plans are becoming a rarity as employers change to other types of retirement plans. If your employer still offers one, understanding your payout options is important. Your income benefit is generally based on a formula that includes the number of years of employment, a final average salary, and a percentage-of-income replacement factor.

Common payout options include the following:

- ✔ **A single life benefit:** This option pays the largest amount over your single lifetime. Upon your death, the benefit stops and your surviving spouse receives nothing.

- ✔ **A reduced benefit guaranteed for a fixed number of years:** Upon your death, your spouse receives the benefit for any remaining years left on the guarantee period.

- ✔ **A reduced benefit guaranteed over your lifetime and your spouse's:** The benefit paid to your spouse on your death may remain the same or be reduced.

At retirement, you and your spouse have to sign a waiver if the option you choose will result in your spouse's receiving a reduction in income that may have a significant impact on his or her standard of living.

Before retirement, you may want to consider a life insurance policy to replace any loss of income to your spouse, depending on the payout option you choose. Evaluate whether the premium for the insurance makes sense in comparison to the additional income you may receive. Make sure the insurance is in place prior to signing the release.

Also ask the following questions about your pension:

- ✔ Is your pension plan integrated with Social Security? Will collecting Social Security reduce the amount of your pension benefit?

- ✔ How financially sound is your pension plan? Can it meet its promised benefits, and if so, how far into the future?

✔ Will you receive a yearly cost-of-living adjustment (COLA) during retirement?

✔ If your employer doesn't withhold Social Security tax, will your Social Security benefits be reduced or eliminated due to the Windfall Elimination Provision (WEP) or the Government Pension Offset (GPO)?

Use Personal Retirement Accounts

Depending on your current age, personal retirement and taxable accounts may be your only retirement income sources. If you've been contributing to these accounts on a regular basis, you hope you'll have enough by the time you retire. How much you can plan to withdraw after you retire depends on when you retire and your asset allocation before and during retirement.

Be aware of these two important age limits that apply to qualified employer retirement plans, such as 401(k) and 403(b) plans, and to traditional IRAs:

✔ Before age 59^1/$_2$, you'll pay a penalty for withdrawing money from your account, except in special circumstances.

✔ Upon reaching age 70^1/$_2$, you generally need to start taking an annual required minimum distribution (RMD).

For additional information on retirement plans, see Strategies #33, #34, and #35. For more info on investment strategies before and after retirement, see Strategies #56 through #59.

Collect Income from Continued Employment or Self-Employment

The definition of retirement has changed over the last 20 years. Retirement is often about having the financial freedom to do what you want. This may mean working part time, opening a small business, or working full time at a job you love.

If you're planning to work past your full retirement age, remember that health issues may derail your plan. Make sure that by a specific age, such as 65 or 67, you're set financially regardless of whether you decide to work. This target age will vary depending on your current health and family history.

#67

Make Sure You're Accumulating Enough

By Ben Jennings, CPA/PFS, CFP

*N*aval aviators (think *Top Gun*) have a tough job: landing a jet that's moving at 150 mph and buffeted by wind and turbulence in a space 20 feet wide and 135 feet long on a carrier deck that's possibly heaving in stormy seas and always moving away at an angle. One tool they depend on is a lens reflecting a colored light *(the ball)* up the target *glide slope* to the ship's flight deck.

Preparing for retirement during an uncertain economy can make you feel like one of those pilots. Experiencing market volatility is stressful. The foundational questions to ask are "Am I still on track to have enough?" and "How much will be enough?"

Determine How Much Is Enough

The answer to how much is enough depends, of course, on the answer to another question: Enough for what?

Estimate retirement spending needs

You can estimate your retirement spending needs by using a couple of approaches: top-down or bottom-up.

Top-down

Common rules of thumb assume some *replacement ratio,* a percentage of your pre-retirement income that will cover your spending needs in retirement. Think of this as the *top-down approach*. The replacement ratio is easy to calculate, but you need to think carefully about adjusting it to your situation.

Replacement ratios often use 70 to 80 percent of pre-retirement gross income. This lower amount reflects that during retirement, you won't have to allocate money for retirement savings, a mortgage you paid off before retirement, payroll taxes, and so on.

Bottom-up

A more refined method for estimating retirement needs is the *bottom-up approach:* Start with your expenses now and consider how they may change in retirement.

Some expenses will, of course, go down:

- ✔ Your mortgage will hopefully be paid off before retirement, but costs such as property taxes will continue.
- ✔ If you have kids, you know how much money they required.
- ✔ You don't typically need life and disability insurance in retirement.

On the other hand, you have additional costs to consider:

- ✔ You may want to spend more on travel, entertainment, or hobbies.
- ✔ Medical insurance previously paid by your employer is a new addition to your budget.
- ✔ Household services and maintenance you do or did yourself may need to be outsourced at some point.
- ✔ Whether or not you use insurance to help, you need some way to account for potential long-term care expenses (see Strategy #63).

Finally, make sure you consider costs you'll incur only periodically:

- ✔ Long-term home maintenance is a big one. Think about roof replacement, painting, major appliance replacement, and so on. A common guideline for annual costs is 1 percent or more of the home's value.
- ✔ You'll want to replace your car from time to time.
- ✔ You may have to pay for special family events, such as weddings, that fall during your retirement years.

Convert current spending targets to future dollars

Whatever your estimated expenses may be, they're likely to cost more in ten years than they do now. So far, you've probably thought of your future expenses in today's dollars. Now you need to adjust for inflation.

You may want to use one of the following two approaches. First, you may use an average rate of increase over time. Be aware, though, that prices for goods and services consumed by Americans over age 62 can be significantly more than average.

Alternatively, you can look at the specific mix of expenses you anticipate in retirement and consider how these may change over time to create your personal inflation rate:

- ✔ A few may stay about the same (long-term care insurance premiums, any mortgage repayments remaining in retirement).
- ✔ Most will increase about with general inflation.
- ✔ Others will go up much faster than inflation. For example, medical costs generally have been going up at about twice the rate of general inflation.

Table 67-1 lists multipliers for various periods of time until retirement, assuming average inflation rates of 3 or 4 percent:

Table 67-1	Calculating Inflation for Your Retirement	
Years Until Retirement	*3% Average Inflation: Multiply Spending By*	*4% Average Inflation: Multiply Spending By*
5	1.16	1.22
10	1.34	1.48
15	1.56	1.80
20	1.81	2.19
25	2.09	2.67
30	2.43	3.24

For example, suppose you're 15 years from retirement, anticipate a 3-percent average annual inflation, and determine you'll need $30,000 in today's dollars. Multiply $30,000 by 1.56, and you see that at 3-percent inflation, your expenses will be $46,800 by the time you reach retirement.

Calculate the assets required

After you determine your total expenses to be covered each year, subtract the portion that future income sources (such as a pension or Social Security) will provide during retirement.

A good tool for determining future Social Security income is your annual Social Security statement. The benefit amounts on these statements are in today's dollars, so just subtract the estimated benefit from your spending target before multiplying by the inflation factor in Table 67-1.

If you use the top-down approach (see the earlier "Estimate retirement spending needs" section), remember that this federal program is designed to favor lower-income earners — the *social* part of Social Security. One reason is the assumption that lower-income earners have reduced opportunities to save and invest during their working lives (so if you do have the opportunity, you need to take it!).

The Social Security Administration estimated in 2007 that a couple, both 65 years old and with a single earner, would receive benefits replacing between 40 percent (assuming high earnings of $86,046) and 60 percent (assuming medium earnings of $38,726) of their pre-retirement income. This estimate seems pretty optimistic; you'd be better off assuming Social Security will replace 25 percent of your pre-retirement family income.

Now you're ready to determine the number:

1. **Determine either a certain percentage of your pre-retirement income or calculate the specific expenses that add up to your desired amount in dollars.**

   For example, perhaps you need 50 percent of your pre-retirement income of $60,000, which would be $30,000. (See the "Estimate retirement spending needs" section.)

2. **Convert that dollar amount to a likely equivalent in future dollars.**

   For example, maybe your $30,000 needs to grow to $46,800 by the time you retire. (See "Convert current spending targets to future dollars.")

3. **Reduce your retirement need by the amount to be provided by Social Security.**

   For example, if Social Security will cover $11,700, or 25 percent of your $46,800, you have to fund $35,100 from your savings.

4. **Multiply that number by 20 and write it down; then multiply it by 25 and write that down.**

   This step calculates the upper and lower ends of the target range for your investment accumulation for retirement. The 20 and 25 factors result from several historical studies that found that initial withdrawal rates between approximately 4 and 5 percent can sustain withdrawals over at least 30 years.

For example, suppose you determine you need $35,100 in the first year of your retirement. Multiply that by 20 for a result of about $700,000. Multiply by 25, and the result is $875,000. This means $700,000 to $875,000 is a good range for total savings. You can withdraw $35,100 from your investments in the first year of retirement, adjust that amount annually for inflation, and have a high degree of confidence you won't run out of money during a 30-year retirement.

Figure Out Whether You're On Track

After you know how much is enough, you have to figure out whether you're saving enough to get you there. You need to know the following:

- ✔ **Your current savings:** Include IRAs, 401(k)s, and taxable and other investment assets. You probably shouldn't include your home equity or other assets that you can't convert to cash in retirement.

- ✔ **How much your investments should earn:** Keep in mind that many market observers may be anticipating investment returns below the long-term historical average in the next few years. For additional considerations, see the nearby sidebar, "Where all the returns are below average."

- ✔ **How much you're saving each year:** This includes not only salary deferrals and after-tax savings but also any employer contributions to your retirement account.

Also consider whether your savings are increasing each year. This tends to be automatic if you're saving a percentage of your income, but you may need to evaluate this number if you target a specific dollar amount each year. If your savings aren't increasing annually, do you anticipate saving more later (for example, when the kids are out of college)?

If you find you need to save more, increase savings by directing at least a portion of your pay raises to savings. This can be a more comfortable way of gradually adjusting your lifestyle to a sustainable level.

By far the easiest way to evaluate needed savings is to use one of the many Web-based investment calculators. The investment goal calculator at www.dinkytown.net/java/InvestmentVariables.html is good. *Note:* Because you express your investment goal in future dollars in this book, you don't need to account for inflation again and can assume 0-percent inflation as a calculator input.

Compare the result from your online calculator to the target you previously determined, and you'll have some idea whether you're on the right track amid the market turbulence.

Allocate Assets at the Current Stage of Your Life

By Garry Good, MBA

*Y*our investment mix should always reflect your financial objectives, time horizon, and risk tolerance. A well-designed portfolio has to be aggressive enough to achieve your financial goals while minimizing the risk of having to sell assets during a bear market.

Take this windmill analogy: Suppose you own a windmill that pumps water from a well. This windmill has two gears. In low gear, the mill rotates with even the slightest breeze — pumping 100 gallons of water every day — slow but steady, never more, never less. In high gear, the windmill pumps water at a much faster space — up to 1,000 gallons per day. However, running the pump in high gear takes a very stiff wind — the windmill may go days without pumping a single drop. Still, over an extended period of time, high gear can always be counted on to average at least 200 gallons per day.

Now consider the following scenarios:

- ✔ You have a 10,000 gallon tank available to collect and store water from your well. Which gear would you select to run your mill?

- ✔ Your storage tank holds only 500 gallons. Also, your essential water needs are a minimum of 100 gallons per day. Is it time to shift gears?

Just as you can select the gear that best matches your storage tank capacity, you have to select the asset mix to match your time horizon.

Like a pump in high gear, an aggressive asset allocation is unpredictable in the short-term but will deliver maximum output given adequate time. Like the large storage tank, time serves as the buffer against uncertainty. Lose this buffer, and you're left with no choice: You have to downshift into a slower, more reliable gear: a more-conservative investment allocation. This strategy tells you how and when to make the switch as you approach retirement.

Decide When to Switch to a More Conservative Asset Allocation

How do you know when to start downshifting your portfolio? And how much change is required? Before answering, you have one more factor to consider: your tolerance for short-term risk. The next three sections cover aggressive, moderate, and conservative investors.

Aggressive investor

For an aggressive investor (with a high risk tolerance), a transition path for your portfolio may look something like Figure 68-1.

Upon retirement, you'll need a reliable income stream — something an aggressive portfolio isn't optimally designed to do. This calls for a less volatile asset mix, but you can't wait until retirement to flip the switch. Converting an aggressive portfolio into income-distribution mode takes a more extensive change. Start the transition early — ten years prior to retirement — to avoid forced selling of securities during a bear market. Keep in mind that market cycles sometimes last several years.

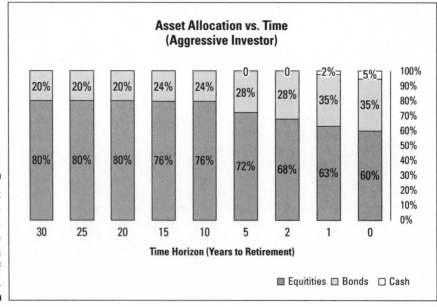

Figure 68-1: A more-drastic change within ten years of retirement.

As you make this transition, note that your personal risk tolerance hasn't changed. You may be tempted to keep the throttle wide open with higher-risk investments; however, you have to let your time horizon trump your attitude about risk.

In the final stage of the process, you'll need to convert enough funds into cash-like instruments to cover retirement expenses over a one- or two-year period. This reserve may seem excessive, but it provides a buffer, giving you more control over when to liquidate assets for income.

Moderate investor

As a moderate investor, you can stomach a loss — within limits — but a more balanced portfolio helps you sleep better at night. After you've developed a moderate portfolio, your transition path to retirement should be a breeze. Compared to the aggressive investor, the required changes are less severe and can begin later. Remember — your risk tolerance has already reduced the volatility in your portfolio. Start the process five years before retiring, as Figure 68-2 illustrates.

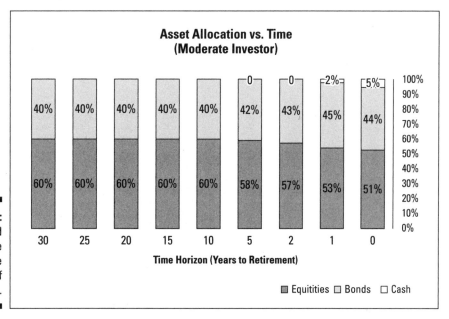

Figure 68-2:
A fairly mild change within five years of retirement.

Conservative investor

As the conservative investor, you enjoy watching the money flow while the market goes strong. Then the money stops coming in — and you go a while without. You begin to think, what if the money flow never starts up again? Do you need a different investment? Does this sound familiar? If so, you can't handle high gear! And your portfolio should look like Figure 68-3.

In this case, your risk tolerance takes precedence over time horizon as a controlling factor in your portfolio design. You may not even need to change the pace — you're already in first gear. There's absolutely nothing wrong with that. A portfolio that exceeds your risk tolerance is like an accident waiting to happen. During a bear market, you'll be pressured to sabotage your plan by selling off assets at precisely the wrong time.

A highly conservative asset allocation 30 years before retirement may make it impossible to amass enough wealth for a comfortable retirement. Make sure you have realistic expectations and that your investment returns will be adequate to achieve your goals. If not, you may be tempted to play catch-up and assume too much risk later on.

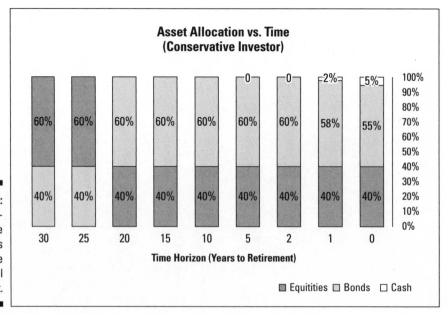

Figure 68-3:
Conserv-
ative
portfolios
receive
minimal
adjustment.

Transition to a More Conservative Asset Allocation

As soon as you have an appropriate transition path for your portfolio, you need a plan to manage the process. Here are some suggestions.

Use new contributions to revise the asset mix

If you're making significant contributions to your retirement savings, you can change your portfolio's asset allocation by simply applying a more conservative mix to all new investments.

Consider the following example: Your current age is 50, and you plan to retire in 15 years. You have $800,000 in current savings, 80 percent of which is equities ($640,000) and 20 percent of which is fixed income ($160,000). Your goal is to steadily transition your asset allocation to a 76-24 split in five years. Your annual contributions, including employer match, total $24,000 per year. The solution? Designate a 50-50 allocation to all new savings. In five years, your overall portfolio (ignoring growth) will stand at $700,000 equities (76 percent) and $220,000 fixed income (24 percent).

Modify your rebalancing plan

One way to change your asset allocation is to incorporate a shift in your asset mix while carrying out a typical portfolio rebalancing program. Normally, *rebalancing* involves swapping funds to restore a portfolio to your original asset allocation targets. Some investors may choose to rebalance on some regular basis — annually is usually sufficient.

Alternatively, you can establish a predetermined deviation trigger, which signals the need to rebalance. For example, if your desired mix is 60-40, you can opt to rebalance whenever your allocation in equities either exceeds 65 percent or falls below 55 percent.

Sometimes during a market decline, your portfolio may even self-adjust to a more conservative allocation. In this event, a corrective change may not be required and you can avoid selling equities during a down cycle. Conversely, you may see equity allocation increase during a period of market growth. This provides a win-win opportunity to benefit from market timing — you'll be selling appreciated stock to reduce your asset allocation below its prior level.

Strategy #77 names a rebalancing plan that can take you through retirement.

#69

Minimize Your Portfolio Risk

- -

By William Keffer, ChFC, CFP

- -

You may be bearing down on retirement with a full head of steam. It's going to be a fast-paced schedule of skydiving, casino trips, and adventure travel for you, right? When it comes to your retirement nest egg, however, you may want to check some of that adventure mentality at the door. Without the right amount of risk in your portfolio and a clear idea of your needs, you may find yourself having to ratchet back your recreation plans — not because you're physically unable but because you can't afford them. In this strategy, you discover how to handle investment risks.

Assess Your Need for Income

You can't assess the risks to your portfolio if you don't know for sure what you need to live on. Therefore, your first step is to assess how much income you'll likely need in retirement.

Identify your basic needs foundation

If you were building a house, would you start by figuring out what kind of doorknobs and decorative lighting you wanted? Hopefully, your first concerns would be a solid foundation and structural design. The foundation of a solid retirement income plan involves knowing your basic living expenses, especially in uncertain times. Even if you're fortunate enough to have substantial savings, it's important to know at a detailed level your basic ongoing living costs.

The old rule of needing 70 to 80 percent of your current income during retirement may or may not apply to you. Do you pay significant job-related expenses like commuting costs, clothing, or professional fees? Yes, these will go down, but things like medical and long-term care insurance and travel and leisure costs will probably go up.

Accept the importance of a (yawn) budget

Fact is, everyone's needs are different, and needs differ from wants and luxuries. Thinking about what you could live without isn't fun, but it's worth taking the time to identify precisely what you need to live on so you can find a way to get a secure income stream or safe assets to support it.

This is where a budget comes in. Look through recent credit card and bank statements. Enter your must-have monthly expenses on a worksheet. Budget tools are available in most personal finance software, or you can do an online search for "budgeting terms." After you enter your current numbers, do a retirement version. Think through it item by item. If your monthly need is greater than your monthly income, the difference must come from your portfolio.

Assess Your Need for Liquidity

Having enough accessible liquid assets on hand when major needs arise is critical, not only to your mental stability but also to protecting your portfolio in uncertain markets. The last thing you want to do is to sell assets in a down market to cover living expenses or a vacation.

Retirement budgeting starts with knowing what you need and when you need it. Basic expenses come first. Make sure you plan for other major expenditures outside your regular budget, such as car replacements, home maintenance projects, or maybe leisure travel. A goal tree that identifies these major liquidity events can help.

Make Sure the Funds Are There

When you know your needs, work on protecting the nest egg you've accumulated. This section explains how to limit investment risks and make sure the money will be available when you need it.

Increase returns while decreasing risk

In an uncertain market, the key to managing risk is diversification. By combining different types of investments, you can get the major benefit of diversification: a relatively high rate of growth, with smaller fluctuations in total value from year to year.

The most common measure of investment risk is called *standard deviation.* Standard deviation measures *volatility,* or how much annual returns deviate from average returns. High volatility means the security's value goes drastically up or down from one year to the next. Consider two baseball players: They have the same number of total bases, but one hits singles every time, while the other swings for the fences, striking out a lot, but also hitting more home runs. Same average, different standard deviation.

Standard deviation — and growth potential — differs for different types of securities:

- ✔ Stocks, which produce the highest long-term returns, have higher standard deviations than bonds.
- ✔ Small company stocks are more volatile but grow more than large company stocks.
- ✔ International company stocks, especially those from emerging markets like India and China, have even higher returns and standard deviations.

The neat thing for investors is that the returns produced by these different types of investments don't move in the same direction at the same time. Their returns aren't correlated. So when stocks are down, bonds may be up. When U.S. markets are in the doghouse, Asian companies' stocks may be booming.

Investing in non-correlated securities produces reduced volatility (or risk) *and* higher returns. Say you have half your money in a U.S. stock fund and the other half in a bond fund. Although the return on the portfolio is simply the average returns of the two funds, the standard deviation, or risk, of the two combined is *less* than the average of the two funds' individual standard deviations.

Manage other risks to your portfolio

In addition to volatility of individual securities, you also face risks related to your life span, market changes, and more. Table 69-1 explains how to minimize risks.

Table 69-1		Risk Management
Risk	*Definition*	*Management Techniques*
Longevity risk	The risk you'll outlive your money	Make sure you have a sensible withdrawal rate. Know what you need for big purchases and for basic expenses. Consider a no-load, low-cost immediate annuity to guarantee an inflation-adjusted lifetime stream of income, at least sufficient to cover basic needs that Social Security and any pension benefits don't cover.
Liquidity risk	The risk that you won't have the cash on hand when you need it, forcing you to sell assets in a down market	Assign chunks of your money to each major goal. Plan to have more accessible liquid assets, such as short-term bonds and cash, in those accounts as the time approaches.

Inflation risk	The risk inflation will outpace the return on your investments, reducing your purchasing power	Long-term inflation is close to 4%; underestimating the effect of price increases can put your portfolio and income stream at risk. Use a realistic inflation factor in your planning. Make sure you have enough equity in your mix to grow your long-term money faster than inflation.
Market risk	The risk that stock and bond markets as a whole will fall	Get a mix of stocks, bonds, and cash that make sense for your risk tolerance and time horizon.
Manager risk	The risk that you'll pick the wrong money manager, your manager will leave, or your actively managed mutual fund will do worse than the market on a risk-adjusted basis	Consider using index mutual funds or exchange-traded funds (ETFs) that attempt to match the performance of their given market sector. Be happy with what the markets give you and enjoy the lower costs.

Follow an investment strategy

When you know the amount for basic living expenses and major goals, use the technique in Table 69-2 to minimize the risk and ensure liquidity for the retirement-funds part of your portfolio.

Table 69-2		**Balancing Risk and Liquidity**		
Account	*Amount*	*Invested In*		*Refill*
Your local bank or credit union	One year's living needs + any goals due this year	50% savings	50% CDs tied to goal dates	From cash reserve account annually
Cash reserve account	Two years' living needs + goals due in two and three years	25% money market	75% high-quality short-term bond fund	From investment portfolio when rebalancing
Investment portfolio	Remainder	Your targeted cash allocation*	Your targeted bond allocation*	From your targeted stock allocation*

*Allocations would be adjusted for bonds and cash held in bank and cash reserve accounts.

#70

Manage Your Qualified Retirement Plan Investments

• •

By Kathy Hankard

• •

*T*raditionally, retirement was a pension plan courtesy of your employer. These days, that's rarely the case. Most folks are responsible for funding their own retirement (with some assistance from Social Security) — and that's just what qualified retirement plans, such as 401(k)s, 403(b)s, and more, were designed to do.

Maybe you've been putting money away in your retirement plan for years. And maybe you've paid attention to how the money was invested — or maybe not. Now's the time to take stock of what you have, determine what you need, and make a plan to get there.

Figure Out What You Have

To determine whether you have enough saved (or whether you're on track to save enough), you first need to know how much you have. Add up the following (and see Strategy #66 for more on retirement income):

- ✔ The vested balance in your current employer plan (if you're not 100 percent vested, you're not entitled to the full balance — if you quit tomorrow, how much would you get?)
- ✔ Money still lingering in an old employer plan
- ✔ Money in IRAs (traditional or Roth)
- ✔ Money in regular, taxable accounts earmarked for retirement

For example, perhaps you have $400,000 in your employer plan, $50,000 in an old plan, $25,000 in an IRA, and $25,000 in other accounts. That gives you a total of $500,000.

Calculate What You Need

Determining how much you have is a lot easier than figuring out how much you'll need. There are a gazillion variables, but follow these steps to get a rough idea:

1. **Determine current living expenses.**

   How much money do you spend each year? If you have no idea, take a look at your tax return and W2. Subtract your actual taxes paid (federal, state, and FICA) from your income. Then subtract any money saved. The remainder is being spent. Here's an example:

   > $100,000 income – $20,000 taxes – $10,000 savings = $70,000

2. **Figure out retirement living expenses.**

   Do you think you'll spend more or less in retirement? Adjust the answer from Step 1 accordingly. (You can say *less* only if you really plan to change your lifestyle — but health care costs will probably take care of that). A paid-off mortgage is a legitimate reason for reduced expenses.

   > $70,000 current living expenses – $12,000 paid off mortgage = $58,000

3. **Determine what you need to provide annually from savings.**

   Subtract your projected Social Security benefit (per your most recent statement) from the answer to Step 2. Also subtract any pensions or other income that'll continue in retirement. That's how much money you'll need to provide each year to fund your retirement.

   > $58,000 retirement living expenses – $20,000 S.S. benefit = $38,000

4. **Take 4 percent of the total you've saved.**

   Use the calculation from the preceding section. The answer is how much your savings could probably provide for you annually.

   > 4% × $500,000 = $20,000

5. **Determine your savings shortage.**

   Take the difference between Step 3 and Step 4, and multiply it by 25. That's about how much *more* you need to save to fund your retirement.

   > ($38,000 – $20,000) × 25 = $450,000

Consolidate Old Plan Assets

If you have money in an old employer plan, you want to roll it into an IRA in most cases. Why? The employer plan probably has a limited set of investment options, and it likely has additional fees that you wouldn't have to pay in an IRA. An IRA has the same tax-deferral benefit.

You can open an IRA at a discount brokerage or a no-load mutual fund company, such as Vanguard, Fidelity, and T. Rowe Price. Note that you can't roll over your current qualified employer plan until you actually quit working for that employer.

Here are some precautions to take when doing a rollover:

✔ Be aware that if you do the IRA rollover with a broker, you'll be charged a commission — up to 5.875 percent of your total account value. Just be sure you ask and know exactly what you're paying.

✔ Be sure you do a direct rollover from your employer plan to your new IRA, or you'll risk owing income tax on the entire amount. Just triple-check with the employer and the new IRA custodian to ensure your rollover is direct. Ideally, the employer and the new custodian will cooperate and do a trustee-to-trustee transfer — so you never actually have access to the money — and therefore can't be taxed or penalized. You never want a rollover IRA check paid directly to you.

✔ Don't invest your IRA rollover in an annuity. The major reason to own an annuity is for tax-deferral. Your retirement accounts are already tax-deferred, so don't pay the extra costs associated with an annuity.

If you have highly appreciated employer stock in a 401(k), a tax strategy known as *net unrealized appreciation* (NUA) may reduce your tax burden. See Strategy #34 for more information. This strategy is complex, so make sure you consult a financial professional.

If you were born before 1936, you may be able to use special ten-year averaging and possibly capital gains treatment on a lump sum distribution from your employer plan. This could result in significant tax benefits and may override the advantages of rolling over your qualified plan into an IRA.

Invest to Supplement Income Needs

By Kevin Brosious, MBA, CPA, CFP

*O*ne of the best ways to save for retirement is through automatic payroll deductions into tax-advantaged retirement plans. These retirement plans are often called *qualified* because of their special tax status. Examples include 401(k)s, IRAs, and SEP IRAs. Because of the special tax status, you're limited on how much you can contribute. Consequently, many people have a significant percentage of their assets outside qualified plans.

For these savings, the goal is to invest in a tax-efficient way while maximizing portfolio growth. Accumulating funds is one thing; keeping them from the tax collector is quite another. This strategy explains how to do both.

Invest with an Eye on the Tax Man

Keep any cash you'll need in three or fewer years in short-term, low volatility investments like short-term CDs or money market funds.

You should be aware of investments that'll harm your portfolio's long-term return if you include them in taxable accounts. If you're in a high marginal federal tax bracket, here's a plan:

- ✔ Put a portion of the money you'll need in three years or less into municipal bond funds. These funds are usually tax-free at the federal level, with some funds also tax-free at the state and local level (triple tax-free).

- ✔ Avoid real estate investment trusts (REITs) and Treasury inflation-protected securities (TIPS). These investments can throw off high taxable dividends. If these investments are appropriate for your portfolio, hold them in qualified accounts. If possible, hold bonds and bond funds in qualified plans, too, because they also generate high tax income.

✔ Use exchange-traded funds (ETFs) instead of mutual funds because the latter have mandatory taxable distributions. If you have to use mutual funds, research carefully to see which funds perform best after taxes.

✔ Use individual stocks only if you can broadly diversify your portfolio and if you have the time and expertise to pick stocks.

To compare the tax-free yield to an equivalent after-tax investment, divide the return of the tax-free investment by 1 minus your marginal tax rate. For example, suppose you're in the 38-percent combined state and federal tax bracket and that an intermediate-term tax-free bond fund currently yields 3 percent. The after-tax equivalent yield is calculated as follows:

$$3 \text{ percent} \div (1 - 38\%) = 4.84\% \text{ equivalent after-tax return}$$

If a taxable bond or bond fund beats that 4.84 percent, invest there instead.

Use Equity Funds for Taxable Investments

In most cases, equity funds are more appropriate for the taxable portion of your portfolio than bond funds. Equity fund returns, which include both capital gains and dividends, are taxed at a maximum federal tax rate of 15 percent (if held for one year or more) and can go as low as zero for taxpayers in the 15-percent or lower bracket. Of course, if you're a retired investor who's currently drawing down your portfolio, keep two to three years' worth of required funds in short-term investment vehicles.

Skipping REITs and TIPS in taxable accounts

REITs and TIPs are outstanding investment choices for most investors but *only* for qualified plans. REIT dividends are nonqualifying dividends, so if you hold them in a taxable account, they're taxed at ordinary income tax rates rather than the maximum dividend tax rate of 15 percent.

TIPS pay semiannual interest, and the principal is continuously adjusted by an amount equal to the consumer price index (CPI). The principal adjustment is payable only when the bond matures, but you owe tax annually on this adjustment. So if you hold TIPS inside a taxable account instead of a tax-advantaged account, you'll pay tax on the "phantom" income (principal adjustment) even though you won't receive any distribution of funds.

Exchange-traded funds (ETFs)

Exchange-traded funds (ETFs) are often a better choice than traditional mutual funds in a taxable portfolio, especially if you're an equity investor. ETFs trade on an exchange, like a stock. In most instances, they're designed to track the performance of an index. ETFs invest in stocks, bonds, commodities, and even currency exchanges. ETFs behave like mutual funds in many ways and also have a couple of advantages:

✔ **Tax advantages:** ETFs have a considerable tax advantage over mutual funds, which is critical when investing outside tax-advantaged accounts. ETFs trade like stock and have similar tax consequences. Unlike most mutual funds, which must declare capital gains on an annual basis, triggering tax consequences for the investor, capital gains on ETFs are typically declared only on the sale of the security. So, like stock, most capital gains (and the associated tax consequence for those gains) can be deferred indefinitely until you want to sell your ETF shares. This tax deferral helps you realize greater compounding and return on your investment.

✔ **Low cost:** ETFs have low annual expenses and no sales fees. Because ETFs trade like a stock, you don't pay a load when purchasing. You do pay normal trading commissions. In addition, ETFs offer some of the lowest annual management expenses in the industry.

Considering that more than 75 percent of mutual funds can't match the performance of their benchmark index, an ETF is a sensible choice for many investors.

After-tax contributions to a 401(k) plan

One investment option is to contribute more to your 401(k) plan. As of this writing, individuals can contribute up to $15,500 pre-tax money per year to their 401(k) or 403(b) plans (or $20,500 if they're age 50 or over). In addition, they can make post-tax contributions up to $46,000 per year.

However, you're better served by making post-tax contributions into ETFs because any distributions from a 401(k) or 403(b) plan are taxed at ordinary income tax rates, versus 15-percent maximum tax rate for capital gains and dividend distributions from your post-tax ETFs. And you have no mandatory minimum distribution required from your post-tax contributions into your ETFs. The same logic applies to funding a nondeductible IRA versus making post-tax contributions into ETFs.

Part VI

Living on Your Investment Earnings and Drawing Down Your Assets

"I just don't know where the money's going."

In this part . . .

In this part, you discover how to maximize your Social Security retirement benefits and any pension benefits you have. You look at the best ways to position your nest egg to provide you with a steady stream of retirement income, whether you're a conservative, moderate, or more aggressive investor. You also discover how to reduce your risk of ever running out of money and how to preserve and transfer assets to your heirs.

Benefits Timing: Make Social Security Work for You

By Tom Nowak, CFP

*U*nlike most investments, your contributions to Social Security weren't exactly voluntary. That tiny issue aside, a great way to make Social Security work for you is to look at it as an investment. Some of the considerations in analyzing investments are evaluating risk, looking at the tax angles, contemplating your time horizon, and controlling your emotions. But one of the most critical decisions in investing is when to buy and when to sell.

The good news is that your *buy* decision has already been made: You're in the program or you aren't. The bad news? The *sell* decision takes some serious thought. For Social Security, the *sell* decision is choosing the date you begin to take benefits. This date may be as early as your 62nd birthday or as late as your 70th birthday. Of course, up until age 70, the later you wait to begin taking benefits, the higher your monthly benefit will be.

Social Security is designed to provide for you in your old age. The built-in incentives to delay starting benefits are significant. Financial planners often provide a source-of-income chart in their planning reports. In many cases, the Social Security component grows to become the largest single source of income in one's later years because Social Security payments have an annual cost of living adjustment. Other income sources either don't keep up with inflation or simply get spent down.

In this strategy, you discover factors that go into the decision of when to start collecting. ***Note:*** As with other investments, Social Security decisions are not one-size-fits-all. The government-sponsored Web site www.ssa.gov is chock full of information that you should become familiar with.

You don't have to apply for Social Security benefits and retire at the same time. Look at your overall plan for income to see what's in your long-term best interest. See Strategy #66 for more information on how to make all your retirement income work together.

Look at the Tax Angles

As with other investments, one of the secrets of success is to understand the tax benefits and the tax traps. Look at the big picture to develop a strategy that avoids unnecessary taxes (as the saying goes, it's not what you earn; it's what you keep — legally). Here are two particular considerations to keep in mind:

- ✔ If you start taking your Social Security payout too early, before your full retirement age (between ages 65 and 67, depending upon your year of birth), you'll be subject to a 50 percent tax on earned income above the allowed limit for the year. In 2008, this limit is $13,560. (Check out *Working after Retirement For Dummies,* by Lita Epstein, for more information.)

- ✔ Social Security benefits may be taxable if your other income — including pensions, wages, interest, and dividends — plus half of your Social Security exceeds a base amount of $25,000 for singles or $32,000 for married couples. The tax may be anywhere from 50 to 85 percent of your Social Security benefit, depending on how much you exceed the base amount.

You can view delaying Social Security benefits as a deferred-income strategy, with the goal of maximizing ultimate return and peace of mind as well.

Sometimes things just don't seem to work out. If your nest egg has lost significant value, you may have to work longer to give it a chance to grow back. If you can't work full time, consider part-time work. If you can't work at all, you probably can't consider delaying your Social Security benefit. See Strategy #76 for ideas on how to allocate your remaining assets for this stage of your life.

If looking at the IRS tax tables makes your eyes glaze over, that's understandable. Just be sure to talk to your tax preparer and financial planner before filing for benefits.

Contemplate Your Time Horizon

The purpose of your Social Security income stream is to provide income when you're older and in less of a position to earn wage income. With any luck, you're in good enough health to be more concerned about running out of money than breath. But consider your health when deciding when to begin taking Social Security benefits:

✔ If your doctor is constantly giving you a hard time about a growing number of risk factors, maybe you're a good candidate for taking benefits as soon as possible (typically age 62).

✔ If there's a reasonable chance that you'll live past 80 ("the new 60"), you should consider delaying benefits for what'll seem like a long time — to age 66, 67, or even 70.

Even if you don't expect to live into your 90s, waiting to start your Social Security benefits until age 70 can have a significant effect if you die before your spouse, particularly if your lifetime earnings were much higher than your spouse's. When you die, your spouse has the choice of continuing with his or her own Social Security benefit or choosing to take the benefits of the deceased spouse. Obviously, if your spouse outlives you by many years or even decades, this can really add up.

Control Your Emotions

Finding reasons to make an emotional decision is easy, especially when it comes to money. Given that over 30 million retirees are currently receiving Social Security payments, there are plenty of stories out there to latch onto. If you're facing a Social Security payout decision in the next five to ten years and already thinking of one of the following reasons for taking an early payout, investigate further:

✔ **You don't think you're likely to live past the break-even age or average life expectancy.** According to government data, about one out of four 65-year-olds alive today will make it past age 90. One out of ten will celebrate a 95th birthday. Consider the role your Social Security check may play in your future.

The *break-even age* is the point at which the higher benefits from waiting until age 70 becomes more than the money you received by starting early. For example, suppose you'd get $11,000 per year at age 62, but you'd get $20,000 per year by waiting until age 70. That means that you received $88,000 by the time you were 70, and the break-even is age 79 ($88,000 divided by the difference between $11,000 and $20,000 is about 9). If you live beyond age 79, all things being equal, you would be better off waiting until age 70 to begin your benefits.

✔ **You don't trust the government to continue paying benefits — maybe you'll buy an annuity instead.** If the government runs into trouble, how do you think company- or insurance industry–guaranteed income promises will fare, keeping in mind that they'd be holding a lot of government bonds in their portfolios?

Future benefits may be linked to your total income, so take this into consideration if you anticipate having a high lifetime income. If a couple thousand dollars per month is a big part of your upcoming retirement income plans, then you'll probably fly under the income limits.

✔ **You'll take the payout early and invest it to get a better return.** Nifty idea, but not thrifty. If you can afford to take the investment risk that'd be necessary to beat the rate of return you get by waiting, you probably don't need to take Social Security early and wouldn't want to for tax reasons. If your full retirement age is 67 (that is, if you were born after 1960), your monthly benefits are reduced by about 30 percent. If you were born between 1943 and 1959, you get an additional bonus of 8 percent per year by delaying your start date past your full retirement age. There isn't a low- to no-risk investment strategy around that can deliver those rates of return.

✔ **You don't want to take withdrawals from your IRAs too soon — they need to grow.** Yes, taking Social Security early may allow your IRA to grow for a few years longer. But after that, the smaller government check will probably require even larger IRA withdrawals.

✔ **Ouch! You already started taking benefits early and wish you'd waited. Isn't it too late?** Go to your Social Security office or www.ssa.gov and use Form 521, Request for Withdrawal of Application, to turn the clock back. You can actually halt your current benefits and, after paying back all you've received interest-free, have them restarted at a higher rate, reflecting your current age.

All the preceding scenarios are well and good, but for many, many people, the argument for cashing in on Social Security early is much simpler and much more emotional: They really need the money now. And that's a great reason. However, consider one point: You'll probably really, really need the larger amount later, so try to postpone benefits as long as possible. Each month you delay between the ages of 62 and 70, the amount you receive for the rest of your life goes up. Future inflation can add to your regret over a premature starting point. Consider that in 1979, 1980, and 1981, annual cost of living increases were 9.9 percent, 14.3 percent, and 11.2 percent, respectively.

Get the Most Out of Your Pension

By Liane Warcup, CFP

Most people who are nearing retirement and have an employer pension are looking forward to a monthly paycheck. Unfortunately, many of those people are fuzzy on the details. More than 44 million workers from a variety of industries (including teachers, state and federal employees, construction and manufacturing workers, financial services employees, and many more) can expect pension income during retirement. Each person's benefits will be different depending on

- The employer's formula for determining benefits
- Whether cost of living adjustments are included
- Which distribution option is selected
- When benefits begin for the retiree

During times of economic uncertainty, understanding and protecting your pension income are doubly important, because during hard times, many companies lay off workers or force workers into early retirement. If you're prematurely forced out of your job along with many others, replacement jobs can be scarce. You may have to take your pension earlier than you want to or earlier than is optimal.

Take a Look at Your Pension

Answer *yes* or *no* to the following questions to see how much you know about your personal pension:

- I have a recent pension benefit statement and I understand what it says.
- I know whether my pension includes cost of living adjustments.
- I know what distribution (payment) options are available.
- I know how soon/late I can begin drawing my pension.
- I know whether my pension provides a disability payment.
- I know my pension's survivor benefits.

If you answered *no* to any of these questions, don't just sit there — talk to your employer to find out what your pension will do for you.

Meanwhile, read on for the basics to understand why knowing your options is so important, especially in difficult times.

Determine Your Benefits

Somewhere in all those documents you glanced at and then filed (or possibly threw away) when you were hired, you can find a formula for calculating your estimated pension benefit. If you can't find this paperwork (called a *summary plan description*), request a copy from your human resources department for your records. One of the most common benefit formulas is based on the total number of years of service multiplied by a percentage of an average of your final years of earnings. Usually, the longer you work at the same company, the larger your current income and the larger your pension income during retirement.

Before you get too excited about this pension income, keep in mind that employers usually design pension benefits to replace about 40 to 60 percent of income, anticipating that Social Security benefits and private savings will cover the difference.

Ask for a pension benefit statement from your employer if you haven't received one in the last year. This statement should be provided annually and should summarize your pension benefit.

Consider Cost of Living Adjustments (COLA)

Receiving a regular income for the rest of your life sounds like a good deal. But does the dollar amount increase each year to compensate for inflation? If it does, stand up and cheer. You have a pension that should keep up with the rising costs of goods and services. Table 73-1 shows the increasing value of a pension with a cost of living adjustment (COLA). As you can see, a little COLA in your pension makes a big difference over time.

Table 73-1	The Effects of COLA on Pension Benefits	
Age	**Pension (No COLA)**	**Pension (3% COLA)**
65	$3,000/month	$3,000/month
75	$3,000/month	$4,032/month
85	$3,000/month	$5,418/month

If you don't already know, find out whether your pension includes cost of living adjustments. This has grave implications on how much money you need to save outside of pension plans for your future retirement. If your expenses already outweigh the combined expected income from your pension and Social Security, and if your pension doesn't have a COLA, the disparity between income and expenses is going to grow rapidly over time. You'll have to make up for that disparity with your savings and other assets.

Know Your Distribution Options (How Much Money and for How Long?)

When you're ready to retire, you may have several pension payment options to consider. Here are the most common:

- **Single life annuity:** You receive monthly income payments for your life only. So if you're married and you die shortly after you retire, your dearly beloved gets to deal with the loss of you *and* your pension unless you have a hefty life insurance policy to make up the difference. This is the largest payment option available. With some pension plans, this is the only option available.

- **Single life period certain:** Payments continue at least for your lifespan or a set number of years (usually 10 or 20 years), whichever is longer. The amount of this payment is less than for the single life annuity because of the guaranteed payment stream for a set number of years.

- **Joint and survivor annuity:** You receive reduced monthly income payments for life. When you die, your spouse receives a survivor benefit for life (usually 50, 75, or 100 percent of your payment).

- **Lump sum payout:** Your employer converts your monthly retirement benefit into a single lump sum payment. If this is an option, you may even get to choose between a full lump sum payment and a partial lump sum combined with a reduced annuity option. Here are some additional issues to ponder:

- You should roll this lump sum into an IRA to defer taxes. If you don't roll your lump sum into an IRA, you pay taxes on the entire amount paid out to you. And if you're younger than 59¹/₂ and you don't roll the funds into an IRA, you'll likely pay a 10-percent penalty in addition to regular income taxes on the lump sum amount. (Exceptions include retiring at age 55 or later, disability, certain medical expenses, and more — consult IRS publication 575, an accountant, or a financial planner for details.)

- If you choose the lump sum, make sure your retiree health insurance coverage (if any) won't change.

- Your lump sum rollover to an IRA must be invested just like all your other financial assets.

- You can purchase your own low-cost annuity with all or part of this money, but make sure that any annuity you pick is at least as good as the pension annuity you've turned down, especially if your pension has a COLA. However, it's highly unlikely that a commercial annuity can compete with your company pension regarding the size of monthly payments and the Pension Benefit Guarantee Corporation (PBGC) guarantee that's available for qualified pension plans.

- Don't even be tempted to go on a crazy spending spree and deplete your nest egg.

So which distribution option should you take? This decision requires you to evaluate your entire retirement income picture. At least consider the following:

- ✔ How much Social Security income you'll receive

- ✔ When to begin your Social Security payments

- ✔ How much, if any, your pension will offset some of your Social Security benefit

- ✔ How much you've accumulated in your personal savings and investment accounts

- ✔ Your estimate of your retirement living expenses

- ✔ If you die, how dependent your spouse will be on your pension

Your choice of payment options is permanent (no pressure!). If these choices make your head spin, consult with a financial planner or two for some pension planning advice. See Strategies #54 and #55 for more information on accumulating money for retirement and making sure it lasts a lifetime (or two).

Get Your Money at the Right Time

Although many pensions are designed to begin paying at age 65, some plans give you a range of choices. Pension benefits may be available as early as age 55 or any time after you retire. Early pension payments will be smaller than if you wait until your normal retirement age (much like early Social Security benefits are reduced). Sometimes you may have great reasons to take advantage of an early payout; examples include locking in healthcare benefits or ensuring a larger survivor benefit.

Some pensions allow you to delay taking payment until long after your retirement. You may find this hard to believe, but some people actually decide to delay their pension payments. People who delay are usually still in the workforce and have earnings pushing them into a higher tax bracket than their future retirement tax bracket. They may wait until they're fully retired because they don't need the pension income while they're still working, and they don't want to pay the higher taxes. Plus, the monthly pension benefit increases with age.

Find out when your pension is available to you. Check with your employer or read the summary plan document to see when you can start your pension payments.

Other pieces of the pension puzzle

The following issues may crop up depending on your situation:

✔ **Incapacitation:** Find out what the rules are if you become disabled before retirement. Some pensions, including Social Security, provide a benefit usually up until age 65, when the regular pension benefit begins.

✔ **Survivorship:** What happens to your pension if you die just *before* you retire? Will your spouse have a pension benefit? How much? If your personal retirement plan is dependent on your pension income, the survivorship question is crucial! If your plan doesn't have decent pre-retirement survivor benefits, you may need to increase your life insurance to cover this risk.

#74

Understand Your Employer Retirement Plan

By Brooke Salvini, CPA/PFS, CCPS

Did you save money in a favorite piggy bank when you were a child? Do you remember the exciting day you finally got to shake out the bank, count your savings, and decide how to spend your money? As a new retiree, you're turning your bank upside down. You still need to be diligent about rebalancing , making smart investment choices, and managing expenses. But you also need to know the ins and outs of shaking loose your retirement savings so you pay minimum taxes and no penalties. This strategy explains how.

Read Up and Talk about It

First, get a copy of your plan summary document, either from your human resources department or benefits coordinator or from a download on your company Web site.

The next step is to schedule an appointment with your human resources department. Ask to have your withdrawal choices fully explained, including possible consequences — that is, taxes and penalties — based on your current age and employment status (retirement isn't necessarily the same as not working, especially if you're a baby boomer breaking all past retirement notions).

Your company's plan may or may not mirror the current tax laws regarding employer retirement plans.

This is also the right time to meet with your financial advisor. Your advisor can help you sort through the various withdrawal options for your retirement savings based your personal goals and needs.

Answer These Questions before You Break the Bank

Especially in uncertain economic environments, you should answer these questions before tapping into your retirement savings:

- ✔ What's your current age?
- ✔ What are your hopes and dreams for retirement?
- ✔ What are your other sources of retirement income?
- ✔ How long do you need your savings to last?
- ✔ How much do you need to live comfortably every month?
- ✔ Do you have an immediate need for a lump sum of money?

Don't expect to answer these questions in five minutes. Everyone has a unique vision of the perfect retirement. A variety of online calculators and resources, such as 360 Degrees of Financial Literacy (www.360financialliteracy.org), can help you answer these questions.

Important ages to keep in mind when planning withdrawals include the following:

- ✔ **Age 50:** Age 50 is the same as age 55 for some types of public safety employees. (If you work in a public service capacity, check with your plan administrator or tax preparer to see whether you qualify).

- ✔ **Age 55:** If you leave your job between 55 and 59$\frac{1}{2}$, you don't pay a 10 percent early withdrawal penalty on 401(k)s and other qualified retirement savings (not including IRAs).

- ✔ **Age 59$\frac{1}{2}$:** The 10 percent early withdrawal penalty expires. (***Note:*** But to withdraw savings from a 457(b), you have to retire or turn 70$\frac{1}{2}$).

- ✔ **Age 62:** This is the earliest age you can obtain Social Security benefits.

- ✔ **Age 70$\frac{1}{2}$ + April 1:** Here, you begin required minimum distributions (RMDs) from employer plans and IRAs (except Roth IRAs). If you're still working and own less than 5 percent of the company, you can delay RMDs from your current employer's qualified plans. (***Note:*** Not all plans allow you to delay RMDs.)

Even though you avoid the 10 percent penalty with proper planning, income taxes will always be payable on retirement savings withdrawals except for Roth IRAs and Roth 401(k)s.

Know Your Options when Leaving a Job

Most near retirees are bombarded with a laundry list of important decisions regarding the future. This can be overwhelming, but don't let that stop you from making smart choices about the savings you've accumulated in the company retirement plan. The next sections cover the three options to consider for your savings when leaving employment.

Leave your money in your employer retirement savings plan

If the plan allows and you're very satisfied with the available investment choices and performance, leave your money right where it is. You can always roll your money to an IRA later.

This is also a good choice if you need maximum protection from creditors because of potential lawsuits, bankruptcy, or other situations. Asset protection for qualified retirement plans is more comprehensive than for IRAs. Borrowing from an IRA isn't permitted, so if this is an important option for you, leave your money in your existing plan (or roll your savings into a new employer's plan).

Also take retirement age into account. At age 55, withdrawals from qualified plans aren't subject to the 10 percent early withdrawal penalty if you're no longer employed by the company. With an IRA, you have to wait until age $59^{1}/_{2}$ to avoid this penalty.

Take a lump sum (or partial) distribution

A lump sum distribution is almost always a bad idea. Because income taxes are due on all distributions (lump sum or partial), a large lump sum distribution will likely force you into a higher tax bracket. This should be your choice of last resort. However, if this is your only way to pay a major expense, you can take a portion of your savings as a lump sum distribution and roll the balance of your savings into an IRA.

If you own highly appreciated company stock in your retirement plan, you can benefit from favorable capital gains tax rates on the net unrealized appreciation (NUA) on the stock. You pay ordinary income tax at the time of withdrawal on the cost of the stock, but when you sell the stock, the NUA is taxed at the more favorable long-term capital gains rate. NUA is a complex tax issue that you should discuss with an accountant or other professional.

Roll your money into an IRA

Most of the time, rolling your retirement plan savings into an IRA is best. IRAs have greater flexibility both with investment choices and withdrawal options. (See Strategy #75 for info on IRA withdrawal options).

The most important thing to remember about a rollover is to request a direct trustee-to-trustee transfer. A direct trustee-to-trustee rollover saves you from unexpected and potentially nasty tax consequences. If you receive the check made out to your new IRA trustee (this happens fairly often), don't worry; this is still a direct rollover — just forward the check on to your new trustee.

Cha-ching! Shaking the Bank

You've decided where to stash your retirement savings, but how much and when should you withdraw? In an uncertain economy, that's the million-dollar question. The longer you can allow your retirement plan savings to grow tax-deferred (or tax-free in the case of Roth contributions), the better.

Many new retirees mistakenly overspend in the early years. Don't deprive yourself, but remember that your retirement could be 30 to 40 years. The cost of the health care you'll probably need in later retirement continues to increase faster than most other expenses.

Determining the correct withdrawal rate for your situation requires many considerations, but a general rule is to withdraw no more than 4 percent of your total savings in any one year. If your investment returns are poor in a particular year, you should revise this percentage downward. And conversely, you can revise your withdrawal upward if you make great returns one year.

Timing your withdrawals from one tax year to the next provides another opportunity to reduce income taxes. For example, if you have unusually high medical expenses in a particular calendar year that qualify as itemized deductions, you may want to take some of your retirement withdrawls in December instead of waiting until January as a way of balancing your income and expenses.

The benefits of tax deferral don't last forever. On April 1 of the year after you turn $70^1/_2$, you have to begin *required minimum distributions* (RMDs) from employer retirement plans and IRAs. However, if you're working at age $70^1/_2$ and you're not more than a 5 percent owner of the company, you can postpone RMDs in that employer's qualified retirement plan until you retire a second time, but you have to take RMDs from all other retirement accounts.

#75

Take Stock of Your Individual Retirement Accounts (IRAs)

By Rick DeChaineau, CSA, CRPC, CFP

After all those years of biting the bullet to put money in your individual retirement account (IRA), it's finally time to begin taking money out. But that's not as easy as withdrawing the amount you want when you want it. This strategy tells you how IRA withdrawals are taxed (or not) and gives you advice on how to best manage your IRA accounts.

Know the Taxes on Withdrawals

Knowing the basics of how IRA withdrawals are taxed can save you money as you deal with uncertainties during your retirement.

Traditional IRA withdrawals

You can take withdrawals from a traditional IRA without penalty after you reach age $59^{1}/_{2}$. You can also take withdrawals before then without penalty under special circumstances. You're required to take withdrawals by April 1 of the year following the year you reach age $70^{1}/_{2}$. To avoid taking two distributions in one year, take the first distribution in the year you reach $70^{1}/_{2}$ and your second distribution the following year.

Your IRA will hold one of the following:

✔ **Only pre-tax contributions:** If you didn't pay income tax on your contribution in the year you made it, you made it pre-tax.

✔ **Only after-tax contributions:** If you did pay income tax on the contribution in the year you made it, you made it after-tax.

✔ **Both pre-tax and after-tax contributions:** If you have an IRA to which you made both pre-tax and after-tax contributions, you have to track both separately so you know how much of the growth is attributed to each portion.

If your traditional IRA contains only pre-tax contributions, you pay ordinary income-tax rates on the entire amount you take out at the time of withdrawal. This includes both the contribution amount and the tax-deferred growth.

If some or all of your IRA includes after-tax contributions, your withdrawals from the after-tax portion of your IRA (or a separate after-tax IRA) will be a proportionate mix of taxable and tax-free money. Here's an example: Suppose you have a traditional IRA with $10,000 of post-tax contributions (your basis). During 2007, you withdrew $10,000. On December 31, 2007, your balance was $90,000.

On IRS Form 8606 (where you report after-tax contributions and calculate how much of your distributions/conversions are taxable) you're asked to total your year-end balance and any distributions or Roth IRA conversions for the year. For 2007, your total was $100,000 ($90,000 balance plus the $10,000 distribution).

Because your $10,000 of pre-tax money (cost basis) in the IRA is 10 percent of the year-end total (of $100,000), 10 percent of your distribution will be tax-free ($10,000 × 0.1 = $1,000) and the other $9,000 will be taxable. Your pre-tax contributions (cost basis) in the IRA are reduced by the $1,000 tax-free distribution and now total $9,000.

The IRS doesn't care whether you have one or a dozen IRA accounts. It looks at all your IRA money (traditional, SEP, and SIMPLE) as one big IRA for purposes of determining the proportion that's tax-free.

Roth IRA withdrawals

Roth IRAs have three big advantages over traditional IRAs. They have no mandatory age at which you must start taking withdrawals, so if you don't need the income, you may never take a withdrawal during your lifetime. The second advantage is that qualified withdrawals from a Roth IRA are tax-free. Third, you don't have to withdraw a required minimum amount at age 70^1/$_2$.

Two sets of criteria determine whether a withdrawal from your Roth IRA is a *qualified* withdrawal. First, the distribution must be one of the following:

- ✔ Made on or after the date you turn 59^1/$_2$
- ✔ Made to your beneficiary after you die
- ✔ Made to you after you become disabled within the IRS definition
- ✔ Used to pay for qualified first-time homebuyer expenses

Second, the five-tax-year rule must be met. This means that you have to wait five years from the year in which you made your first contribution before you can withdraw the earnings on your contributions without penalty.

You can withdraw the amount of your contributions from a Roth IRA at any time.

Match Account Contents with Tax Treatment

During retirement, your IRA and Roth IRA will likely hold only a portion of your retirement assets. Your first step in managing your taxable income is to ensure the right assets are in the right accounts. This assumes you already have various types of other taxable investment accounts. Do *not* pull money out of an IRA just to create the other account types.

Because your traditional IRA withdrawals will be taxed as ordinary income, you'll want to hold ordinary-income assets, such as bonds, CDs, and so on, in your IRA.

Your personal (taxable) accounts should hold investments that are eligible to be taxed at the (currently) lower long-term capital gain and qualified dividend rates. Examples of these investments include stocks and equity mutual funds. Tax-free assets, such as tax-free municipal bonds, also belong in your personal account.

If you intend for your children to someday inherit your Roth, you can invest more aggressively in your Roth account.

Balance Your Account Actions for Minimal Tax Impact

If you want to pay the least amount of income tax in retirement (doesn't everyone?), you may want to balance taxable income from your personal account with income from tax-exempt assets. If you need more income than you're receiving from your employer retirement plan and your IRA withdrawals, you may want to balance that taxable income with withdrawals from your Roth IRA. You don't want to prematurely take out money that can otherwise continue to grow tax-deferred or tax-free. Finding the right balance takes some planning.

The following steps help you figure out how to best integrate IRA and Roth IRA withdrawals with the rest of your income:

1. **Figure out how much income you'll need each year.**

   See Strategy #55 for details.

2. **Identify how much income you'll receive from various non-IRA sources, such as your**

   - Pension

   - 401(k), SIMPLE, SEP

   - Deferred compensation plan

   - Annuity

   - Rental property

   - Personal (non-qualified) investments

   - Other

   Do you have a shortfall? If so, how much will you need to withdraw from your IRA/Roth IRA each year? When you're 70$\frac{1}{2}$ and older, you'll be required to take a minimum amount of distribution from your qualified retirement plan assets and your traditional IRA. These distributions will be counted as part of your taxable income.

3. **Tally how much of that income is taxable and what your tax bracket is.**

4. **Determine the mix of traditional IRA (taxable) and Roth IRA (tax-free) income to withdraw, keeping in mind the amount of your required minimum distribution, if applicable.**

   If you don't need to tap your traditional IRA for current income, look at what effect the required minimum distributions (RMDs) will have on your taxes when you turn 70$\frac{1}{2}$. If you have a large IRA balance, taking withdrawals before 70$\frac{1}{2}$, or converting amounts to a Roth IRA to reduce your RMDs later, may make sense.

Whatever your current situation, review these estimates annually because tax laws and your investment balances change.

To Convert or Not to Convert? That Is the Question

As of the writing of this book, you're allowed to convert money from the following accounts into a Roth IRA if your modified adjusted gross income (MAGI) isn't more than $100,000:

- ✔ IRA
- ✔ Qualified pension, profit-sharing, or stock bonus plan (including a 401(k) plan)
- ✔ Tax-sheltered annuity (403(b) plan)
- ✔ Deferred compensation plan of a state or local government (section 457(b) plan)
- ✔ Pension

Beginning in 2010, this income limit is lifted, and you'll be able to convert money from your IRA to a Roth no matter how much you make. You'll even be able to spread the taxes on the conversion between 2011 and 2012!

But wait! Converting traditional IRA money to a Roth means you'll pay tax on the converted amount now to get tax-free withdrawals later. Is this a good idea? As you know from figuring out how to balance your traditional IRA and Roth withdrawals, your tax brackets — now and when you're taking required minimum distributions (RMDs) — will drive this decision.

If, when you start taking RMDs, you estimate you'll be in the same tax bracket or lower than you're in now, don't convert. However, experts feel that tax rates are unlikely to go lower and very likely will go up in the future, which makes converting to a Roth IRA more attractive.

If you're able to reduce your future tax bracket by withdrawing or converting to a Roth now — without pushing yourself into a higher bracket by doing so — do it!

With money in a Roth IRA, you'll have the tools to manage your IRAs to minimize your tax bill. This is a big benefit in uncertain times.

Use Your Taxable, Partially Taxable, and Non-Taxable Investments Wisely

By Jeff Alderfer, CFP, AIF

*A*fter you spend a lifetime accumulating a tidy nest egg, you get to figure out how to spend it. It's not as simple as just buying all you need and some of what you want. You need to pay attention to which investments you spend now, which you spend later, and which you're going to leave to your children. What's more, uncertain times can affect taxes as well as investing, so you need a plan that considers both. Without one, you're probably going to give more money to Uncle Sam than you need to. So in this strategy, you discover how to spend the money you've invested while minimizing the taxes you have to pay.

Separate Your Money into Tax Buckets

Sometimes it's easier to explain finances by using a bucket brigade rather than a spreadsheet. If you're like most people, your investment buckets are scattered about: an IRA here, a couple of old 401(k)s there, a taxable broker- age account, a money market account, and maybe an annuity. And here's where the bucket concept makes things easier: Don't think about all the dif- ferent accounts you have — just think about which tax bucket your money is in. Following are the only three tax buckets:

✔ **Bucket #1, the tax-free bucket:** This bucket contains all the accounts that will never be taxed. Specifically, this bucket includes Roth IRAs and Roth 401(k)s. No matter how much money you take out of this bucket in retirement, you won't have to pay income taxes on it.

Because this bucket contains only tax-free money, you can take out as much or as little as you want in retirement, with no tax liability.

✔ **Bucket #2, the tax-deferred bucket:** The taxes have been deferred for the accounts in this bucket. Some specific accounts include traditional IRAs, 401(k)s, 403(b)s, tax-deferred annuities (variable and fixed), 457(b) plans, and some other more exotic retirement accounts. See Strategies #33, #34, and #35 for more information about retirement accounts.

In general, any money you withdraw from your traditional IRA, 401(k), 403(b), or annuity is taxed as ordinary income, so you're taxed in whatever federal tax bracket you're part of (as determined by your family income). If you've made non-deductible contributions to your traditional IRAs or 401(k)s, these contributions will be taxed only on the growth, because you've already paid taxes on the contributions. If you have any of these hybrids, be sure you carefully document the contributions. But in general, plan on paying income taxes on any withdrawals from any account in the tax-deferred bucket.

✔ **Bucket #3, the taxable bucket:** This bucket contains accounts that receive no special tax treatment, and it includes brokerage accounts, money market accounts, and savings accounts. Here you pay taxes as you go, on a yearly basis.

The rules for taxation are the same as they were during your working years — that is, long-term capital gains and dividends are currently taxed at the more favorable rate of 15 percent. (See Strategy #32 for a more thorough explanation of taxable investments.)

Consolidating all the accounts within each bucket makes your life considerably easier. For example, you can roll all your 401(k)s and traditional IRAs (inside Bucket #2) into a single, monster, traditional IRA. Not only does this strategy make it easier to track your investments, but it also reduces the blizzard of paperwork you receive for each of the smaller, individual accounts. Taking this step doesn't change your tax liability, but it does make your life simpler!

Spend the Money in Your Buckets

After you figure out which tax bucket holds each of your investments, it's time for the fun part: How should you spend your money? Here's a good general guideline:

✔ **Bucket #1, the tax-free bucket:** Use the money in this bucket *last*. It'll never be taxed, and if you never get around to spending it, your heirs can spend it tax-free as well.

✔ **Bucket #2, the tax-deferred bucket:** Okay, pay attention here. Years ago, financial advisors used to recommend that you leave your tax-deferred accounts untouched as long as possible to let them compound free of taxes. However, given the very real prospect of higher tax rates in the future, drawing down these funds sooner rather than later may be beneficial — even though this advice goes against the conventional wisdom of deferring taxes as long as possible (the mantra of all Certified Public Accountants). Drawing money from this bucket gives you the added benefit of reducing the amount of your nest egg that will be subject to required minimum distributions (RMDs) when you turn $70\frac{1}{2}$.

✔ **Bucket #3, the taxable bucket:** Although tax rates are likely to climb in the future, capital gains taxes (those taxes that are due when you sell an investment) are likely to remain lower than ordinary income taxes. And these assets receive a "stepped up" basis when you die, so if you never get around to them, your heirs can likely enjoy more favorable taxation as well.

To hedge your bets (or "diversify your risk" in financial planner–speak) in uncertain times, plan to initially take money out of Bucket #2 and Bucket #3 each year of your retirement. One clever way to apply this strategy is to draw from your tax-deferred (Bucket #2) accounts first, until reaching the upper limit of your current federal tax bracket (remember to include any taxable Social Security payments), and then draw the remainder of your spending from your taxable accounts in Bucket #3 (taxed at the more favorable long-term capital gains rate). This way, you're maxing out the lower tax bracket with Bucket #2 and then using Bucket #3 to round out your spending needs.

Here's a brief example:

Total funds available in retirement:

Tax Bucket #1:$100,000 in a Roth IRA

Tax Bucket #2:$100,000 in a traditional IRA

Tax Bucket #3:$100,000 in a brokerage account

Total funds needed: $12,000 per year

Assume your pension/Social Security income puts you just $7,000 below the top of the 15-percent federal tax bracket. Using this strategy, you withdraw $7,000 from your traditional IRA, which fills up that 15-percent tax bracket. Then, to provide the rest of the money you need, you sell $5,000 worth of your brokerage account assets — on which you owe just 15 percent of the capital gains. If you were to instead withdraw the entire $12,000 from your traditional IRA, that extra $5,000 would be taxed at the rate of 25 percent.

Let Your Kids Spend the Money: Estate Planning Issues

Although some people hope to pass on just as they feed their very last dollar into the vending machine, they'll probably have at least some money left over when they go. Current estate laws treat each tax bucket differently. Here's a snapshot:

- ✔ **The tax-free bucket:** One of the best reasons to leave money in Bucket #1 for as long as possible is this: When you pass, your heirs won't have to pay any income taxes on any of the money from this bucket. They'll have to withdraw the inherited funds over their remaining lifetime(s), but the money will be tax-free!

- ✔ **The tax-deferred bucket:** If your heirs inherit any money from Bucket #2, they'll have to pay ordinary income taxes on any money they withdraw. The rate they pay depends on their individual tax brackets when they withdraw the funds. So if you have two kids and two IRAs (one traditional, one Roth), consider how you can fairly divide them up.

- ✔ **The taxable bucket:** Taxable investments have an extra bonus. When you die, the value of these assets will be "stepped up" to the value at your date of death. Then, when your heirs eventually sell the assets, they'll be taxed only on the increase in value since your death. As an added bonus, they'll be taxed at the more favorable long-term capital gains rate, currently 15 percent. Thus, if you have any highly appreciated assets, you may want to hold on to them, if possible, and let the kids inherit them.

Allocate Assets in the Active Stage of Retirement

By Kay Conheady, CFP

*W*ith good health, you'll be active and living independently for the majority of your retirement. You may plan to travel, spend time with family and friends, pursue your favorite hobbies, volunteer, or even start your own business. To fund those dreams, you now need to structure your nest egg to provide regular income that meets the following criteria:

✔ It adequately supplements pension and/or Social Security income to fund your desired standard of living.

✔ It'll be there in both good and uncertain economic time periods throughout your retirement.

✔ It lasts as long as you need it to.

This strategy explains how to get your portfolio management off to a good start as you begin tapping into your nest egg.

Understand Retirement Uncertainty

Knowing which uncertainties will impact the success of your retirement can help you better plan and manage your assets and your income. Here are several risks you need to consider:

✔ **Longevity risk:** The risk that you'll run out of dollars before you run out of breaths

✔ **Inflation risk:** The risk that the cost of everything will go up faster than your income

- ✔ **Market risk:** The risk that you'll have to sell investments when they're down in value in order to produce needed income

- ✔ **Timing risk:** The risk that you'll experience large investment losses in the first three to five years of retirement

Your best defense is to hold off on retiring until you have a comprehensive plan to protect against these four risks. Asset allocation is your primary tool to manage them. Monitoring your plan and making periodic adjustments is also part of the process.

Decide Whether to Use Annuities

Allocating some of your nest egg to an immediate annuity creates a stream of income you can't outlive. Such a strategy can help overcome longevity risk. (For info on fixed and variable annuities, see Strategies #19 and #22.) If you're married, buy a joint and survivor benefit so the surviving spouse will continue to receive income.

Before putting your all or a portion of you nest egg into an annuity, even one that'll keep pace with inflation and fully fund your desired standard of living, understand that with an annuity, you give your money to an insurance company in exchange for the promise of a lifetime income. Once initiated, or *annuitized,* annuity income can't be stopped or changed, even if you no longer need that income or need additional money for unexpected expenses. Be sure to read the annuity policy and ask questions about how the policy works.

Deciding how much of your nest egg to allocate to an annuity is a real challenge. You have to assess the following to make a wise decision:

- ✔ The probability that you'll burn through your assets prematurely

- ✔ Your tolerance for investment risk

- ✔ The long-term trend of the stock market

If the probability of exhausting your assets prematurely is high, your tolerance for investment risk is low, or the stock market appears to be peaking or in the early stages of a downswing, consider allocating 60 to 80 percent of your nest egg to an immediate annuity.

Allocate Your Nest Egg to Stocks, Bonds, and Cash

Longevity and inflation risk mandate that you allocate at least some of your nest egg to risky assets — stocks and bonds. These assets can help you stay ahead of inflation, although their returns aren't guaranteed. At the same time, investing in stocks and bonds can increase the uncertainties that may cause your accounts to decrease in value. This section explains how to find — and keep — the right balance.

Decide on your target balance

The first asset allocation decision you have to make is how much to invest in stocks versus bonds and/or cash. As an early stage retiree, a reasonable cash-bond-stock allocation is to keep

- ✔ Three years' worth of annual income in cash
- ✔ Three to five years' worth in bonds
- ✔ The rest in stocks

Using this strategy provides you with income for seven years. You get the opportunity to sell stocks when they're up in order to replace cash and bond assets that are used up by income withdrawals. Meanwhile, the bonds and cash investments help protect you against the large losses the stock market occasionally delivers. Bonds often provide positive returns when stocks are performing negatively, which helps reduce the negative impact on your total investment portfolio.

In early retirement, an allocation of 45 to 60 percent of your portfolio in stocks is reasonable. Allocating more than 60 percent to stocks in the early stages of retirement increases the risk of experiencing large losses, and allocating less than 45 percent increases the risk of depleting your portfolio due to feeble growth.

Diversify your investments

After you choose your overall allocation, you have to actually choose your investments. Here are few bond suggestions:

✔ Diversify and buy lots of different types of bonds, keeping your investment in high-yield bonds relatively low.

✔ The majority of your bonds should be intermediate maturity — between five and ten years. Avoid owning too many bonds or bond funds with maturity dates longer than ten years because these tend to fluctuate in value more dramatically than intermediate- and short-term bonds.

✔ Consider putting 15 to 40 percent of your bond allocation in bonds designed to provide inflation protection. (See Strategy #18 for more information.)

Your stocks should make up 60 percent or less of your total portfolio. As you choose stocks, make sure you adequately diversify into the different classes of stocks, including the following (see Strategies #42 through #45 for more info on diversifying your stock portfolio):

✔ Domestic and foreign

✔ Small and large cap

✔ Growth and value

Generally, growth stocks tend to be riskier than value stocks, international stocks tend to be riskier than domestic stocks, and small company stocks tend to be riskier than large company stocks.

For the cash portion of this portfolio, pursue the highest interest rates available, short of tying up your money in long-maturity CDs. Check out Strategy #17 to help you decide which cash savings vehicles to use during retirement.

Rebalance your investment portfolio

Because you'll be regularly depleting the cash portion of your investment portfolio, you need to periodically adjust the amounts you have in bonds and stocks so that the percentage of each in your total portfolio equals your target asset allocation.

Rebalancing within a taxable account can have potentially expensive tax ramifications. For taxable accounts, you may want to seek the help of a financial advisor who's experienced in retirement investing and taxation.

However, rebalancing within a 401(k) or IRA has no immediate tax ramifications, so the decision to rebalance is much simpler. For early stage retirees who've allocated three years of nest-egg withdrawals to cash and another five years to bonds, the concern is when to replenish the cash reserve. Here are three principles to remember for rebalancing:

- ✔ **Cash:** Replenish your cash stash at least every two years back to the three-year amount. To increase your cash, liquidate bond assets when stocks have performed poorly or use stock assets if they've done well.

- ✔ **Bonds:** Replenish your allocation to bonds back up to three to five years' worth of living expenses when the amount falls below two years' worth. If your bond portfolio exceeds five years' worth of withdrawals, divert assets first to cash and then to stocks to reestablish the target balance.

- ✔ **Stock:** Make sure your stock allocation stays between 45 and 60 percent of your total portfolio. It's better to have more than five to seven years' worth of living expenses in bonds and cash if necessary to keep your stock allocation in check.

If you find that you can no longer maintain at least 45 percent of your portfolio in stocks after restocking your cash and bond reserves, this is a red flag that you may be consuming your nest egg too quickly. Do a comprehensive review of your retirement income plan to see what adjustments you need to make.

If you experience large losses in the first two to five years of retirement, you need to redesign your retirement income plan. You may want to reconsider the role of immediate annuities in your plan. Seek help from an experienced financial planner if your confidence is shaken.

Allocate Your Assets for the Slow-Down Stage of Retirement

By Kay Conheady, CFP

*I*f you've been taking income from your nest egg for a while, it may no longer be growing at a rate that outpaces or even equals inflation. Your annual withdrawals have likely steadily grown to meet your inflating expenses, which may have doubled since the beginning of your retirement.

Reevaluate and determine whether you need to change the asset allocation of your investment portfolio. To intelligently assess your asset allocation, first do the following:

- ✔ Review your health and prospects for longevity (and those of your spouse).
- ✔ Review how well your nest egg has been doing and whether you can expect it to last as long as you do.
- ✔ Re-estimate your future expenses for
    - Everyday living
    - Healthcare and the potential need for long-term care
    - Unmet retirement dreams
- ✔ Revisit your goals for leaving an inheritance to your heirs.
- ✔ Assess your ability and desire to continue managing your investments.

After you do this review, you should have all the insights you need to make good asset allocation decisions.

Revisit the Four Elements of Retirement Uncertainty

Strategy #77 discusses four elements of retirement uncertainty. Three of the four are still important for those in the slow-down stage of retirement:

✔ **Longevity risk:** Your updated retirement income plan can tell you whether this challenge is still a major consideration for you. Evaluating whether you'll outlive your money is a bit easier at this stage because you're planning for inflation, investment returns, and living expenses for fewer years.

✔ **Inflation risk:** As you revise your retirement income plan, pay special attention to inflation trends for the goods and services you need going forward — especially healthcare, long-term care, major home mainte-nance or remodeling, and other large periodic expenses.

✔ **Market risk:** Your asset allocation strategy for your updated retirement income plan will continue to address the risk that you'll have to sell investments when they're down.

Large investment losses that occur during early retirement are compounded over time, so avoiding them is imperative; however, when you're well into retirement, timing risk isn't a major concern anymore.

Next, look at the key asset allocation decisions you first explored in active retirement (refer to Strategy #77 for details).

Rethink Income Annuities

If you decided against the purchase of an immediate annuity during the active stage of your retirement, you may want to reconsider your decision now. If your updated retirement income plan indicates that you face a high probability of living longer than your assets will last, an immediate annuity may provide the lifelong income that meets your needs.

Next, decide whether to purchase an annuity with an income stream that increases each year to protect against inflation. Because you face fewer years of compounding inflation than you did when you first retired, an annually increasing income isn't as essential as it was then. Look at the current rate of inflation to see whether it's been trending up or down over the last sev-eral years. And look at the rate of inflation for healthcare and long-term care services; these costs increase by a higher rate than the cost of normal goods and services.

Assess the value of immediate-income annuities in regard to your current financial realities and goals. If you can afford to purchase the amount of annu-ity income you need, including an inflation benefit, you reduce the impact of the other three elements of retirement uncertainty. You may place a high value on the peace of mind you get from a guaranteed income.

If you can't afford to purchase the level of income you need with inflation protection, evaluate how close you can come to meeting your current needs if you avoid the additional cost of the inflation protection. And if you decide against investing in an income annuity, you need to continue to invest wisely. See Strategies #19 and #22 for more on annuities.

Examine Your Stock, Bond, and Cash Asset Allocations

As you enter the slow-down stage of retirement, determine whether and how you should change your investment portfolio to better suit your circumstances.

When thinking about your asset allocation for the slow-down stage of retirement, keep the following in mind:

- **Cash and bonds:** Your first concern is still to secure the cash flow you need over the next eight or so years; set this amount aside in cash and bonds.

- **Stocks:** Depending on your age and life expectancy, you may want to go from seeking inflation-beating investment returns to achieving inflation-matching investment returns. This method allows you to reduce your allocation to stock investments within your portfolio. Reducing your overall stock holdings to 35 to 40 percent of your portfolio is perfectly reasonable.

All the principles of rebalancing discussed in Strategy #77 still apply. In fact, you should be even more vigilant and disciplined here because you have less time to make up for mistakes. Replenish the cash with your profits from the stocks as you get them so you're protected when the markets disappoint.

For the most part, the advice about bonds and bond funds from Strategy #77 holds. Look for bonds that seek to provide inflation-matching returns (or better); your bond allocation should include 50 to 60 percent of these bonds. Keep a portion of your stocks in all the major categories, but favor the more-conservative categories of U.S. (versus foreign), large company (versus small company), and value (versus growth) stocks.

Allocate Your Assets During the Late Stage of Life

· ·

By Kay Conheady, CFP

· ·

*H*opefully, you're able to continue living independently during your later years. If, however, you need help taking all your medications on schedule, getting up and going in the morning, fixing your meals, or maintaining your home, consider long-term care. Whether you receive this care in your own home, an assisted living residence, or a skilled nursing home, your outflow of cash is likely to increase considerably, and you may be more concerned than ever about outliving your assets.

Now is a good time for a financial review. Your nest egg has probably been slowly shrinking as you've been withdrawing an ever-increasing income to keep up with inflation. You may have reached the point where you're taking withdrawals of income faster than your nest egg is growing. With good planning and investment management, you've been able to survive ups and downs in the economy; but if the cost of long-term care is now the most pressing uncertainty you face, this strategy can help.

Assess Your Assistance Needs

Before focusing on your investments and whether you need to make changes to your allocation strategy, assess your situation:

- Determine what your needs for assistance are.

- Figure out who's available and willing to be involved with your care. Family? Friends? Acquaintances?

- Determine what kinds of care should be provided by professionals.

- Investigate available federal and state government programs and what kinds of services they provide.

- Determine how your living environment does and doesn't support your continuing to live where you are.

- Look at what kinds of modifications to your home or what kinds of technology would help you to remain where you are.

> ✔ Look at other living alternatives and compare the cost of staying where you are to the cost of living in another environment.

Use this information to determine whether your income sources will continue to cover your living expenses (and your spouse's) and whether you can cover long-term care expenses with your income. Then figure out how much more you need from other resources to meet your needs. Other resources may include the following:

> ✔ Medicare and/or Medicaid, depending on the services you need, your health status, and whether you qualify financially for Medicaid

> ✔ Long-term care insurance benefits if you have such a policy and meet the requirements for receiving benefits (see Strategy #7)

> ✔ Annuities or life insurance that includes benefits to cover long-term care if you meet the requirements for receiving benefits

> ✔ The equity you've built up in your home

Tailor Your Asset Allocation Strategy to Your Savings

You need to keep at least three years' worth of upcoming living expenses in cash and replenish it at least every two years. Factor in the cost of long-term care that other resources can't cover. If you're still in your home, factor in any large expenses for home modifications and/or assistive technology devices or systems.

After you calculate how much to allocate to your cash stash, you'll know how much of your nest egg is left over. Explore your asset allocation challenges by analyzing the two common scenarios outlined here.

Scenario 1: Your nest egg is modest relative to your anticipated needs

If you determine that your nest egg is adequate relative to your anticipated future income needs, you can now

> ✔ Sell your riskier investment holdings

> ✔ Buy securities such as CDs and bonds (especially inflation-tracking bonds) that have relatively stable values

At later stages of life, the potential reward of investing in risky assets is no longer worth the risk. The higher returns you may enjoy from risky investments won't significantly extend how long your nest egg lasts, but investment losses, large or small, can significantly shorten it.

Scenario 2: Your nest egg is sizable relative to your anticipated needs

If you have plenty of available resources, consider yourself fortunate! Then consider the following:

- ✔ You're free to continue to invest for growth to build your legacy for heirs and charitable intentions.

- ✔ Assets reserved for your remaining needs should be invested conservatively, whereas assets you anticipate passing on to your heirs can be invested up to 100 percent in stocks. A good asset allocation may be 20 to 30 percent stocks, 30 to 40 percent bonds, and 30 to 40 percent cash.

- ✔ Rebalancing and vigilance are still necessary.

Get Help with Long-Term Care Planning

Working with a financial planning professional who's knowledgeable about planning for and financing long-term care may be helpful. (For more info on long-term care, see Strategy #63.)

Look for the following local resources to work with when planning for your long-term care needs:

- ✔ **Area agency on aging:** Your local area agency on aging can help you find nearby programs and services that can meet some of your needs.

- ✔ **Medicaid office:** Medicaid offices can help if your resources are dwindling and you suspect you may need to rely on Medicaid to pay for services. Work with your local office well ahead of time so you know current qualification requirements and can best plan how to meet them.

You can find more information from the U.S. Administration on Aging, Department of Health and Human Services, at www.eldercare.gov or 1-800-677-1116.

#80

Preserve Assets to Pass on to Your Heirs

By John Vyge, CFP

*I*f you want to leave assets to your heirs, you have to balance your need for current income with preserving your assets. If you play it too safe, your portfolio won't keep pace with inflation. If you take too much risk, wild fluctuations in the stock market may shrink your nest egg. After you put your assets in the right place, then you can implement wealth preservation strategies to guide your future financial decisions.

Put Your Assets in the Right Place

One way to preserve assets for your heirs is to draw retirement income from fixed-income securities. Having a sufficient base of these types of assets, which aren't subject to the fluctuations of the stock market, allows you to put other assets in more growth-oriented investments. Here are some fixed-income options:

- **Individual bonds:** Individual bonds provide regular interest payments, but you need to be willing to hold the bonds until they mature. Bond mutual funds also pay interest regularly, but they fluctuate in value, so you have no guarantee you'll have a specific amount on a specific date. Consult an investment advisor before building a bond portfolio. (Also read Strategy #18 on government bonds and Strategy #27 on individual bonds.)

- **Certificates of deposit (CDs):** A CD is one of the safest ways to earn interest and avoid loss of principal. However, a CD often pays an interest rate that's less than the inflation rate. (For more information on CDs, see Strategy #17.)

- **Money market accounts:** A bank money market account may pay a slightly higher rate of interest than some CDs, but it still may not protect against inflation. Mutual fund companies offer a variety of money market funds, which also pay interest regularly. (For more information on how these accounts and funds work, see Strategy #17.)

Also consider the value of tax-deferred accounts. Not only do tax-deferred retirement accounts save you from current taxes, but they can also protect you in the event of bankruptcy.

Draw Down Your Assets Wisely

At some point, you're probably going to need to spend some of that money you've saved and invested over the years. The whole point of putting that money away was to enjoy it during retirement, right? This section offers some tips on how you can spend your money wisely while protecting the balance for your heirs.

Whose time horizon? Asset allocation

The appropriate mix of equity and fixed-income investments is important. The assets you'll use for retirement income will be targeted for income and safety of principal. A smaller percentage will be geared towards growth (you may live a long time!).

If you have enough to see you through retirement (including possible emergencies and long-term care), you can allocate the remainder based on your heirs' time horizons. If you'll be leaving money to young grandchildren with years before college, you can invest that money more aggressively. If your heirs are adults with financial pressures, put the money in more stable investments.

What comes first? Redemption order

Choosing the accounts from which to withdraw money can make a difference in what's left for your heirs. Here are some guidelines:

- ✔ If you have taxable accounts, balance the preservation-for-heirs goal against how much you'll pay in taxes along the way. Investments in a taxable account may receive an increase in cost basis when they pass to your heirs. This may enable your heirs to sell these investments and pay little or no capital gains tax.

- ✔ If you have a very large IRA, 401(k), or other tax-deferred account, you may want to delay taking income until your required beginning date after you reach age $70^1/_2$ and then take only the required minimum distribution. If the transfer is structured properly, IRAs can pass to heirs who can then take income out over their lifetimes.

✔ Your Roth IRA is a wonderful vehicle for your heirs to receive because it provides tax-free growth and withdrawals. But remember, the Roth IRA beneficiary has to take withdrawals based on his or her life expectancy, so all the money can't be left to continue to grow.

If you have no Roth IRA because you never qualified for one, a law allows anyone at any income level to convert traditional IRAs to Roth IRAs in 2010. Although you'll pay tax on the taxable portion of the IRA, you can spread the tax liability over 2011 and 2012 under certain conditions. Be sure to calculate the tax cost of converting to a Roth IRA before making the move.

Plan Your Estate

When you die, your estate will be decreased by your existing debt, final expenses (medical, burial, and so on), attorney's/probate fees, and maybe estate taxes. You can minimize or avoid some of these costs, depending on the estate planning strategies and documents you use. You should consult a competent estate planning attorney before acting, but knowing some of your options can help you start the planning process now.

Estate and gift taxes

Most people won't end up paying any federal estate tax under the current system. But given the uncertainty of estate tax laws after 2010, planning between now and then can be challenging. Basic information includes the following:

✔ **Unlimited marital deduction:** You can give an unlimited amount to your spouse, free of estate and gift taxes. However, when the remaining spouse dies, the estate may be subject to federal and/or estate taxes, depending on the size of the estate at his or her death.

✔ **Annual gifting:** You can give up to $12,000 per year per person to as many people as you like, without triggering any gift tax.

✔ **Lifetime exclusion:** Up to $2,000,000 of your estate is exempt from Federal Estate Tax in 2008. This exemption amount increases to $3,500,000 in 2009 and will be unlimited in 2010 for one year only. Congress has been working on legislation to provide permanent estate and gift tax rules before 2010. According to 2008 laws, up to $1 million in gifts during your life are also exempt from Federal Gift Tax.

Probate

Probate is a process used to validate your will and make sure your wishes are carried out. Your estate pays the costs, which can run as high as 5 to 6 percent or more of your gross estate at death, depending on where you live.

Owning property within a revocable living trust can avoid the costs of probate and may leave more assets for your heirs. Work with an estate-planning attorney to see what your options are.

Family limited partnerships

If you own assets such as real estate or business interests that you believe are going to grow, you may consider using a family limited partnership. A *family limited partnership* consists of general partners and limited partners, all of whom are family members. The general partners — typically you and your spouse if you're married — run the partnership. The limited partners, your heirs, have an ownership interest in the assets held by the partnership but have no control over any of the assets while you're alive.

When you die, your heirs become the general partners and take control of the assets. If the partnership is structured properly, only today's value of those assets will be included in your taxable estate at death. Work with an experienced estate-planning attorney if you're interested in this tactic.

Life insurance

If you want to ensure that you leave an inheritance to your heirs, life insurance may be a good solution. Or if you have a sizeable estate that may be subject to estate taxes, life insurance may fulfill your needs.

To avoid having the insurance benefit included in your taxable estate, consult an attorney about the benefits of using an *irrevocable life insurance trust* (ILIT). By having an ILIT own the life insurance, the death benefit can be excluded from your taxable estate at death and provide money to pay estate taxes.

#81

Know Which Types of Investments You Need for Retirement Income

By Martha Schilling, AAMS, CRPC, ETSC, CSA

*W*hen you get to retirement, you have a little wiggle room in your lifestyle. You've paid down debt, the children are out on their own, and now is the time for golf, leisure, and other hobbies. Make sure you manage your income, because taking money out of equities or other investments on a periodic basis *without* having a plan can reduce your portfolio by as much as 50 percent in a volatile market.

In this strategy, you find out how to segment your funds into categories for near-term, mid-term, and long-term availability. You want safety for now, balance for the near future, and continued growth for later. This mix helps you weather current and future volatility with the least impact on your funds over the long term.

Keep Safe Investments for What You Need Now

After you determine your fixed and variable monthly expenses (see Strategy #40 for assistance), figure out how much money you'll need after collecting Social Security, pension, and annuities. Knowing your expected shortfall helps you determine how much you need to take from your portfolio each month. When you know how much you need, you can determine how much risk to take and what kinds of securities you need to invest in.

Any money you need within two to three years shouldn't be in stocks. Use money market funds, short-term bond funds, CDs, and U.S. Treasury bills and notes for near-term spending. (See Strategies #17 and #18 for more on these types of investments.) As you spend down these assets, replenish them with the funds from your mid-term assets. This safety net keeps you from having to sell stocks in falling markets and jeopardizing your long-term plan.

Maintain Your Balance

The mid-term segment of your plan should be the balanced portion of your portfolio. It should have laddered bonds that mature as needed or bond funds/exchange-traded funds (ETFs) that provide monthly income. Include higher-yielding real estate investment trusts (REITs), preferred securities, and dividend-paying stocks or stock mutual funds. The income from these vehicles pours into your money markets to replenish the short-term funds you're drawing down.

Go for Growth for Longer-Term Needs

With the remainder of your funds, maintain a well-diversified portfolio that includes the major asset classes in U.S., international, and emerging market equities to reap the rewards of alternating classification stars. Use this growth to periodically replenish the securities you use for the mid-term segment. Think of your investments as having a waterfall or cascading effect. As the pool at the bottom gets drained, you pour out a little from the top-growth tier into the mid-term pool, which overflows into the pool on the bottom. Allow the funds at the top to continue to grow as you spend down other assets, and you provide an inflation-protected income stream for your later use in retirement. When times are tough for stocks, you can always use up the mid-term securities a little faster than you'd like. That gives you time to wait for the stock market to rebound, thus avoiding selling into a bad market.

Employer-sponsored retirement accounts such as 401(k) and 403(b) plans often have high annual fees and limited choices. A trustee-to-trustee rollover to an IRA with a discount broker can give you better investment options and lower costs. Determine your target percentages and rebalance annually.

Always Think "Tax Return"

One overlying consideration at all three investment levels is taxation. Distributions from Roth IRAs and income from municipal bonds are tax-exempt. On the other hand, distributions from traditional IRAs are subject to ordinary income tax liability, which is currently as high as 35 percent. Taxable accounts face favorable long-term capital gains rates, which are currently 15 percent. You should manage your distributions to minimize the tax bite.

Part VII
The Part of Tens

The 5th Wave

By Rich Tennant

@RICHTENNANT

BRAIN TWISTER PUZZLE

"That reminds me — I have to figure out how to save for retirement <u>and</u> send these two to college."

In this part . . .

Every *For Dummies* book includes a Part of Tens, which consists of top-ten lists of important information the authors think you should have. In this part, we give you ten tips for building a solid financial foundation and ten ways to minimize risk.

Ten Tips for Building a Solid Financial Foundation

*G*etting your financial household in order once and for all helps prepare you financially for all the potentialities you may face in your lifetime. With a solid financial foundation, you can withstand just about every bout of market turmoil or financial crisis that may be heading your way. Here's how to set yourself up for success:

- **Establish adequate cash reserves.** In the event of a downturn in the markets, a family emergency, or loss of income, nothing is as comforting as having adequate cash reserves to get you through those rough times.

- **Invest in your ability to earn money.** One of the biggest — if not *the* biggest — assets you have is your ability to earn money. In uncertain times, invest in yourself. Continue to sharpen your axe, whether you're securely employed, between jobs, temporarily retired, or permanently retired. Often, the easiest way to reduce the stress and strain on your investment nest egg is to continue to earn money, even for a short period of time.

- **Give yourself credit.** Managing your debt wisely — by minimizing or eliminating debt — reduces personal and financial stress. Building an excellent credit history provides you with options to access money if and when you need it.

- **Insure your income.** If you're not yet retired, make sure you have adequate disability insurance. If you need your paycheck to survive, you need disability insurance, just in case you can't earn that paycheck due to a prolonged illness or injury. If others (such as your spouse or family) depend on your income, you also need adequate life insurance to replace your income if you die prematurely.

- **Provide for healthcare expenses.** Make sure you have medical insurance and consider whether long-term care insurance is right for you.

- **Cover your assets.** Periodically review your homeowner's or renter's insurance, automobile insurance, and liability insurance to make sure you're adequately insured.

✔ **Diversify your investment portfolio.** One of the best things you can do to minimize the majority of investment risks is to effectively diversify your portfolio.

✔ **Monitor and rebalance.** After you establish the proper diversification for your investment portfolio, spend a little time on it once or twice a year. Make sure you're monitoring your investment portfolio's performance relative to its peers on a risk-adjusted basis, and be sure to rebalance your portfolio back to your original target allocation.

✔ **Plan for certainties in life.** Many of the major events that occur in your life shouldn't come as surprises. Maybe the timing is a surprise, but the event itself shouldn't blindside you. Think about these potential events. Is your car on its last leg? Do you have children who you want to help through college? Would you like to be able to retire and maintain your standard of living someday? These events are near certainties. The details or timing may be fuzzy, but these events will most likely occur. Prepare in advance — as much as possible — for these eventualities.

✔ **Get help.** If you're unsure of where to turn for personal help and direction about your personal financial situation, be proactive. Get help sooner rather than later. With time on your side, you have many more options.

Ten Tips to Minimize Risk

You face a variety of risks in your financial life. Some of these risks can and should be avoided. Others can be transferred to an insurance company. And some risks are a normal part of your investing life. The following list identifies the primary risks and the most common suggestions of ways you can best handle these risks:

- ✔ **Understand risk.** Possibly the best thing you can do for yourself is understand investment and financial risks and discover which ones can be transferred through insurance and which ones may be minimized by different investment strategies. Understand history and plan for the future.

- ✔ **Be aware of volatility in the financial markets.** Check your risk profile and select a portfolio allocation that lets you tolerate all market climates. Then diversify your portfolio across a broad mix of investments that aren't all subject to the same risks.

- ✔ **Watch out for inflation.** Invest in equities (stocks, mutual funds, or exchange-traded funds) that tend to do well during inflationary periods, such as consumer staples (toothpaste and toilet paper), energy, real estate, and alcohol and tobacco. Put some of your fixed income allocation into Treasury inflation protected securities (TIPS).

- ✔ **Set goals.** Determine where you are now and what you need to realize your goals. Periodically review your status and make adjustments as necessary.

- ✔ **Have a plan for unexpected expenses.** Even the best of plans can be derailed by unexpected financial issues. Think through all the potential what-if scenarios in your life and explore how you can best handle these issues. Adequate cash reserves, ample liquidity, a steady income, and good insurance can get you through the majority of life's financial emergencies.

- ✔ **Maintain liquidity and flexibility.** Avoid unnecessary expenses. Avoid all consumer debt, and build up a comfortable emergency reserve. Have a line of credit available for true emergencies only. Maintain a great credit score.

✔ **Control costs.** When you think of investments, keep in mind three primary factors that influence total returns:

- • The returns provided by the markets

- • Income taxes

- • Investment expenses

The latter two factors can make up a significant chunk of your total return. You have little control over what the markets provide; however, you have a great amount of influence over the taxation and expenses on your investments. Exercise that control!

✔ **Make sure your retirement money lasts.** As for the risk of outliving your money, you have a few options. You may be able to accumulate gobs of money so this isn't a concern. For everyone else, strongly consider working and postponing Social Security retirement benefits until full retirement age, or better yet, age 70. If you're lucky enough to have a defined benefit pension plan, do the same. If you don't have a pension plan, consider taking a portion of your nest egg at retirement and purchasing an immediate annuity to provide you with guaranteed income for the rest of your life. Long-term healthcare can also devastate your finances, so consider buying long-term care insurance.

✔ **Wisely tap into retirement income.** Have a plan for drawing down your assets in retirement (see Part VI). This plan can help you minimize taxes, make sure money is available to fund the distributions, and maximize any remainder for your heirs.

✔ **Hedge your risks.** Investors often achieve hedging by purchasing insurance to protect themselves from risks they can't afford to bear; however, insurance isn't available or appropriate for all risks that you face in your financial life. Hedge most of your financial risk with insurance. In select circumstances, you may want to hedge a portion of your investment portfolio with stock options (see Strategy #28).

Index

• G •

BUSINESS, CAREERS & PERSONAL FINANCE

Accounting For Dummies, 4th Edition*
978-0-470-24600-9

Bookkeeping Workbook For Dummies†
978-0-470-16983-4

Commodities For Dummies
978-0-470-04928-0

Doing Business in China For Dummies
978-0-470-04929-7

E-Mail Marketing For Dummies
978-0-470-19087-6

Job Interviews For Dummies, 3rd Edition*†
978-0-470-17748-8

Personal Finance Workbook For Dummies*†
978-0-470-09933-9

Real Estate License Exams For Dummies
978-0-7645-7623-2

Six Sigma For Dummies
978-0-7645-6798-8

Small Business Kit For Dummies, 2nd Edition*†
978-0-7645-5984-6

Telephone Sales For Dummies
978-0-470-16836-3

BUSINESS PRODUCTIVITY & MICROSOFT OFFICE

Access 2007 For Dummies
978-0-470-03649-5

Excel 2007 For Dummies
978-0-470-03737-9

Office 2007 For Dummies
978-0-470-00923-9

Outlook 2007 For Dummies
978-0-470-03830-7

PowerPoint 2007 For Dummies
978-0-470-04059-1

Project 2007 For Dummies
978-0-470-03651-8

QuickBooks 2008 For Dummies
978-0-470-18470-7

Quicken 2008 For Dummies
978-0-470-17473-9

Salesforce.com For Dummies, 2nd Edition
978-0-470-04893-1

Word 2007 For Dummies
978-0-470-03658-7

EDUCATION, HISTORY, REFERENCE & TEST PREPARATION

African American History For Dummies
978-0-7645-5469-8

Algebra For Dummies
978-0-7645-5325-7

Algebra Workbook For Dummies
978-0-7645-8467-1

Art History For Dummies
978-0-470-09910-0

ASVAB For Dummies, 2nd Edition
978-0-470-10671-6

British Military History For Dummies
978-0-470-03213-8

Calculus For Dummies
978-0-7645-2498-1

Canadian History For Dummies, 2nd Edition
978-0-470-83656-9

Geometry Workbook For Dummies
978-0-471-79940-5

The SAT I For Dummies, 6th Edition
978-0-7645-7193-0

Series 7 Exam For Dummies
978-0-470-09932-2

World History For Dummies
978-0-7645-5242-7

FOOD, GARDEN, HOBBIES & HOME

Bridge For Dummies, 2nd Edition
978-0-471-92426-5

Coin Collecting For Dummies, 2nd Edition
978-0-470-22275-1

Cooking Basics For Dummies, 3rd Edition
978-0-7645-7206-7

Drawing For Dummies
978-0-7645-5476-6

Etiquette For Dummies, 2nd Edition
978-0-470-10672-3

Gardening Basics For Dummies*†
978-0-470-03749-2

Knitting Patterns For Dummies
978-0-470-04556-5

Living Gluten-Free For Dummies†
978-0-471-77383-2

Painting Do-It-Yourself For Dummies
978-0-470-17533-0

HEALTH, SELF HELP, PARENTING & PETS

Anger Management For Dummies
978-0-470-03715-7

Anxiety & Depression Workbook For Dummies
978-0-7645-9793-0

Dieting For Dummies, 2nd Edition
978-0-7645-4149-0

Dog Training For Dummies, 2nd Edition
978-0-7645-8418-3

Horseback Riding For Dummies
978-0-470-09719-9

Infertility For Dummies†
978-0-470-11518-3

Meditation For Dummies with CD-ROM, 2nd Edition
978-0-471-77774-8

Post-Traumatic Stress Disorder For Dummies
978-0-470-04922-8

Puppies For Dummies, 2nd Edition
978-0-470-03717-1

Thyroid For Dummies, 2nd Edition†
978-0-471-78755-6

Type 1 Diabetes For Dummies*†
978-0-470-17811-9

---

* Separate Canadian edition also available
† Separate U.K. edition also available

Available wherever books are sold. For more information or to order direct: U.S. customers visit www.dummies.com or call 1-877-762-2974.
U.K. customers visit www.wileyeurope.com or call (0)1243 843291. Canadian customers visit www.wiley.ca or call 1-800-567-4797.

INTERNET & DIGITAL MEDIA

AdWords For Dummies
978-0-470-15252-2

Blogging For Dummies, 2nd Edition
978-0-470-23017-6

**Digital Photography All-in-One
Desk Reference For Dummies, 3rd Edition**
978-0-470-03743-0

Digital Photography For Dummies, 5th Edition
978-0-7645-9802-9

**Digital SLR Cameras & Photography
For Dummies, 2nd Edition**
978-0-470-14927-0

**eBay Business All-in-One Desk Reference
For Dummies**
978-0-7645-8438-1

eBay For Dummies, 5th Edition*
978-0-470-04529-9

eBay Listings That Sell For Dummies
978-0-471-78912-3

Facebook For Dummies
978-0-470-26273-3

The Internet For Dummies, 11th Edition
978-0-470-12174-0

Investing Online For Dummies, 5th Edition
978-0-7645-8456-5

iPod & iTunes For Dummies, 5th Edition
978-0-470-17474-6

MySpace For Dummies
978-0-470-09529-4

Podcasting For Dummies
978-0-471-74898-4

**Search Engine Optimization
For Dummies, 2nd Edition**
978-0-471-97998-2

Second Life For Dummies
978-0-470-18025-9

**Starting an eBay Business For Dummies,
3rd Edition†**
978-0-470-14924-9

GRAPHICS, DESIGN & WEB DEVELOPMENT

**Adobe Creative Suite 3 Design Premium
All-in-One Desk Reference For Dummies**
978-0-470-11724-8

**Adobe Web Suite CS3 All-in-One Desk
Reference For Dummies**
978-0-470-12099-6

AutoCAD 2008 For Dummies
978-0-470-11650-0

**Building a Web Site For Dummies,
3rd Edition**
978-0-470-14928-7

**Creating Web Pages All-in-One Desk
Reference For Dummies, 3rd Edition**
978-0-470-09629-1

**Creating Web Pages For Dummies,
8th Edition**
978-0-470-08030-6

Dreamweaver CS3 For Dummies
978-0-470-11490-2

Flash CS3 For Dummies
978-0-470-12100-9

Google SketchUp For Dummies
978-0-470-13744-4

InDesign CS3 For Dummies
978-0-470-11865-8

**Photoshop CS3 All-in-One
Desk Reference For Dummies**
978-0-470-11195-6

Photoshop CS3 For Dummies
978-0-470-11193-2

Photoshop Elements 5 For Dummies
978-0-470-09810-3

SolidWorks For Dummies
978-0-7645-9555-4

Visio 2007 For Dummies
978-0-470-08983-5

Web Design For Dummies, 2nd Edition
978-0-471-78117-2

Web Sites Do-It-Yourself For Dummies
978-0-470-16903-2

Web Stores Do-It-Yourself For Dummies
978-0-470-17443-2

LANGUAGES, RELIGION & SPIRITUALITY

Arabic For Dummies
978-0-471-77270-5

Chinese For Dummies, Audio Set
978-0-470-12766-7

French For Dummies
978-0-7645-5193-2

German For Dummies
978-0-7645-5195-6

Hebrew For Dummies
978-0-7645-5489-6

Ingles Para Dummies
978-0-7645-5427-8

Italian For Dummies, Audio Set
978-0-470-09586-7

Italian Verbs For Dummies
978-0-471-77389-4

Japanese For Dummies
978-0-7645-5429-2

Latin For Dummies
978-0-7645-5431-5

Portuguese For Dummies
978-0-471-78738-9

Russian For Dummies
978-0-471-78001-4

Spanish Phrases For Dummies
978-0-7645-7204-3

Spanish For Dummies
978-0-7645-5194-9

Spanish For Dummies, Audio Set
978-0-470-09585-0

The Bible For Dummies
978-0-7645-5296-0

Catholicism For Dummies
978-0-7645-5391-2

The Historical Jesus For Dummies
978-0-470-16785-4

Islam For Dummies
978-0-7645-5503-9

**Spirituality For Dummies,
2nd Edition**
978-0-470-19142-2

NETWORKING AND PROGRAMMING

ASP.NET 3.5 For Dummies
978-0-470-19592-5

C# 2008 For Dummies
978-0-470-19109-5

Hacking For Dummies, 2nd Edition
978-0-470-05235-8

Home Networking For Dummies, 4th Edition
978-0-470-11806-1

Java For Dummies, 4th Edition
978-0-470-08716-9

**Microsoft® SQL Server™ 2008 All-in-One
Desk Reference For Dummies**
978-0-470-17954-3

**Networking All-in-One Desk Reference
For Dummies, 2nd Edition**
978-0-7645-9939-2

**Networking For Dummies,
8th Edition**
978-0-470-05620-2

SharePoint 2007 For Dummies
978-0-470-09941-4

**Wireless Home Networking
For Dummies, 2nd Edition**
978-0-471-74940-0

OPERATING SYSTEMS & COMPUTER BASICS

iMac For Dummies, 5th Edition
978-0-7645-8458-9

Laptops For Dummies, 2nd Edition
978-0-470-05432-1

Linux For Dummies, 8th Edition
978-0-470-11649-4

MacBook For Dummies
978-0-470-04859-7

**Mac OS X Leopard All-in-One
Desk Reference For Dummies**
978-0-470-05434-5

Mac OS X Leopard For Dummies
978-0-470-05433-8

Macs For Dummies, 9th Edition
978-0-470-04849-8

PCs For Dummies, 11th Edition
978-0-470-13728-4

Windows® Home Server For Dummies
978-0-470-18592-6

Windows Server 2008 For Dummies
978-0-470-18043-3

**Windows Vista All-in-One
Desk Reference For Dummies**
978-0-471-74941-7

Windows Vista For Dummies
978-0-471-75421-3

Windows Vista Security For Dummies
978-0-470-11805-4

SPORTS, FITNESS & MUSIC

Coaching Hockey For Dummies
978-0-470-83685-9

Coaching Soccer For Dummies
978-0-471-77381-8

Fitness For Dummies, 3rd Edition
978-0-7645-7851-9

Football For Dummies, 3rd Edition
978-0-470-12536-6

GarageBand For Dummies
978-0-7645-7323-1

Golf For Dummies, 3rd Edition
978-0-471-76871-5

Guitar For Dummies, 2nd Edition
978-0-7645-9904-0

**Home Recording For Musicians
For Dummies, 2nd Edition**
978-0-7645-8884-6

**iPod & iTunes For Dummies,
5th Edition**
978-0-470-17474-6

Music Theory For Dummies
978-0-7645-7838-0

Stretching For Dummies
978-0-470-06741-3

Get smart @ dummies.com®

- Find a full list of Dummies titles
- Look into loads of FREE on-site articles
- Sign up for FREE eTips e-mailed to you weekly
- See what other products carry the Dummies name
- Shop directly from the Dummies bookstore
- Enter to win new prizes every month!

* Separate Canadian edition also available
† Separate U.K. edition also available